Praise for **INSTANT REPLAY**

"In my life as a writer and reader, there are only a few books that I've read over and over again for the sheer pleasure of the experience. Jerry Kramer's *Instant Replay* is the only sports book among them. I loved it when I was a teenager, and I love it still today."
— DAVID MARANISS, author of *When Pride Still Mattered*

"One of the great sports books of all time." — BILLY CRYSTAL

"This was the book that started it all—for athletes telling their stories, for sportswriters going in depth, for great athletic tales being bound between the covers. Dick Schaap's classic is timeless. Required reading for anyone who loves sports or sportswriting."
— MITCH ALBOM, bestselling author, columnist for the *Detroit Free Press*

"It's forty-five-wind-chill-degrees-below in Green Bay, Wisconsin. Dallas leads the Packers in the last quarter of the final playoff of the season. Driving the length of the field in the game's final desperate minutes, Green Bay is stopped by a wall of Cowboys at their goal line. Quarterback Bart Starr grabs the ball, charges at the mass of bodies, dances around Jerry Kramer's perfect block, and suddenly he's in the end zone. He's done it—winning Green Bay its third straight title in a row, a first, on the coldest day of this or any other year. And I was there. I saw it all through tear-frozen eyes. And it was almost as exciting as the book *Instant Replay*, Kramer and pal Dick Schaap's bestseller that tells how it came to happen." — D. A. PENNEBAKER, filmmaker

"As a girl who loved sports, I began to understand the fascinating world of the professional athlete and the magic of wonderful sportswriting from the pages of *Instant Replay*. I also soon realized I had found a hero in a man who later would become a mentor and friend, the great Dick Schaap."

— CHRISTINE BRENNAN, *USA Today* sports columnist

"*Instant Replay* is as timely today as it was twenty years ago. Dick Schaap and Jerry Kramer put a frame around the sport of football when it was played without today's glamour, glitz, and big business. When I read it twenty years ago I did not want it to end, and now it doesn't have to. *Instant Replay*'s honesty is as compelling today as it was then. It is still a must-read for fans and people who make sport their profession." — RICHARD LAPCHICK

"First the writer George Plimpton stepped into the world of pro football. Next Dick Schaap wrote NFL All-Pro Jerry Kramer into the world of literature. And the partnership of sports and books was in motion. Schaap established a literary genre for the ages."

— JOHN A. WALSH, ESPN executive editor

INSTANT REPLAY

INSTANT REPLAY

The Green Bay Diary of Jerry Kramer

JERRY KRAMER and DICK SCHAAP

DOUBLEDAY NEW YORK LONDON TORONTO SYDNEY AUCKLAND

PUBLISHED BY DOUBLEDAY

A previous edition of this book was originally published in
1968 by The New American Library, Inc. It is here reprinted
by arrangement with Jerry Kramer and the estate of
Dick Schaap.

Published in the United States by Doubleday, an imprint
of The Doubleday Broadway Publishing Group, a division
of Random House, Inc., New York.
www.doubleday.com

Insert photos copyright © 2006 by Vernon and John Biever;
except photo on insert page 2 (top), which is courtesy of
Jerry Kramer

Photo on page 295 courtesy of Trish McCleod Schaap

Lines from *The Madman* by Kahlil Gibran. Published by
Alfred A. Knopf, Inc., in 1918.

Book design by David Goldstein

CATALOGING-IN-PUBLICATION DATA IS ON FILE WITH THE
LIBRARY OF CONGRESS

ISBN-13: 978-0-385-51745-4
ISBN-10: 0-385-51745-9

PRINTED IN THE UNITED STATES OF AMERICA

10 9 8 7 6 5 4 3 2 1

FIRST DOUBLEDAY EDITION

For Vince and for my teammates

CONTENTS

FOREWORD

What may well be the most famous play in the history of the National Football League took place on the last day of 1967 at Lambeau Field in Green Bay. The temperature was thirteen below, the field was frozen solid—the game is known in NFL mythology as the Ice Bowl—yet for nearly sixty minutes the Green Bay Packers and the Dallas Cowboys played one of the great championship games in NFL history. With sixteen seconds to go, the Cowboys held a 17–14 lead, but the Packers were on the Cowboys' one-foot line. It was third down. The footing was dreadful. Rather than settling for a field goal and a tie, with overtime to follow, Green Bay quarterback Bart Starr decided to go for the win. He called a quarterback sneak, to be run behind his right guard, Jerry Kramer, who was facing the ferocious Dallas defensive tackle Jethro Pugh. Let Kramer tell it:

I slammed into Jethro hard. All he had time to do was raise his left arm. He didn't even get it up all the way and I charged into him. His body was a little high, the way we'd noticed in the movies, and, with [Ken] Bowman's help, I moved him outside. Willie Townes, next to Jethro, was down low, very low. He was supposed to come in low and close to the middle. He was low, but he didn't close. He might have filled the hole, but he didn't, and Bart churned into the opening and stretched and fell and landed over the goal line. It was the most beautiful sight in the world, seeing Bart lying next to me and seeing the referee in front of me, his arms over his head, signaling the touchdown. There were thirteen seconds to play.

Kramer's perfectly executed block immediately became a signal moment in American sports history, up there with Bobby Thomson's home run and Jesse Owens's four gold medals and Joe Louis's knockout of Max Schmeling. It is a moment that lives not merely in the grainy films of that epic game but also in Kramer's own words. By unlikely but entirely happy coincidence, Kramer had been persuaded to keep a diary of his 1967 season by Dick Schaap, an uncommonly gifted and convivial journalist. Schaap knew that Kramer was intelligent, literate, observant, and thoughtful, and Schaap suspected—rightly—that Kramer could provide a unique view of pro football from its innermost trenches: the offensive line.

As it turned out, The Block, as it came to be known, provided the dramatic climax for the book that resulted, *Instant Replay*, which was published in 1968 and became a national bestseller, but the book didn't need The Block to be recognized at once for what it remains to this day: the best inside account of pro football, indeed the best book ever written about that sport and that league. There's much to be said on behalf of Roy Blount Jr.'s

About Three Bricks Shy of a Load (1974), a knowing and amusing examination of the Pittsburgh Steelers as they stood perched on the brink of greatness, but no book matches the immediacy of Kramer's or its intimate knowledge of the game and the punishment men undergo to play it.

My own admiration for *Instant Replay* was reluctant but then wholehearted. Since the founding in 1960 of the American Football League—known to sportswriters one and all as "upstart"—I had been a supporter of its challenge to the established (and smug) NFL. I was still smarting after the whacking the Packers had administered to the AFL champion Oakland Raiders in the second Super Bowl, played in January 1968. To me the Packers under Vince Lombardi were like the New York Yankees under Casey Stengel: methodical, ruthless, unbeatable, and on all counts unlovable. But when I read *Instant Replay* later in 1968, Kramer and Schaap forced me to reconsider that, not merely because Kramer himself emerged from its pages as entirely likable and admirable but also because their portrait of Lombardi brought out the human side of a man who, from a distance, seemed like a martinet, pure and simple.

Astonishingly, considering the great success and high reputation it enjoyed, *Instant Replay* has been out of print for years. This seems even more astonishing after a second (or third, or fourth) reading, because the book has lost absolutely nothing over almost four decades. It is funny, smart, evocative, honest, and unpretentious. Its prose is Kramer's, dictated into a tape recorder and regularly mailed to Schaap as the season progressed. Schaap's role was "to organize, to condense, to clarify, and to punctuate," but he "did not have to polish Jerry Kramer's phrases or prompt his thoughts." All in all, it's as good a job of collaboration between unprofessional writer and professional journalist as

I can recall reading, and it is as vivid and engaging now as it was in 1968.

So this new edition of *Instant Replay* is especially welcome. It arrives at a time when professional football has replaced baseball as the country's most popular sport, if not as the national pastime. The game has accumulated enough history by now so that past triumphs (and failures) can be viewed with some perspective. The Green Bay team on which Kramer played was the second pro-football "dynasty"—the first being the Cleveland Browns of the early to mid-1950s—and it has achieved a degree of mythic status that no other pro-football team has enjoyed before or since. In part this is because the Packers were then, as now, the only small-city team in the National Football League, in part because they so emphatically dominated the league, in part because they were an uncommonly appealing group of men, and in large part because they were coached by Vince Lombardi.

Not merely do we now have this opportunity to reacquaint ourselves with those storied Packers in this best of all pro-football books, thanks to Kramer we can hear as well as read about what it was like to be a Packer in the mid-1960s. Not long ago he found, in his garage, tape recordings he had made for Schaap during the 1967 season. He has edited them, supplemented them with his own interviews with several of his former teammates, and released them as a two-CD set called *Jerry Kramer's Inside the Locker Room: The Lost Tapes of the 1967 Championship Season.* They must be listened to carefully, as ambient noise in the locker room is considerable (it includes the pronounced sound of toilets flushing), but players can be heard giving each other low-key pep talks before the Super Bowl against the Raiders, followed by Lombardi's own brief and subdued but emphatic speech to the team. Kramer's interviews with the old vets are revealing and often delightful, especially a hilarious conversation with Doug Hart about the semifinal NFL championship game against the Los Angeles Rams, coached by the tight-sphinctered George Allen.

Kramer was thirty-one years old during the 1967 season. He'd been with the Packers since graduating from the University of Idaho in 1958 (his signing bonus was $250). He played for eleven seasons, was All-Pro six times, and in 1970 was selected for the NFL's All-Fifty-Year Team. Inexplicably, and absolutely unjustly, he has yet to be elected to the Pro Football Hall of Fame. He retired after the 1968 season and moved to Idaho, where he continues to pursue various business ventures with considerable success. From that vantage point he was able for a time to look with pride to Atlanta and Tennessee, where his son Jordan played linebacker in the early 2000s for the Falcons and the Titans.

The league in which Jordan Kramer played bears only limited resemblance to Jerry Kramer's. For one thing, it's much bigger: It absorbed the AFL in the 1970s and added expansion teams thereafter, doubling from sixteen teams to thirty-two. Black players, a distinct if prominent minority in Kramer's day, dominate the league today. Television contracts and media attention have multiplied exponentially. So too have coaching staffs and player rosters, and salaries—at least for the relatively small number of players who achieve star status and enjoy long careers—have gone through the roof; the check that players competed for in the 1967 and 1968 Super Bowls—$25,000 per man—wouldn't even come close to buying the kind of car that the typical NFL celebrity drives these days. Not merely are there more coaches, but they are a more controlling presence than they were in Kramer's era; most plays are now sent in from the sidelines, and few quarterbacks enjoy anything approximating the play-calling freedom that Lombardi entrusted to Starr.

Yet the game is still the game, and the pressures faced by the men who play it remain the same. Training camp is hell—"We started two-a-day workouts today, and the agony is beyond belief. Grass drills, agility drills, wind sprints, everything. You wonder why you're there, how long you're going to last"—and the possibility of serious, career-ending injury is always present. Competition is strenuous and endless, with a long line of fresh young talent all too eager to send the veterans packing. Each week's game is a new opportunity to make a mistake that costs the team a win. Readers who would like a close and well-informed look at the strains under which today's players labor may want to supplement *Instant Replay* with *Wedded to the Game* (2006) by Shannon O'Toole, the wife of a man who played on the NFL's margins for several years and who knows, from firsthand and sometimes painful experience, that most players are journeymen and that life in the league is scarcely as easy as we outsiders assume it to be.

Kramer was keenly aware of the costs the game exacted and the pressures it imposed. "At times," he writes, "you really wonder about football, if you need it, what makes you drive yourself, what makes you go through with all that pain." Later he says, "It takes a great deal to play this game. It takes a lot of pride and a lot of determination and a lot of hustle and a lot of sacrifice, and you have to be in the right frame of mind. You can't do it halfway." The game did reward him with what was, for the time, a handsome income and, following The Block and then the publication of this book, with a considerable measure of celebrity, but in the end he concludes that "for me the main lure of football is the guys, my teammates, the friendship, the fun, the excitement, the incredibly exhilarating feeling of a shared achievement."

For the men who played for the Packers of the 1960s, all the game's built-in pressures were compounded many times over by the presence of Lombardi. He, not Kramer, is the real protagonist of *Instant Replay*, and he is a formidable figure indeed, "a cruel, kind, tough, gentle, miserable man whom I often hate and often love and always respect." He "thinks of himself as the patriarch of a large family, and he loves all his children, and he worries about all of them, but he demands more of his gifted children." He is "a psychologist" or "a child psychologist," and he knows how to build each of his players up to maximum performance:

> In 1959, his first year, he drove me unmercifully during the two-a-days. He called me an old cow one afternoon and said that I was the worst guard he'd ever seen. I'd been working hard, killing myself, and he took all the air out of me. I'd lost seven or eight pounds that day, and when I got into the locker room, I was too drained to take my pads off. I just sat in front of my locker, my helmet off, my head down, wondering what I was doing playing football, being as bad as I was, getting cussed like I was. Vince came in and walked over to me, put his hand on the back of my head, mussed my hair and said, "Son, one of these days you're going to be the greatest guard in the league." He is a beautiful psychologist. I was ready to go back out to practice for another four hours.

There were times when Kramer wanted to choke the life out of Lombardi, times when the man left him utterly confused: "He screams at you, hollers at you, makes life unbearable until you're about ready to quit, and then he starts being real nice to you and makes your life enjoyable for a while." But Kramer's final judgment is the one that matters: "I loved Vince. Sure, I had hated him at times during training camp and I had hated him at times during the season, but I knew how much he had done for us, and I knew how much he cared about us. He is a beautiful man, and the proof is that no one who ever played for him ever speaks of him afterward with anything but respect and admiration and affection. His whippings, his cussings, and his driving all fade; his good qualities endure."

More than anything, Lombardi made the Packers into something that's surprisingly rare in the world of team sports: a *team*. Whether it's playing football, baseball, or basketball, what we call a "team" usually is a loose conglomeration of people more motivated by individual than collective goals. It's hard to persuade a group of adults to put team above self, but Lombardi was able to do it:

> We're all different. We all have our own interests, our own preferences, and yet we all go down the same road, hand in hand. Maybe, ultimately, we're not really friends, but what I mean is that no individual on this club will go directly against another individual's feelings, no matter what his own opinion is. . . . There's no friction, no division into cliques. Certainly we have different groups—the swingers, the family men, the extremely religious young men—but everyone respects everyone else's feelings.

Maybe that sounds a little old-fashioned now, yet early in the twenty-first century the dominant team in pro football, the New England Patriots, has been Lombardi's kind of *team*. Its coach, Bill Belichick, isn't cast in the Lombardi mold, but he gets Lombardi results by chanting the same mantra: "All for one and one for all." Now as then it's a winning formula, as *Instant Replay* makes abundantly—and instructively—plain on every page. In that respect as in so many others, *Instant Replay* remains as pertinent today as it was in 1967. It's funny, too, and smart and, in the end, more moving than one might expect a book about football to be. That, of course, is because it's about a lot more than football.

JONATHAN YARDLEY
Washington, D.C.
2006

Jonathan Yardley is the book critic and a columnist for the *Washington Post*. He is the author of six books and the winner of a Pulitzer Prize for Distinguished Criticism.

INTRODUCTION

This is Jerry Kramer's book. These are his thoughts, his impressions, his words. He is, I believe, an observant, perceptive, and articulate young man who happens to be a tremendous professional football player.

Here is how he kept his diary: At least two nights every week, sometimes four and five and six nights, from the start of training to the end of the football season of 1967, he spoke into a tape recorder, preserving his daily actions and reactions. Often, on days when he was too fatigued or too busy or too dispirited to face the recorder, he took notes for reference. He mailed the tapes to me each week, and the transcriptions ran well beyond 100,000 of his words. Additionally, I spent a total of four weeks in Green Bay and three weeks on the road with Jerry

Kramer and the Packers, reviewing and amplifying the transcriptions.

At the end of the season, we took two weeks to go over the diary, adding background and explanations, but never modifying the essence, never changing the mood to suit later developments, never tampering with the spontaneity and immediacy that make this diary, in fact as well as title, an instant replay.

One note about the language of the book: Football players, in their locker rooms, use approximately the same language that an educated army platoon would employ in its barracks. Like soldiers, the players use words they would not dream of using in the home or among strangers. The harshness of the language varies, of course, from man to man. Among the Green Bay Packers, for instance, Bart Starr and Carroll Dale shy away from all obscenity; Vince Lombardi limits his to the few words that lend emphasis to his habitually impassioned speeches. Jerry Kramer himself is fairly typical; he is neither appalled nor amused by obscenity. In his diary, he has retained only the minimum necessary to reflect each situation accurately and honestly. He has avoided using obscenity simply for shock value.

My job, with this diary, was to organize, to condense, to clarify, and to punctuate. I did not have to polish Jerry Kramer's phrases or prompt his thoughts. If anyone suspects that I placed words in Jerry Kramer's mouth, he credits me with too much courage. I would never put words in the mouth of anyone three inches taller and sixty-five pounds heavier than I.

DICK SCHAAP
New York City
April 1968

PROLOGUE

They sat in front of me, an audience of college presidents and college deans, gathered at a banquet in Milwaukee a few years ago, and as I looked down from the speaker's rostrum I could tell they were waiting tolerantly to hear what a professional football player could possibly say to them. I could hardly resist one line: "Before this dinner, I rode up in the elevator with several of you gentlemen, and I want to tell you I was amazed to discover that you people can actually talk and carry on a civilized conversation."

I was, of course, twisting the cliché, turning upon those educators the line I had heard too many times about professional football players. Nothing irritates me more than the implication that we're some sort of subhuman beasts, trained animals clawing each other for the amusement of modern Romans. I'm not trying to suggest that pro football players as a group are the intellectual equals of, say, the staff of *The Paris Review*. But I've sat with lawyers and with politicians and with writers, and, frankly, when I want an interesting conversation, I'd just as soon chat with a bunch of pro football players. At least the players are willing to discuss something besides football.

I guess the editor of *The Paris Review,* George Plimpton, feels the same way. He'd rather go to a football training camp than to a literary cocktail party, and I can't blame him.

Not that I have anything against literature, or against cock-tails, for that matter. I like to read—poetry, philosophy, novels, almost everything. I don't think my reading habits are excep-tional—I certainly don't pretend to be a scholar—but every time a reporter comes to my room in training camp or to my home and sees my books, he seems impressed (The Beast reads!), which makes me suspicious about the reading habits of reporters.

Like almost every professional football player, I'm simply not a one-dimensional figure. I'm a businessman much of the time. I own part of the American Archery Company in Wisconsin and part of the Packer Diving Company in Louisiana. I'm the host of a syndicated TV show once a week during the football season, and I'm involved in half a dozen advertising ventures. I follow the stock market. I keep looking for new opportunities for investments.

Still, most of all, I'm a professional football player. I joined the Green Bay Packers in 1958, fresh from the University of Idaho, and during my rookie season we were the worst team in pro foot-ball. Over the past eight seasons, we've been the best team in pro football. Not coincidentally, our head coach for the past eight sea-sons has been a man named Vincent Thomas Lombardi, a cruel, kind, tough, gentle, miserable, wonderful man whom I often hate and often love and always respect. I've played next to great foot-ball players in Green Bay; sixteen of my teammates have been named to one or another of the All-Pro teams during the past nine years. I managed to make the All-Pro teams four years myself.

I've worked hard at professional football, and professional football has worked hard on me. During my life, I've submitted, not always cheerfully, to a total of twenty-two operations, most of them major, many of them the direct result of football injuries. I was given up for dead once; everyone, including my doctors, feared that I had cancer. I've got lasting scars from the top of my head to my ankles; for all my stitches, my teammates call me "Zipper." I've been told at least three different times that I would never be able to play football again, but I've kept coming back to play.

Why? I'm not sure. That's one of the reasons I've decided to keep this diary of my 1967 football season. I'm thirty-one years old now, and I have no pressing need for the money, much less the aches and scars, I'll earn during my tenth professional season. But perhaps, by setting down my daily thoughts and observations, I'll be able to understand precisely what it is that draws me back to professional football.

I want to show exactly what it's like for me — an offensive lineman, a right guard, definitely not one of the glamour positions — to struggle through a professional football season. I want to show what my teammates are like in all their dimensions. I want to show what it's like to push yourself almost beyond endurance for a coach who considers pain only something that you must shrug off.

And I want this diary to have a happy ending. After all, this isn't *Hamlet*, and I'm not Shakespeare. I'm a professional football player.

JERRY KRAMER
Green Bay, Wisconsin
February 1967

NO.	NAME	POS.	HT.	WT.	AGE	COLLEGE
26	Adderley, Herb	DB	6–0	200	28	Michigan State
82	Aldridge, Lionel	DE	6–4	245	26	Utah State
44	Anderson, Donny	HB	6–3	210	24	Texas Tech
57	Bowman, Ken	C	6–3	230	24	Wisconsin
12	Bratkowski, Zeke	QB	6–3	210	34	Georgia
83	Brown, Allen	TE	6–5	235	24	Mississippi
78	Brown, Bob	DE	6–5	260	26	Arkansas A., M. & N.
40	Brown, Tom	DB	6–1	195	26	Maryland
60	Caffey, Lee Roy	LB	6–3	250	26	Texas A. & M.
88	Capp, Dick	TE	6–3	235	23	Boston College
34	Chandler, Don	K	6–2	210	33	Florida
56	Crutcher, Tommy Joe	LB	6–3	230	25	Texas Christian
84	Dale, Carroll	E	6–2	200	28	V.P.I.
87	Davis, Willie	DE	6–3	245	32	Grambling
86	Dowler, Boyd	E	6–5	225	29	Colorado
55	Flanigan, Jim	LB	6–3	240	21	Pittsburgh
81	Fleming, Marvin	TE	6–4	235	25	Utah
68	Gillingham, Gale	G	6–3	255	23	Minnesota
33	Grabowski, Jim	FB	6–2	220	23	Illinois
75	Gregg, Forrest	OT	6–4	250	33	Southern Methodist
43	Hart, Doug	DB	6–0	182	28	Arlington State
13	Horn, Don	QB	6–2	195	22	San Diego State
50	Hyland, Bob	C	6–5	250	21	Boston College
27	James, Claudis	E	6–2	190	23	Jackson State
21	Jeter, Bob	DB	6–1	205	30	Iowa
74	Jordan, Henry	DT	6–3	250	32	Virginia
77	Kostelnik, Ron	DT	6–4	260	27	Cincinnati
64	Kramer, Jerry	G	6–3	250	31	Idaho

NO.	NAME	POS.	HT.	WT.	AGE	COLLEGE
80	Long, Bob	E	6–3	205	24	Wichita
85	McGee, Max	E	6–3	210	35	Tulane
30	Mercein, Chuck	FB	6–2	225	24	Yale
66	Nitschke, Ray	LB	6–3	240	30	Illinois
22	Pitts, Elijah	HB	6–1	205	28	Philander Smith
89	Robinson, Dave	LB	6–3	240	26	Penn State
45	Rowser, John	DB	6–1	180	22	Michigan
76	Skoronski, Bob	OT	6–3	245	33	Indiana
15	Starr, Bart	QB	6–1	190	33	Alabama
63	Thurston, Fred	G	6–1	245	33	Valparaiso
73	Weatherwax, Jim	DT	6–7	260	24	Los Angeles State
23	Williams, Travis	HB	6–1	210	21	Arizona State
36	Wilson, Ben	FB	6–1	230	27	Southern California
24	Wood, Willie	DB	5–10	190	30	Southern California
72	Wright, Steve	OT	6–6	250	25	Alabama

Coaches

NAME	TITLE	AGE	COLLEGE
Vince Lombardi	Head Coach	54	Fordham
Phil Bengtson	Defensive Coach	54	Minnesota
Jerry Burns	Defensive Backfield Coach	40	Michigan
Dave Hanner	Defensive Line Coach	37	Arkansas
Tom McCormick	Offensive Backfield Coach	37	College of the Pacific
Bob Schnelker	Offensive End Coach	39	Bowling Green
Ray Wietecha	Offensive Line Coach	39	Northwestern

INSTANT REPLAY

PRELIMINARY SKIRMISHES

I drove downtown to the Packer offices today to pick up my mail, mostly fan mail about our victory in the first Super Bowl game, and as I came out of the building Coach Lombardi came in. I waved to him cheerfully—I have nothing against him during the off-season—and I said, "Hi, Coach."

Vince Lombardi is a short, stout man, a stump. He looked up at me and he started to speak and his jaws moved, but no words came out. He hung his head. My first thought—from force of habit, I guess—was I've done something wrong, I'm in trouble, he's mad at me. I just stood there and Lombardi started to speak again and again he opened his mouth and still he didn't say anything. I could see he was upset, really shaken.

"What is it, Coach?" I said. "What's the matter?"

Finally, he managed to say, "I had to put Paul—" He was almost stuttering. "I had to put Paul on that list," he said, "and they took him."

I didn't know what to say. I couldn't say anything. Vince had put Paul Hornung on the list of Packers eligible to be selected by the Saints, the new expansion team in New Orleans, and the Saints had taken him. Paul Hornung had been my teammate ever since I came to Green Bay in 1958, and he had been Vince's prize pupil ever since Vince came to Green Bay in 1959, and it may sound funny but I loved Paul and Vince loved Paul and everybody on the Packers loved Paul. From the stands, or on television, Paul may have looked cocky, with his goat shoulders and his blond hair and his strut, but to the people who knew him he was a beautiful guy.

I stood there, not saying anything, and Lombardi looked at me again and lowered his head and started to walk away. He took about four steps and then he turned around and said, "This is a helluva business sometimes, isn't it?"

Then he put his head down again and walked into his office.

I got to thinking about it later, and the man is a very emotional man. He is spurred to anger or to tears almost equally easily. He gets misty-eyed and he actually cries at times, and no one thinks less of him for crying. He's such a man.

JUNE 15

Practice starts a month from today, and I'm dreading it. I don't want to work that hard again. I don't want to take all that punishment again. I really don't know why I'm going to do it.

I must get some enjoyment out of the game, though I can't say what it is. It isn't the body contact. Body contact may be fun for the defensive players, the ones who get to make the tackles, but body contact gives me only cuts and contusions, bruises and abrasions. I suppose I enjoy doing something well. I enjoy springing a back loose, making a good trap block, a good solid trap block, cutting down my man the way I'm supposed to. But I'm not quite as boyish about the whole thing as I used to be.

A couple of months ago, I was thinking seriously about retiring. Jimmy Taylor, who used to be my roommate on the Packers, and a couple of other fellows and I have a commercial diving business down in Louisiana. Jimmy, who comes from Baton Rouge and played for Louisiana State University, is a great asset to the business; he's such a hero in Louisiana I wouldn't be surprised if he ended up as governor. We've been building up the company for three years now, and this year, with Jimmy playing for the Saints—he played out his option here and jumped to New Orleans—we should really do well. He'll be able to entertain potential customers, wine them and dine them and take them to the Saints' games.

I thought of retiring so that I could devote more time to the company. And I would have retired, I believe, or at least tried to shift to the New Orleans team, if a deal hadn't come through with a man named Blaine Williams, who's in the advertising business in Green Bay. We're getting portraits made of all the players in the National Football League, and we're selling them to Kraft Foods to distribute on a nation-wide basis. It can be a very lucrative thing for me, so I decided I'd better stay here in Green Bay and keep an eye on it.

Coach Lombardi heard that I was thinking about retiring—he hears everything—and he suspected I was going to use this as a wedge to demand more money. That wasn't what I had in mind, not this time.

Still, I haven't heard a word from Lombardi about a contract for this year.

JULY 5

Pat Peppler, the personnel director of the Packers, phoned today and asked me if I wanted to discuss my contract. I told him I wanted $27,500, up from $23,000 last year, and I said it isn't as much as I deserve, of course, but I'll be happy with it and I won't cause any problems, any struggle.

I mean it. I know I'm worth more than $27,500, but I don't want a contract fight over a few thousand dollars. I can remember what happened in 1963.

That was the year after I kicked three field goals in the world championship game against the New York Giants, and we won the game by three field goals, 16–7. During the 1962 season, I kicked extra points and field goals, and I was named All-Pro offensive guard, and, in general, I had a pretty good year. I came in wanting a sizable raise, and Coach Lombardi started out with the standard 10 percent he offers when he wants to give a guy a raise. I said I wanted nearly 50 percent, from $13,000 up to $19,000, and he hit the ceiling and said absolutely not. He said he'd give me $14,500 or maybe $15,000.

In the back of my mind, I was thinking about playing out my option—the one-year professional football contract allows a man to play out a second year at the same salary and then become a free agent, the way Jimmy Taylor did last year—and jumping to Denver in the rival American Football League. Denver wanted me badly.

Coach Lombardi, with his spy system, found out what I was thinking about. He has a real thing about loyalty, and he got doubly upset. He called me into his office and offered me $15,000 and said, "Look, I'm going to give you fifteen, but you have to take it today. Tomorrow, it'll be down to fourteen." I didn't take it.

I started training camp without a contract, and Vince made

practice almost unbearable. Every block I threw, every move I made, was either slow or wrong or inadequate. "Move, Kramer, move," he'd scream, "you think you're worth so damn much." And the contract negotiations weren't kept at any executive level. They were held at lunch and dinner, at bedtime and during team meetings, and the rest of the coaches joined in, all of them on my back, sniping at me, taking potshots at me. I got bitter, I got jumpy, and then a lot of the other guys, my teammates, began to tease me, to ride me, and the teasing didn't sound like teasing to me because I was getting so much hell from all angles.

And then I almost exploded. We have a ritual the day before a game. The offensive linemen get together with the defensive linemen and throw passes to each other. We take turns playing quarterback, and you get to keep throwing passes until one of them is incomplete. It's a silly little game, but it loosens us up and it's fun. Every lineman's dream, of course, is to be a quarterback. So, in 1963, the day before an exhibition, we were playing this game, and I stepped up for my turn to play quarterback and Bill Austin, who was our line coach, yelled, "No, get out of there, Kramer, you can't be a quarterback."

I said, "Why not?"

And he said, "Just 'cause I said so."

There was no reason, except for the contract, and this burned me up. Later, Austin approached me in the lobby of the hotel we were staying in, and he said, "Jerry, I want to talk to you."

I said, "Look, you sonuvabitch, I don't want to talk to you at all. I don't have a word to say to you. I don't want to have anything to do with you. Stay away from me."

I was out of my head a little bit.

Bill said, "Now, now, don't be like that."

"I mean it, Bill," I said. "Stay away from me." I stopped just short of punching Austin.

That night, Coach Lombardi put me on the kickoff team, the suicide team, which is usually reserved, during exhibition games, for rookies. "The kickoff team is football's greatest test of courage," Lombardi says. "It's the way we find out who likes to hit."

I knew how dangerous the kickoff team could be. In 1961, when I was kicking off for the Packers, I had to be on the kickoff team, of course. I kicked off once against the Minnesota Vikings, the opening play of the game, and when I ran down the field, I ran straight at the wedge in front of the ballcarrier. The wedge is made up of four men, always four big and mobile men, more than 1,000 pounds' worth. One of the guys from the Minnesota wedge hit me in the chest and another scissored my legs and buckled me over backwards and then the ballcarrier stumbled onto me and pounded me into the ground and a couple of other guys ran over me and stomped me in deeper, and the result was a broken ankle. I missed eight games in 1961.

And then in 1963, for that exhibition, I found myself on the kickoff team again. I took out all my fury on the field. I was the first man down the field on every kickoff, I hit everyone who got in my way, and after the game Lombardi came up to me and said that he wasn't the vindictive type, that we could get together and settle the contract. I signed the next day for $17,500.

Pat Peppler told me today he would check with Coach Lombardi about my demand for $27,500.

JULY 7

Pat Peppler called back. "You can have $26,500," he said.

"If I wanted $26,500," I told him, "I would have asked for $26,500. If I'd said $44,500, I suppose Lombardi would have come back with $43,500. I want $27,500 without any fuss, without any argument."

JULY 10

"OK, it's $27,500," Pat Peppler said today. "Stop by and sign."

I'm going to forget that I ever thought about retiring. I'm going to forget that I've got a lot of money coming in. I'm going to forget that I don't really need football anymore.

I've decided to play. Let's get on with it.

BASIC TRAINING

Practice began officially yesterday for everyone except the veteran offensive and defensive linemen. We don't have to report until 6 P.M. tomorrow, Saturday, but I couldn't wait. I had to go over to the stadium this morning. It's not that I'm anxious to start the punishment, but I figured one workout today and one tomorrow would help me ease into training. Monday, we start two-a-days, which are pure hell, one workout in the morning and one in the afternoon, and if I don't get a little exercise, the two-a-days'll kill me.

Naturally, I saw Vince this morning. He asked me how I was, and, before I could tell him, he said, "You look a little heavy."

I guess I am. I was up around 265 a few weeks ago, and I'm 259 now, and I'd like to play somewhere between 245 and 250. I'm not too worried about my weight. I know I've got the best diet doctor in the world. His prize patient right now is a rookie tackle named Leon Crenshaw, from Tuskegee Institute, who reported to training camp a week ago weighing 315 pounds. Dr. Lombardi has reduced him to 302.

I started off the day by trotting three laps around the goal posts, a total of almost half a mile, not because I love running, but because Coach Lombardi insists upon this daily ritual. As long as he's been here, we've had only one fellow who didn't run his three laps, a big rookie named Royce Whittenton. When Green Bay drafted Whittenton during the winter of his senior year in college, he weighed about 240. When the coaches contacted him in the spring, he weighed 270. They told him they didn't want him to come to camp any heavier than 250, and he reported in the summer at 315 pounds. He made one lap and half of another around the goal posts and then he couldn't go any farther. Lombardi cut him from the squad before he even took calisthenics.

We had one of our little "nutcracker" drills today, a brand of torture—one on one, offensive man against defensive man—which is, I imagine, something like being in the pit. The defensive man positions himself between two huge bags filled with foam rubber, which form a chute; the offensive man, leading a ballcarrier, tries to drive the defensive man out of the chute, banging into him, head-to-head, really rattling each other, ramming each other's neck down into the chest.

The primary idea is to open a path for the ballcarrier. The secondary idea is to draw blood. I hate it. But Coach Lombardi seemed to enjoy watching every fresh collision.

Lombardi thinks of himself as the patriarch of a large family, and he loves all his children, and he worries about all of them, but he demands more of his gifted children. Lee Roy Caffey, a tough linebacker from Texas, is one of the gifted children, and Coach Lombardi is always on Lee Roy, chewing him, harassing him, cussing him. We call Lee Roy "Big Turkey," as in, "You ought to be ashamed of yourself, you big turkey," a Lombardi line. Vince kept saying during the drill today that if anyone wanted to look like an All-American, he should just step in against Caffey.

"Look at yourself, Caffey, look at yourself, that stinks," Lombardi shouted. Later, Vince added, "Lee Roy, you may think that I criticize you too much, a little unduly at times, but you have the size, the strength, the speed, the mobility, everything in the world necessary to be a great football player, except one thing: YOU'RE TOO DAMN LAZY."

During the nutcracker, Red Mack, a reserve flanker for us last year who weighs 179 pounds soaking wet, lined up against Ray Nitschke, who weighs 240 pounds and is the strongest 240 pounds in football. Ray uses a forearm better than anyone I've ever seen; when he swings it up into someone's face, it's a lethal weapon. Red should have lined up against someone smaller. Ray's used to beating people's heads in, and he enjoys it, but he looked down at Red Mack and he said, "Oh, no, I can't go against this guy."

Red looked up at Ray and said, "Get in here, you sonuvabitch, and let's go."

They went at it and Ray almost killed him. Red fired off the line and Ray hit him with a forearm and knocked him to his knees, knocked him groggy. When he got up, Red just shook it off, the stubborn little bastard.

Lombardi was in beautiful mid-season form. He kept chewing rookie Bob Hyland, our number-one draft choice, a 250-pounder from Boston College. Hyland's an offensive lineman, both a center and a guard, and he looks like he's going to be a fine football player. But right now he's got a bad stance. "Look at that stance,

Hyland," Vince screamed. "What can you do from that stance? You can't do anything. You can't go right. You can't go left. You can't block. The only thing that stance is good for is taking a crap."

JULY 15

I went to jail today. I started an eight-week sentence in Sensenbrenner Hall, which is a student dormitory at St. Norbert College in West De Pere, Wisconsin, a ten-minute drive from Lambeau Field in Green Bay. Eight weeks a year, since 1958, I've lived in this dormitory; I deserve an honorary degree from St. Norbert.

The whole thing is a pain in the ass. The worst part is that you're completely a captive of Lombardi and of football. It's not like you put in two hours in the morning, two in the afternoon, and two in the evening. You're required to attend breakfast at 7 A.M., ride in the bus over to the stadium, ride back in the bus, eat lunch, go over to the stadium and back again, dinner, meeting, curfew. If you're lucky, you get an hour and a half or two hours a day to do whatever you want.

I'm in Room 207, the same room I've had for five or six years, and now that Jimmy Taylor's gone, I'm rooming with Donny Chandler, a place-kicker for six months a year and an Oklahoma businessman for six months a year. Our room is neither spacious nor gracious. It is exactly like every other room, perfect for college sophomores, but adequate, barely adequate, for pro football players. Our beds are about six feet long and three feet wide. My head hangs over one end, my feet hang over the other, and my arms hang over both sides.

We each have a closet, a dresser and a desk, and everything is jammed. I've moved in a modest wardrobe, fifteen or twenty pairs of slacks, a dozen Bermuda shorts, two dozen sports shirts, and several pairs of shoes and sandals. I'm a little more clothes-conscious than most of the players, although the guys do care about clothes. We're in the public eye a lot, and we have to dress well.

The room is wired completely for sound. Donny brought in a portable television set and I brought in a stereo system and a dozen records. I've also got a handful of books and, most important, my cribbage board. Cribbage is the national pastime here; I usually support myself in the game.

For obvious reasons, we try not to spend too much time in the rooms, except for playing cribbage and sleeping. We do get our share of sleep. Curfew, which means in bed with lights out, is 11 P.M. six nights a week and midnight on Saturday. The married players whose families are in town are allowed to sleep at home Saturday nights, but my wife and our three children are out in Idaho, visiting relatives, so I have to sleep in the dorm every night. The curfews are strictly enforced; Lombardi runs this place like a penal institution.

I still remember Lombardi's first year, 1959, which was also the first year I roomed with Taylor. At eleven on the dot one night, Vince came by our room and Jimmy was sitting on the edge of his bed, with his socks and his shorts on.

Coach said, "Jimmy, what time you got?"

Jimmy whipped out his watch and said, "I've got eleven o'clock sir."

"Jimmy, you're supposed to be in bed at eleven, aren't you?" Coach said.

"Yes, sir," said Jimmy.

Coach said, "Jimmy, that'll cost you twenty-five dollars."

Jimmy looked at me open-mouthed and I raised my eyebrows a little bit and I said, "Ooh, this guy's pretty serious."

The next day, Ray Nitschke was in the phone booth two or

three minutes after eleven and it cost him $50. (Our fines, incidentally, usually go to charities, like the St. Norbert building fund.) We began to believe right then that Lombardi was very, very serious about everything he said.

After about three weeks, a few of us decided we had to test Lombardi. Paul Hornung asked me if I wanted to sneak out of the dorm after curfew. It was very difficult to talk me into it; it took Paul about three seconds. At 11:30 we began our big getaway. Paul's roommate, Max McGee, said he was going with us, and the three of us started sneaking down the hall.

"Wait," said Max. "Let's get Ringo."

Jim Ringo was our captain then, and we figured if he was with us and we got caught, we wouldn't get fined as much.

I said, "Great, get Ringo."

Ringo happened to be rooming with Dave Hanner, who is one of our coaches now, and Dave said that he had a psychological problem, that he couldn't sleep alone, so he joined us.

When the five of us passed Bill Quinlan's room, Quinlan woke up and said, "I'm going with you." Quinlan's roommate, Dan Currie, told us he was afraid of the dark; he came along, too.

Then there were seven of us crazy little creatures, running up to 280 pounds apiece, sneaking down the hall, tippy-toeing, our shoes in our hands. We made it outside, and, of course, we had no plans. We just wanted to sneak out to see if we could get away with it. We went to the local pizza parlor, and naturally everyone in the town knows every Packer by sight and knows what time we're supposed to be in bed. We sat around eating pizza and giggling like schoolgirls till two or three in the morning. Then we snuck back in the dorm, and we thought everything was beautiful. No repercussions, no fines, nothing. Later, we discovered that Vince knew everything, knew exactly who had gone out and where we had gone and how late we had stayed; he was just holding back his fire until he could catch us in the act.

"People have been phoning me saying that they've seen some of you guys out after curfew," he announced, "but I don't pay any attention to those crank calls."

A few weeks later, Max McGee tried to sneak out alone, and Lombardi caught him, and the following day, at a team meeting, where we try to bring everything out in the open, Lombardi said, "Max, that'll cost you $125. If I catch you again, it'll cost $250."

Perhaps a year or two went by before Max got caught again. And again we had a meeting, and again the emotion, the wrath, the screaming, the hollering, a typical Lombardi production. "Max," Vince shouted, "that'll cost you $250. If you go again, it'll cost you $500."

Max doesn't scare easily.

Another year passed, and Max, a shrewd Texan who loves life, got away with a few. Then one night he snuck out and the Wisconsin state police, who are strict around here, caught him speeding. Max promised them the world if they would keep the ticket out of the newspapers, but they didn't. When the item appeared, Max could hear Coach Lombardi screaming from the training room clear to the dorm: "MAX! MAX!"

The inevitable meeting followed. "MAX!" Vince said. "That's $500." Coach was really shaking; he was very, very upset. He seemed to be fighting a losing battle, and Lombardi does not like to lose at anything. "MAX!" he yelled, "I said that'll cost you $500 and"—Vince turned purple—"if you go again, it'll cost you a thousand." The room was totally silent, hushed. Lombardi stopped shaking and actually managed to grin a little. "Max," he said, softly, "if you can find anything worth sneaking out for, for $1,000, hell, call me and I'll go with you."

You can imagine the temptation it is to sneak out, fifty or sixty healthy young men locked up for two months, in a college dorm. Women, of course, look better every day, and more remote. (Henry Jordan, our great tackle, once spent ten minutes staring at a girl down the far end of the practice field, saying how pretty she looked, and then, finally, he said, "Hey, that's old Olive"—his own wife.) When your teammates start looking good to you, you know you'd better start drinking a lot of soup. Nobody's ever proved it, but we've always suspected that they stock the soup in training camp with saltpeter.

At 6 o'clock tonight, we had our first official training camp meal. I sat with Forrest Gregg, Lee Roy Caffey, and Doug Hart, three Texans with Texas appetites. Gregg and Caffey and I are all over 250 pounds, a little more than we should weigh, and we have to watch what we eat. Doug Hart, a defensive back, weighs about 182 pounds, and if he eats a fantastic amount for a week, he goes up to 182 and a half. Doug had a piece of prime ribs that was as big as all of ours put together. I swear it must have weighed four or five pounds. It was three to four inches thick and about eight inches across, and it had two ribs in it. It was the largest piece of meat I've ever seen, and Doug ate the whole thing, along with some carrots and peas and fruit and butter and rolls and a couple of glasses of milk. I sat there with a very small portion of meat and a little dish of peas and one glass of iced tea, and I ate real slow, to make me feel like I was getting a lot more.

After dinner, Lombardi conducted our first meeting of 1967, and he stressed the tremendous challenge facing the Packers this year. We've won the National Football League championship two years in a row, and since the NFL playoff system was instituted in 1933 no team has ever won three straight championships. We had a similar opportunity in 1963, after we'd won in 1961 and 1962, but then we finished second in our division. Only five other teams have won two straight NFL playoffs, and no other team has done it twice. The challenge of winning a third straight championship is just as important to the players as it is to Lombardi. It's one of the few things that we have left to accomplish, and we want it. We want it badly. We have a lot of pride.

Vince reviewed the training rules and the club rules and the league rules, all of which I think I've heard a million times. He warned us against fraternizing with unknown individuals; they could be gamblers. "You don't sit down and have a drink with somebody if they come up and want to chat," he said. "If they say they're from your home town, and you don't know them, don't associate with them. As simple as that. And don't talk about injuries to anyone, not to your neighbor, not to your father, not to your brother. Don't even tell your wife. Keep your mouth shut."

We've got a saying posted on the wall in our locker room: WHAT YOU SAY HERE, WHAT YOU SEE HERE, WHAT YOU HEAR HERE, LET IT STAY HERE WHEN YOU LEAVE HERE. Vince means that, very, very much, especially when you're talking to the press.

He lectured for a while about the importance of conditioning, about his desire to have every man in top physical shape. "Fatigue makes cowards of us all," he said, quoting his favorite source, himself. "When you're tired, you rationalize. You make excuses in your mind. You say, 'I'm too tired, I'm bushed, I can't do this, I'll loaf.' Then you're a coward." He said that when we don't use our ability to the fullest, we're not only cheating ourselves and the Green Bay Packers, we're cheating the Lord; He gave us our ability to use it to the fullest. "There are three things that are important to every man in this room," Lombardi said. "His religion, his family, and the Green Bay Packers, in that order." Vince means just what he says, but sometimes I think he gets the order confused.

Then Lombardi tried to impress upon all of us, especially the rookies, that every man in the room theoretically was a rookie, that everyone had to prove himself, that no one had his position sewn up. Of course, you look around the room at people like Bart Starr, our quarterback, who was the Most Valuable Player in the NFL last year, and you think that's silly. Nobody's going to take his job away from Bart. But you've got to remember that every day there are young guys out looking for your job, bright-eyed, bushy-tailed, flat-bellied, whippy-wristed college boys.

It seemed strange not to have Paul Hornung and Jimmy Taylor at the first meeting. Paul was here ten years, Jimmy nine, and for several years they gave us the best one-two running attack in pro football.

"We're going to miss Paul Hornung," Lombardi said. "We're going to miss Paul a great deal. He was a leader and he added a lot of spice to professional football. We're all going to miss him."

And then Vince said, "We will replace the other fellow."

He does have a thing about loyalty.

JULY 16

Today was an easy day, our annual picture day, when the publicity photos are taken of all the players. The photographer set up one shot of me and Fuzzy Thurston and Forrest Gregg and Bob Skoronski, the regular offensive guards and offensive tackles. When we posed, Ron Kostelnik, who plays defensive tackle, started laughing at us.

"What's this?" he said. "The over-thirty club?"

Kostelnik's cocky because he's only twenty-seven. Gregg and Skoronski are thirty-three, Fuzzy's thirty-two, and I'm thirty-one; we've each put at least ten years in pro football. We're certainly not young by football standards; we're practically doddering. But it's impossible to overestimate the value of experience in this sport. We have eleven Packers with ten or more years in the NFL; the only other teams with so many veterans are the Cleveland Browns and the Baltimore Colts. Yet, over the past three seasons, with all the old men in our lineups, the three most successful teams in the NFL have been the Browns, the Colts, and the Packers.

Some people say that we're getting too old, that experience can't compensate for our loss of speed and agility, but I refuse to believe it. Sooner or later we'll have to retire and make room for younger men, but I doubt we've reached that point yet.

After the picture session, we had our first major cribbage workout of the year. Lee Roy Caffey and I played against Max McGee and Tommy Joe Crutcher. Tommy Joe's our fourth linebacker, a solid reserve behind Caffey, Nitschke, and Dave Robinson. Tommy Joe's from McKinney, Texas, and he's an intelligent young man, but to amuse himself—and the rest of us—he deliberately plays the country boy. He wears a pair of boots that have to be forty years old; I don't know what holds them together. And he loves to use country sayings. Today, when he was playing Lee Roy, Lee Roy said, "If I could only get a cut," and Tommy Joe snapped back, "If a frog had wings, he wouldn't whomp his ass every time he jumped." When he lost to Lee Roy, Tommy Joe allowed, "I ain't seen nothing like that since Cecil Barlow's cow got caught in the brush." He's beautiful.

JULY 17

We started two-a-day workouts today, and the agony is beyond belief. Grass drills, agility drills, wind sprints, everything. You wonder why you're there, how long you're going to last. The grass drills are exquisite torture. You run in place, lifting your knees as high as you can, for ten, twenty, sometimes thirty seconds. When

Lombardi yells, "Down," you throw yourself forward on your face, your stomach smacking the ground, and when he yells, "Up," you get up quick and start running in place again. We call the exercises "up-downs," and when Vince is in a good mood, he gives us only three or five minutes of them. If he's upset, he'll keep going till someone's lying on the ground and can't get up, till everyone's on the brink of exhaustion.

You try to block out all the pain, all the gasping breaths, block it all out of your mind and function as an automaton. Just up and down and up and down and move and keep moving and legs up and when you feel like you can't get up, like you can't possibly make it, then you've got to get up. You've got to make it. You've got to think, "Get up." We did seventy up-downs this morning, and the only thing that kept me going was that I looked around and saw some of the other guys my age looking worse than me. Then I figured I wasn't going to die.

We've never had anybody die during grass drills, but we had a rookie a few years ago who really couldn't bear the pain.

"What do you do around here to get in shape, Kramer?" he asked me. "I can't take it."

"You just got to push yourself, kid," I said. "If you get a little pain, you just can't think about it. Go on. Don't stop."

"But man," he said, "I see visions out there."

"What do you mean, visions?" I said.

"Visions, man," he said. "I see people walking around in the air."

He got cut a few days later.

We did more than half an hour of exercises today, and afterward Ben Wilson, the big fullback we acquired over the spring from the Los Angeles Rams, told me that the Rams' total exercises consisted of about our first five minutes. Everything we did after that was over and above what he'd ever done with the Rams.

No other team in pro football works as hard as we do. Of course, no other team wins so often, either.

In the morning, we had another lovely nutcracker drill, and I jumped in against Kostelnik, who's about 275 right now, then against Bob Brown, who's close to 280. With pads on, they've got to weigh at least 290 apiece. By the time we finished the nut-cracker, I had two scratches on my forehead and the blood was trickling down between my pretty blue eyes and my tongue was bleeding and Lombardi was smiling. Everything was copasetic, as far as he was concerned.

I ate a little lunch, took a nap, and went back to suffer some more. The second or third play of a scrimmage, Fuzzy Thurston, who's been my running mate at left guard for nine years, hurt his knee and hobbled off the field. Fuzzy's one of my closest friends on the team—on the banquet circuit, he always says, "There are two good reasons the Packers are world champions; Jerry Kramer's one of them, and you're looking at the other"—but I cursed him up one side and down the other and called him a phony. I knew that he wasn't a phony, that he wasn't trying to con anybody, that he really had hurt his knee, but I still couldn't for-give him for leaving me out there alone. The guy who stepped in to take his place was young Gale Gillingham, a rookie last year. Gilly bought 300 head of Black Angus and a thousand-acre ranch in Minnesota after the Super Bowl victory, and he resembles an Angus himself. He's thick-shouldered, powerful, strong. He stepped in and began running plays for Fuzzy and then he ran the wind sprints. For the last nine years, I've been the fastest lineman on the club, and now Gillingham is the fastest lineman on the club. I cursed him for his youth, for his vigor, for his vitality, for all the things I'd lost, and I wondered how much longer I'd be able to play professional football.

After the afternoon session, we had about an hour free, and

Donny Chandler and Zeke Bratkowski, our number-two quarterback, and I went over to the Century Bowling Alley. We go to the
alley every chance we get, but as far as I know, Max McGee and
Doug Hart bowled the only game any Packer ever bowled there.
Li'l Brother beat Max, 97–96, and won $50. We go there mostly
because they serve good cold pop. It's brown pop, and it's got a
head on it.

The only thing that keeps you going is a little relaxation, a few
moments of the civilized world. At times, you really wonder about
football, if you need it, what makes you drive yourself, what
makes you go through all that pain. You look at the people who
come out to watch you practice and you see them in their cool
summer shirts, their golf slacks and their sunglasses, and you wonder, "Why in the world do I beat my head against a 280-pound
lineman for six months every year?"

I don't know, and I guess I never will.

JULY 18

We've got about thirty-five rookies here in camp and no more
than half a dozen of them can possibly make the team. I've taken
a particular interest in one of them, a boy named Dick Arndt.
Dick's from my college, the University of Idaho, and my high
school, Sand Point High School in Idaho. When I joined the Packers in 1958, he was just starting the eighth grade. When I was All-
Pro in 1962, he won the Jerry Kramer Award as the best blocker
on the Sand Point High School team. Now he's twenty-two, weighs
275 pounds, and he's looking for my job. It doesn't make me feel
any younger.

One of the other rookies came over to me today and told me
he had just received a letter from his wife. He was upset because
she told him things at home weren't going quite as well as they ex-

pected. It brought back to me the difficulties a rookie faces trying to make a pro football team. It's not only the newness of the whole system, learning the plays and the players. There's also the attitude among the veterans, the feeling of togetherness that makes the rookie feel like an outsider. He's away from home, away from a familiar setting, and often away from a wife he's just been married to for a little while. It's a miracle that any of them make it. In the past, we've had lots of rookies "domino" out on us, just pack up in the middle of the night, sneak out the door and go home. The strain is brutal, going through all the incredible torture we go through and wondering if you're going to make the club.

The attitudes of the individual rookies are a study. We've got some good, hard-working ones, like this big tackle Crenshaw, who loses four or five pounds every day, and a couple of fast running backs, Claudis James and Travis Williams, but some of them are so cocky it's unbelievable. There's no question in their minds about making the club. They think they're going to be All-Pro the first year.

And then there's the other extreme. One of them got up tonight after dinner, when we always make the rookies sing, and he sang, "I feel so breakup, I want to go home. . . ." I think that's just about the way he felt. He knows he's too light for his position, he doesn't move well enough, he doesn't have a chance of making this club. Next week he'll be back home in Boston or wherever it is.

JULY 19

It's impossible to put into words exactly how horrible I feel. I ache beyond description. We set a record in up-downs this morning. We did seventy-five or eighty of them, to the point where big Leon Crenshaw could barely stand up. His legs were wobbling, his tongue was hanging out, he was just about to fall down when we'd stop and rest a few seconds and then we'd go again.

It was hot, miserably hot, above 90. Until now, we've had a little cloud, a little haze, a little cool breeze, but today the heat just descended upon us and made everything even more unbearable than usual. Guys were hiding by the fence at the end of the field or under the photographer's tower, anywhere, just to get a little bit of shade.

I started thinking back to the high country, which is one of my favorite spots on this world, the high country in Wyoming or British Columbia or Idaho. I grew up in the high country in Idaho and I've gone grizzly-bear hunting in the high country in Wyoming and British Columbia, and my greatest pleasure in these places is to climb for half a day, looking for grizzly, and to come upon a mountain spring. The water has trickled its way out from underneath an ice pack and run through its subterranean tunnels to get to this place where it just seems to spring out of a rock. This water is so unbelievably cold and sweet, almost as if it had sugar in it. I started telling the guys about it today—about being up in the high country with the beautiful, crystal-clear, sweet water rolling out from under a rock—and they wanted to beat me to death.

Fuzzy Thurston was sneaking us ice. They keep ice out on the practice field in case of fractures and sprains and things like that, so Fuzzy put some chips of ice in a towel and stuck it under his sweat jacket and hobbled out to us on his bad knee and gave us the ice, and it was like the sweetest thing I ever tasted.

Somebody once said that a person lives from want to want, or from pain to pain, or something like that. I don't know exactly what he said, but I know what he meant. When you want it desperately, the smallest pleasure, a sip of Pepsi, a sliver of ice, can be so beautiful. You savor it so much. It tastes so fantastically delicious. I can take a sip of Pepsi and almost go into an ecstatic state.

It just is unbelievable, the pleasure you get when you're so hot and so dry and so tired, and you get ice-cold Pepsi and you just roll it around in your mouth, and it's like one of the sweetest things that ever happened to you.

JULY 20

Lombardi put us through grass drills again this morning, another agonizing session, and at lunch today, standing in line waiting for his food, Leon Crenshaw crumpled up and passed out and lay on the floor groaning. We threw an ice pack on him and tried to cool him off a little bit, but we couldn't move him. He couldn't even sit up. Finally, someone called an ambulance, and they hauled Leon off to the hospital. He was totally dehydrated, totally exhausted. He's lost twenty-five pounds since he's been in training camp.

We had our first full-scale scrimmage today, and little by little we're starting to take shape as a football team. We're still missing six of our players. Two of the best rookies, Bob Hyland and linebacker Jim Flanigan, are practicing with the College All-Stars, and three of our veterans, Donny Anderson and Jim Grabowski and Bob Long, are finishing up six-month tours in the Army. Fuzzy's swollen knee kept him out of the scrimmage. When he dropped his hat the other day—gave up his position—Gale Gillingham picked it up and I don't know if Fuzzy'll ever get it back, the way Gilly's going. He looks more and more like an Angus every day. We had starting drills this morning—a practice to see how fast the offensive linemen move once the ball is centered—and Gilly was beating everybody by about three yards. Forrest Gregg looked at me and shook his head. "Jerry," he said, "I guess we might as well give up, we might as well stop trying to beat him, 'cause we ain't going to do it."

Lombardi was not terribly pleased with the first scrimmage, and he did not hide his feelings. "Some of you people are fat," he said at the meeting tonight. "You're fat in the head and fat in the body. You're out of shape. It's an absolute disgrace the way you came into camp. That $25,000 you all made at the end of last year for winning the Super Bowl made you all fatheaded. You're lazy."

He trotted out another of his pet sayings: "The harder you work, the harder it is to surrender." I can't argue with him; often during the season, when we're in a crucial situation, we look back and we remember how hard we worked all through July and we think, "Is that all going to be for nothing?" It really is true that the harder you work at something, the harder it is to quit.

"If you quit now, during these workouts," Vince said, "you'll quit in the middle of the season, during a game. Once you learn to quit, it becomes a habit. We don't want anyone here who'll quit. We want 100 percent out of every individual, and if you don't want to give it, get out. Just get up and get out, right now.

"Your whole life is ahead of you. Most of my life is behind me. My life now is the Green Bay Packers.

"Today we have the beginning of a damned good football team. You looked a little sluggish out there, but toward the end of the scrimmage, it began to look like we may have a damned good football team.

"Gentlemen, we are going to have one."

We will, too, if he has to kill us.

JULY 21

Leon Crenshaw went back to work today, back to grass drills and wind sprints. They kept him in the hospital for only four or five hours, gave him some intravenous injections and sent him back to training camp. Leon's one of about half a dozen Negro rookies trying out for the team, and I was thinking today that when I joined the Packers in 1958, there was only one Negro on the whole team. Now we have eight Negroes in the starting line-ups alone, and four of them made All-Pro last year.

We've got a lot of Southerners, too, most of them Texans, and there's no friction on the field, not even a hint of prejudice. You've got to give Lombardi the credit. The first year he came to Green Bay, we had an exhibition game in the South; the hotels had already been booked—separate accommodations for Negroes and for whites—so he couldn't do anything about that. But when the restaurant where we were eating our team meals told Vince that the Negro players had to enter and leave by the back door, he made certain that every man on the team entered and left by the back door. The next year, when we had to play another exhibition in the South, we all stayed and ate together at an Air Force base. Vince doesn't care what color a man is as long as he can play football, as long as he can help us win, and all the players feel the same way. That's what being a Green Bay Packer is all about—winning—and we don't let anything get in the way of it.

A few years ago, there was some feeling among the white guys that the colored guys weren't so tough under pressure, or something ridiculous like that. I don't see how you can generalize about any group of people, Negroes or Eskimos or Indians or lawyers or soda jerks. Our guys have destroyed that myth about toughness under pressure. They don't make football players any tougher than Dave Robinson, our linebacker, or Willie Davis, our defensive end, or Willie Wood, our safety. Next to Lombardi, in fact, Wood scares his own teammates more than anybody else does. Wood even scares Ray Nitschke. "I hate to miss a tackle," Ray says, " 'cause if I do, I know I'm gonna get a dirty look from Willie. He'll kill you with that look."

Wood, who comes from Washington, D.C., and has spent his

off-seasons working with juvenile delinquents, was a little sensitive when he came to Green Bay in 1960, a little wary. He was looking for signs of discrimination. Once he realized that his teammates accepted him for what he was—a hard-nosed football player—he relaxed. He became a leader. He's one of the guys the rookies turn to for guidance.

We rarely think in terms of race. The way we look at it, guys like Wood and Herb Adderley and Lionel Aldridge aren't Negroes—they're Packers; they're teammates. One night several years ago, Max McGee, from Texas by way of Louisiana, lent his new Cadillac to Nate Borden, the one Negro on the Packers in the late 1950s. Driving back to camp in a rainstorm, Nate skidded and crashed through the window of a furniture store. He phoned Max and told him, apologetically, what had happened. "Well, Nate," said Max, "how much furniture did we buy?"

When Nate was with Dallas in 1960 and the Cowboys played us in Green Bay, we all chipped in and bought him a plane ticket from Green Bay to Dallas so that he could stay in town with us an extra day.

The subject of race generally comes up only in kidding ways. Elijah Pitts—he's our regular halfback, and we call him "ZaSu" and "Gravel" and "Olive" and every kind of pit—likes to sneak up behind me in practice and whisper, "Burn, baby, burn." And after the Watts riots two years ago, Marv Fleming, who lives in California, told us he could get us all good buys on color television sets; he's walking around camp this year with matchbooks labeled "Muhammad Fleming." I once got Marvin a bow and some arrows from my company and took him bow-hunting with me. After a couple of hours, he turned to me and said, "Jerry, it's all coming back to me how to do it—just like my great-great-granddaddy did it."

Marv can take the kidding, too. Once he said to McGee, "Max, I hear you've opened a restaurant over in Manitowoc."

Max said, "That's right, Marvin, why don't you come over for dinner sometime?"

"You serve colored people?" Marv said.

"Sure," said Max. "How do you like them cooked?"

I know it's not great humor, but we're football players, not comedians.

Nobody on the Packers is more popular, among the players and the fans, than Willie Davis, the captain of the defensive unit. Willie's the best storyteller on the team; he can imitate almost anyone. For years he's had the nickname of "Doctor," and once a few of us asked him how he got the name. "Women gave it to me in my youth," said Willie. "They all called me 'Doctor' because I made 'em feel so good." Ever since then, we've called him "Dr. Feelgood."

Willie once walked up to Henry Jordan, a big Virginian who's also on the defensive line, and said, "Henry, do you believe in that segregation stuff?"

"No, Willie," said Henry, "I don't."

Willie brightened. "You don't believe in segregation? Then you must believe in integration."

"Nope," said Henry.

"You don't believe in segregation," said Willie, "and you don't believe in integration. Henry, what do you believe in?"

Henry smiled. "Willie," he said, "I believe in slavery."

Henry was only kidding, I think.

Lombardi chewed on us again tonight. Sometimes he seems to hate everybody without regard to race, religion, or national origin. First, he compared the Packers to a large corporation, like

General Motors or IBM or Chrysler, and he said that a large business cannot tolerate mistakes. "We've got seventy people here in camp now," he said. "If the ones we have can't do the job, we'll get some more."

We held a blitz drill this morning, a drill in which our offensive backs and center try to pick up blitzing linebackers, and Lombardi said the drill was an absolute disgrace. "If you don't do better tomorrow," he said, "then you're not going to get Sunday off. Nothing says you have to have a day off. I give you a day off, and if you don't perform, you don't get a day off."

He went on to say that some of our veterans still weren't in shape, weren't putting out, weren't working as hard as they should. "Some of our All-Pros last year look like hell," he said. "Some of our defensive backs are ducking tackles, actually ducking tackles. We want men here, not just players. Players are a dime a dozen."

Henry Jordan doesn't seem able to make up his mind whether or not he wants to play. Henry's been All-Pro five times, but he's thirty-two now and he's having trouble pushing his body, getting himself in the right frame of mind. He hasn't been working nearly as hard as he could. "Henry," Coach Lombardi asked him tonight, "you ready to play? You going to quit? Or what is it?"

Henry said, "I don't know."

"Well, you better damn well find out in a hurry," Vince said. "Your condition is an absolute disgrace. You ought to be ashamed of yourself."

JULY 22

I found out this morning Henry Jordan quit last night. After the meeting, he went to Phil Bengtson, the defensive-line coach, and turned in his play book, the black, loose-leaf notebook in which we record our plays. Henry told Phil he thought he'd had all he wanted.

Phil had a long talk with Henry and persuaded him to stay in the dorm overnight, and then this morning Coach Lombardi had a long talk with Henry and so did several of the players. It wasn't money that was bothering Henry; it wasn't any one thing in particular. It was just a general letdown in enthusiasm, a feeling that the rewards of football simply weren't worth the pains anymore. A lot of veterans go through the same thing. It takes a great deal to play this game. It takes a lot of pride and a lot of determination and a lot of hustle and a lot of sacrifice, and you have to be in the right frame of mind. You can't do it halfway.

After the talks, Henry decided to stick it out. He's going to try to give it 100 percent from here on in and see if he can do it. I know how he feels. Henry honestly believes he is the best defensive tackle in pro football (he may be the smallest too; by midseason, he's usually down to about 240 pounds); once he decides he wants to play, his pride alone will make him great. We need him. We need him just around the locker room. A year ago, he decided to try some special tonic to bring back all the hair he's lost, and he had to go into the shower each day wearing a pretty flowered shower cap. Some of the rookies were wondering what kind of a team they were trying out for.

Henry joined the rest of us for the workouts this morning, and I guess Lombardi was in a playful mood. He started off complimenting us on our nice sun tans. "Look at the sun tans you're getting," he said. "Isn't that beautiful? Just like a health spa here."

Coach Lombardi smiled. "You know," he said, "a lot of people pay a lot of money to get sun tans like you've got."

The sun was beating down on us, the temperature was close to 92 degrees and, with a heavy scrimmage coming up, none of us was too enthusiastic about our wonderful tans. "Hey, Coach,"

Dave Robinson said, "I've had this tan of mine all my life and I didn't spend a dime for it." Robby spat. "But I've been paying for it ever since I got it," he said.

We scrimmaged, still without Fuzzy and Andy and Grabo and Long and the two All-Star rookies, and Marv Fleming suffered a slight shoulder separation. Naturally, the coaches allowed Marv to finish out the scrimmage. Under normal conditions, meaning anywhere except in the Green Bay Packer training camp, Marv's injury would be called a shoulder separation, and the guy would either have it operated on or set or something. But, in our camp, it's just a slight separation, just a small one, just enough for Marvin to get strapped up and keep hitting the sleds and hitting the dummies.

Coach Lombardi never takes second place when it comes to Oral Roberts or any of the rest of the healers. He can just walk into a training room filled with injured players, and he'll say, "What the hell's wrong with you guys? There's nobody in here hurt." And the dressing room will clear immediately. And all the wounded will be healed.

JULY 23

No practice today, thank God. I thought Sunday would never come. To relax, Don Chandler and I played a golf match against Max McGee and Zeke Bratkowski, our room against their room. Max and Zeke, the old men of the club at thirty-five, have been buddies for ten years, ever since they were pilots together in the Air Force.

We had a time trying to decide how many strokes Max and Zeke ought to give Don and me. We were all lying about how bad we were. Finally, we found an impartial judge, Bart Starr, who people around here consider no less saintly than the pope himself. We knew Bart would never do anybody any wrong, so we let him fix the strokes. Zeke shoots in the middle 70s, I'm around 80, and Max, who's erratic, and Don usually score in the 80s. Bart ruled that they had to give us just three strokes. It wasn't enough. They beat us for about $50 apiece, but it was worth it, just to get away from football.

The coaches made some cuts in the squad today. They dropped seven men, bringing us down to a total of sixty-one, twenty-one more than we can carry during the season. Six of the men who went were rookies; the seventh was Red Mack, the flanker we picked up last season after he was cut by the Atlanta Falcons, the team with the worst record in the league. I remember what a thrill it was for Red to come from a team like that to a team like the Packers, and I'll never forget the look on his face after we won the Super Bowl. He was walking around the locker room in his jockstrap, hugging everybody, tears just running down his face, and he was saying, "This is the greatest moment of my life. I just want to thank every one of you guys."

Red's a hard-nosed guy, the way he threw himself against Ray Nitschke in that first nutcracker drill, and he's spent six years in the NFL. I think he suspected he might go. He just packed up and left without saying good-bye. I don't think he wanted to face anybody. He left me a note saying he'd probably see me at one of the games during the season.

Dick Arndt, the big boy from Idaho, survived the cut without much difficulty. He's a nice kid, with a real good attitude, a real willingness to work, and I'm pretty sure that if he doesn't make our club, he'll play somewhere in the league. The coaches tried him out first at offensive guard, then at offensive tackle, and now they're going to give him a shot at defensive tackle. I'll try to help him, try to give him a few pointers, because I've played against defensive tackles for ten years and I know how they can give a guard the most trouble. But the situation's touchy. First, when Dick was playing offense, he was competing against, besides me, Fuzzy Thurston and Forrest Gregg and Bob Skoronski, and these guys have been my friends for ten years. How am I going to coach this kid to take their jobs? I like the kid and he's close to me and I'm going to try to help him, and yet if I help him too much, these guys are going to start looking at me out of the corners of their eyes. Now, with Dick playing defensive tackle, Henry Jordan's my neighbor and he's been there ten years. I don't think there's any danger of Henry getting cut, now that he's made up his mind to play, but there could be if this kid came on strong, looked great. Then Henry'd never forgive me. The whole relationship between veteran and rookie is strange. You can help to a certain extent, but you can't go overboard.

Arndt's shown one sign of progress. He's earned a nickname. We call him "Herman," from Herman in *The Munsters*.

JULY 24

The drills and the scrimmages seem to follow one after one, day after day, and they all melt into one another. Even the day off didn't help. A fan gave me a ride this morning up the hill to the dressing room from the practice field, and he asked me what time we practice in the afternoon and I couldn't tell him. All I know is that when everyone else moves, I move, and when everyone else files out of the dorm, I file out, and when everyone else gets on the bus, I get on the bus. I get dressed with everyone else and I leave the locker room with everyone else. I really don't know what time it is, what day it is, what year it is. I don't know anything at all.

We sat in a meeting tonight and went over plays and I began thinking, "How many years have I been sitting here in the same damned room in the same damned meeting on a hot summer night looking at plays?" It's been eighteen years, four years in high school, four years in college, and ten years with the Packers. It seems like every hot summer night as far back as I can remember I've been watching coaches draw O's and X's, and I don't know if I ever knew any other existence. I guess maybe this was all I was made for.

My mind drifted, away from O's and X's. Where would I be without football? I didn't choose a profession; it chose me. In high school, I didn't study often, but I wasn't a bad student. I finished in the top fifth of my class. I liked to read even then and, because I was interested in astronomy and in physics, I took every math course and every science course. I thought of joining the Air Force.

The first time I thought seriously about football, I was a sophomore. A coach from the University of Idaho visited Sand Point to talk to our coach and a few of our seniors. I was sitting on the bench and he patted me on the head and said, "You're the kind of boy we want to have at the University of Idaho one of these days."

It was unusual for anyone to notice a sophomore, and, for the first time, I began thinking about college. My family didn't have much money; my father always had to struggle. Nobody else in the family went to college and, without a football scholarship, I couldn't have gone, either. Once I thought of college, I started thinking about playing pro football. I saw the movie, *Saturday's Hero*, with Crazy Legs Hirsch, and I became a Los Angeles Rams fan. In my high-school yearbook, in fact, it says that my ambition was to play professional football for the Los Angeles Rams.

In my senior year, colleges began to recruit me, partly for my football and partly because I broke the state record in the shot put. A bunch of schools wrote to me, but the only ones that really interested me were Washington State College, the University of Idaho, and the University of Washington. I eliminated Washington

State fairly early, but by the time I graduated from Sand Point, I still hadn't chosen between Idaho and Washington.

One of my classmates, Kenny Armstrong, a basketball player, had decided to go to the University of Washington, and as soon as we finished high school, he took a job in Seattle, painting fences—just the sunny side, I think—for a couple of dollars an hour. The university offered to find me a similar job. I happened to mention the offer to someone who had gone to the University of Idaho. The same night, a representative from Idaho came to my home—he'd driven about one hundred and thirty miles—and said he had a job for me in Moscow, the site of the University. I figured I wanted to see both schools anyway, so I took a ride to Moscow. The Idaho people put me on a plane, flew me to Boise, got me a job in a sawmill and a room in a boarding-house and hid me, absolutely hid me. The University of Washington looked everywhere for me. They flew Kenny Armstrong to Boise two or three times in a private plane, but he couldn't find me. I made up my mind I was going to the University of Idaho. My father made up his mind, too; he told me not to talk to anyone from Washington. The Idaho people told me to save my money from my summer job, but, naturally, I spent it all on clothes. At the end of the summer, I went home to Sand Point to pack my winter clothes and move to Moscow.

Kenny Armstrong flew in from Seattle. "It's all settled," he said. "You're going to Idaho and I'm going to Washington. We won't see each other much. Let's go over to Spokane tonight, see a movie and celebrate." We drove down to Spokane, some sixty miles, and he suggested we visit a prominent University of Washington alumnus. I knew I shouldn't, but I agreed to join him. "Why don't you two fly to Seattle this evening, take in a movie and watch practice tomorrow?" the alumnus said. I couldn't resist the chance to fly around.

The next day, the Washington coach took me to practice and made me feel like a big shot. Bert Rose, who's now general manager of the New Orleans Saints, was then the public relations man for the University of Washington. "We guarantee we'll make you All-American in three years," he promised. "We'll push you. We'll do everything we can."

School was starting at Washington a week later than at Idaho, so the Washington people offered to send me on a salmon-fishing trip for a week. They promised me a job in Alaska for the summer. It all sounded beautiful. "My folks want to see me play," I said, "and it's a long way from Sand Point to Seattle." The Washington people said they'd fly my folks free to every home game.

"I'd better speak to my father," I said. "I can't tell him I'm in Seattle. I better go back and talk to him."

The Washington people told me they couldn't get me a flight out of Seattle. They said everything was booked up.

"I got to go," I said. "I'll take a bus or hitchhike or walk."

Finally, they double-checked and put me on a flight to Spokane. There were about four people on the plane. I got home and spoke to my father and he told me I was definitely going to Idaho. He said that if he wanted to see a football game, he could drive there. He made up my mind for me, and I wasn't really upset. I was just happy to be going to college.

The first week at Idaho, I wasn't so happy. I didn't get the job I'd been promised, and I felt cheated. I called Kenny Armstrong in Seattle. "These guys are putting it to me," I said. "I'm not happy."

Kenny telephoned one of the Washington football coaches, who called me and said, "Get in your car and leave. We'll transfer you. We'll have somebody get your clothes. We'll do everything. Just get in your car right now and leave."

I was in the Sigma Nu house at the time, and I guess one of the brothers overheard my conversation. Less than ten minutes after I got off the phone, the Idaho football coach was at the fraternity house. "What's going on?" he said. We got everything straightened out, and I decided to stay at Idaho.

I started in engineering, and in one of my first classes, a professor asked, "Are any of you people in here football players?"

I told him I was.

"It should either be football or engineering," he said.

"I'm in college on a football scholarship," I said.

"Then I recommend that you get out of engineering," he said.

He was an ass for telling me that. I could have stayed in engineering. I could have shifted into a five-year or even a six-year course. I really wanted to be an engineer. But he told me to get out, and I didn't know any better, so I got out of engineering and just drifted for a while, wondering what course to study. I didn't want to go into phys ed. so, finally, I settled on business administration. It wasn't difficult. I skipped a lot of classes and sort of wandered through school. Football seemed bigger and bigger, and I began thinking of myself as a football player first and as an individual second.

I met my wife, Barbara, at a freshman orientation class the first week of school, dated her during my freshman and sophomore years and married her during my junior year. Our first son, Tony, was born the following year. Barbara knew nothing about football when we met, and she really doesn't know too much more now, but she always encouraged me to do what I wanted to do.

I played good football at Idaho. I was never hurt, never missed a single practice. We didn't have too many bodies, and I averaged about 58 minutes a game my junior and senior years. Our best record was four victories, four defeats, and a tie during my senior season, and I made second-team All-Pacific Coast Conference. I might have been All-American at Washington, but I wouldn't have played quite so much football.

During my final year, a few pro football teams wrote to me, requesting my vital statistics. I don't think I ever actually met a pro scout; they didn't bother watching the University of Idaho those days. I was picked by Green Bay in the fourth round of the draft, higher than I'd expected, and I was also drafted by Vancouver in the Canadian league. The Packers were my first choice. I told Lisle Blackbourn, who was then the Green Bay coach, that I wanted a starting salary of $8,000 plus a bonus. We argued. Eventually, I agreed to a salary of $7,750 and a bonus of exactly $250. Just the other day, I heard Gale Gillingham complaining about the contract he signed a year ago. "What kind of bonus did you get?" I asked.

"Fifty," Gilly said. "Fifty thousand. I should have gotten a lot more."

In 1958, I was very happy to get $250.

"Flakey," Bob Long, and "Grabo," Jim Grabowski, reported for practice today, and to make them feel right at home, Vince saved a few extra grass drills and wind sprints for them. Grabo's a little underweight, at 211, because he's been going through Ranger courses in the Army, but we don't have to worry about him. He looks as if he's ready to move into Jimmy Taylor's old job.

We had a good long song session after dinner tonight. Leon Crenshaw, who's got a beautiful deep voice, sang some soul music for us, and then Dick Arndt, who's got the worst voice God ever gave a human being, sang the Idaho alma mater, and I helped him out on the chorus. "Dr. Feelgood," Willie Davis, climbed up on a chair and told everyone about a trip he had taken to New York. Willie wore a black mohair suit and a shirt and tie, and the doorman at his hotel mistook him for an African diplomat they were expecting. The doorman grabbed Willie's attaché case and held an umbrella over his head, and he got the full red-carpet treatment until he looked around and said, "Man, what in hell is going on?" The doorman threw the attaché case back at him.

Then Fuzzy took over. He always sings "He's got the whole world in his hands," always referring to Coach Lombardi. When Paul Hornung came back to camp after being suspended for a year for betting on his own team, Fuzzy got up and sang, "He's got the gamblin' man, in his hands." Often he sings, "He's got the greatest guards, in his hands," and, "He's got the greatest quarterback, in his hands." But tonight Fuzzy led off with, "He's got Henry Jordan, in his hands," and the dining room broke up laughing, and Henry laughed, too, and he wasn't embarrassed anymore about his temporary decision to quit.

JULY 25

I think I'm going to live. Just one more day of two-a-days and then we settle down to normal brutality. Vince is driving us like a madman; he never lets up. It's hard to resist hating him, his ranting, his raving, his screaming, his hollering. But, damn him, he's a great coach.

I spend a lot of time thinking about him these days; I don't have much choice. I wish I could figure him out. I guess, more than anything else, he's a perfectionist, an absolute perfectionist. He demands perfection from everyone, from himself, from the other coaches, from the players, from the equipment manager, from the water boys, even from his wife. Marie Lombardi joined us at a team dinner before one game last year, and the dessert was apple pie. Marie asked the waiter if she could have a scoop of ice cream on her pie, and before the waiter could answer, Vince jumped out of his seat, red in the face, and bellowed, "When you travel with the team, and you eat with the team, you eat what the team eats."

He pays such meticulous attention to detail. He makes us execute the same plays over and over, a hundred times, two hundred times, until we do every little thing right automatically. He works to make the kickoff-return team perfect, the punt-return team perfect, the field-goal team perfect. He ignores nothing. Technique, technique, technique, over and over and over, until we feel like we're going crazy. But we win.

He seems so unfeeling at times. A few years ago, we played the 49ers in San Francisco and I got banged up something terrible. My ribs were killing me. The next day, the team doctor gave me a shot or two of novocaine, and Vince told me to shake it off. We stayed on the west coast all week, and the following weekend I played the full game against the Los Angeles Rams. When we got back to Green Bay, I went to see my own doctor and he told me that I had two broken ribs, that they had been broken for at least a week.

On Tuesday, I showed up at practice and I went up to Vince and I said, "Hey, Coach, you know I played that whole game Sunday with two broken ribs." I thought he'd pat me on the head or say, "Nice going," or something like that. Instead, he just looked at me and said, "I guess they don't hurt anymore."

Yet, in 1964, when I almost died with all my intestinal ailments, Lombardi visited me in the hospital and he told me not to worry, that the Packers would pay my salary in 1964 and 1965 even if I couldn't play and that the club would pay all my hospital bills. He does things like that. His players are his children, and he nurses them when they're sick and scolds them when they're bad and rewards them when they're good.

But his personal feelings, I suspect, end up running second to his professional feelings, which are summed up in another one of his favorite sayings. "Winning isn't everything," he tells us. "It's the only thing."

JULY 26

Two-a-days ended today. I was sure the last twenty-four hours that I had leukemia or polio or some incurable disease because it was such an effort to raise my arm, such an effort to walk, such an effort to climb three or four stairs—not flights of stairs, just stairs. I was so tired I could hardly lift my arms to comb my hair. I was certain that at any moment it was all over for me.

My little six-foot-by-three-foot bed felt like heaven after lunch today, and the cold pop at the Century Bowling Alley tasted so sweet after the afternoon workout. I felt human again.

Donny Anderson, our second-year halfback who wants to grow up to be Paul Hornung, came in from the Army today, and he began telling me about all the business deals he's getting into. When Donny signed with us in 1966, he received a contract worth something like $600,000, including bonus and salaries. He told me today how he negotiated the contract. He started off by talking to Lombardi, and Vince told him that Green Bay would meet any other offer he had. Then he went to Bud Adams, the owner of the Houston Oilers in the American Football League, and Adams told him the same thing. So Donny told Adams that Green Bay was offering him x dollars, and Adams topped it, and then Donny went to Lombardi and told him that Houston was offering y, and Lombardi topped it, and it just kept going back and forth, getting higher and higher. "Hell," Donny said, "at the end, I just couldn't think of anything else to ask for. I couldn't think of anything else I wanted."

I never heard of an offensive lineman having a problem like that.

We had our annual intrasquad game tonight, the offense vs. the defense, in front of more than 30,000 people. We ate breakfast at ten o'clock and the big pregame meal at four, and spent the rest of the day just sitting around, killing time, telling war stories.

It's awfully hard to get ready for the intrasquad game. In order to play pro football, you've got to have a bit of hate in your heart, hate for your opponent. It's not easy for me to hate Henry Jordan, who's my neighbor, and Willie Davis, who's my friend, and I had to play against them tonight. Everybody's always glad when the game's over.

The game is doubly demanding physically, too, because the defense knows your plays almost as well or even better than you do. The other day, I missed a play in practice and Henry Jordan said to me, "Jerry, y'awl supposed to crossblock on that 37, ain't you?"

I said, "How'd you know, Henry?"

"I been watchin' those plays for ten years," he said. "I oughta know them by now."

It's one of those nights when you really can't win. If the offense looks good, Lombardi screams at the defense. If the defense looks good, he screams at the offense. It's impossible for the whole team to look good in his eyes.

Before the game, a man came over to the dorm with a weight-lifting machine he'd invented. He was planning a brochure about the machine and he wanted some of our guys to pose for pictures. I said, "How much?"

"All the guy's got is $150," said Chuck Lane, our publicity director.

I said, "Apiece?"

"No," said Chuck. "For everybody."

He wanted five of us, and that amounted to $30 apiece, and I told him what he could do with his machine. I had just finished posing with seven of the other guys for the 1966 Associated Press All-Pro team, and I guess I was feeling uppity. I growled at the man for offering me $30 because I was feeling pretty valuable.

Maybe half an hour earlier, I'd been sitting in my room and Donny Anderson had come in and he'd said, "Jerry, these hair-tonic people want me to do a commercial for them, and do you think $7,000 is enough?"

That's more than a quarter of my whole salary, and I said, "Yeah, Donny, that doesn't sound like a bad deal to me."

Now here's a guy offering me $30 for a commercial. The guy finally got Forrest Gregg to pose for $40. "What the hell," Forrest said, "I might as well." Forrest had heard Donny Anderson talking about the $7,000 hair-tonic commercial, and he said, "I've been in this league eleven years, and in eleven years I haven't even made $1,000 for all the commercials put together."

I went over to the locker room a little early and went through my ritual. Everyone has his own superstitions. One of mine is that when I tape up my long socks, I've got to use a new roll of tape, and nobody else can use the same roll. I can't take a half-used roll, and once I've used my share, the roll's got to be thrown away. I don't know why. It just has to be that way.

The offense won the game, which wasn't surprising, since the defense never gets the ball, except on punts and interceptions and fumbles. The score was 10–0, but that wasn't quite enough points for Lombardi, and he had a mild hemorrhage after the game. He said the offensive line looked like Maude Frickert and her crew.

My roomie, Don Chandler, missed two field goal attempts, and he felt pretty low. Kicking is a lonely chore; you don't have an opportunity to take out your emotions on anyone else. When I get real upset, real nervous, real emotional, I just hit one of those 280-pound defensive tackles, and all my jitters disappear.

JULY 28

Lombardi, whose generosity knows no bounds, gave us off till noon today, to recuperate from the game last night. Chandler was still feeling blue this morning about missing those field goals, but Zeke and Max and I talked him into renewing the golf match. On the seventh hole, Don pushed his drive into the adjoining fairway and a man walking up the fairway caught the ball right in his head. He needed about eight stitches to stop the bleeding, and Chandler was so shook up he could hardly talk, except to thank all of us profusely for talking him into a golf match.

We worked out after lunch, and Vince suspected that some of us were a little tired. "There's too many deadasses out there," he screamed. "Move. Move. Move." I wish he weren't so excitable.

JULY 29

Lombardi's lungs were going all day long today. "This is a game of abandon," he told the backs, "and you run with complete abandon. You care nothing for anybody or anything, and when you get close to the goal line, your abandon is intensified. Nothing, not a tank, not a wall, not a dozen men, can stop you from getting across that goal line." He stared at the backs hard. "If I ever see one of my backs get stopped a yard from the goal line," he said, "I'll come off that bench and kick him right in the can."

Vince was a little gentler on the rookies; he knows exactly who can take what. "Some of you boys are having trouble picking up your assignments," he said. "It's a tough task. You've got so many plays to learn, so many moves to learn. If you make a mistake, if you drop a pass or miss a block, anything like that, hell, forget it. If we had a defensive back here who felt bad every time he got beat on a pass pattern, he wouldn't be worth a damn. Take an education, but don't dwell on it. Don't let it affect your play. You will drop passes. You will make mistakes." Then he added, "But not very many if you want to play for the Green Bay Packers."

Vince found time to discuss the singing in the dining room, too. "The singing absolutely stinks," he said. "It's lousy. I don't give a damn what you sing, but I want to hear you. I want to see what kind of a man you are." He does, too. He can judge a man by his singing performance. If a man has the guts to stand up in front of fifty or sixty guys and try to carry a tune, especially if he's got a bad voice, the same man is likely to handle himself well in a crucial situation in a ball game. At least he's got poise.

I had dinner tonight with Bob Brault, the doctor who seemed to spend all his time operating on me in 1964 and 1965. He's some guy, a young guy, thirty-five, thirty-six, a heart surgeon. I was one of his first patients in Green Bay. Our team physician sent me to Bob and recommended that Bob operate on me. I had a hard spot just below my breast bone, above my stomach, and the doctors were 95 percent certain it was cancer. They were going to go in and remove as much of my intestines as they could, hoping they'd save me.

We had exploratory surgery and found a large tumor growing on the liver, a nonmalignant growth called actinomycosis, something like a fungus, about the size of a grapefruit. While I was waiting in Bob's office one day, I opened a medical book and read that actinomycosis in the intestinal tract was invariably fatal. He told me the book was outdated. Dr. Brault cut my tumor open and packed it and drained it, and I started to get better, but a few weeks later, when I was about to rejoin the team, I discovered another lump growing down inside my groin, near the bottom of my abdomen. I went out to the Mayo Clinic, and they operated on me and resected my intestine and found I had a leak in it, and they didn't know why. They operated again and put it back together, and four days later I developed postoperative pneumonia and four days after that the intestine burst again, and they rushed me back up to surgery. They performed a colostomy and attached a plastic bag to my side, which I had to live with for several months. Around the end of 1964, I went home and I was down from 255 pounds to 205. A month or so later, I returned to the Mayo Clinic, and they said the wound in my intestine was still draining, and they still didn't know why. They sent me home and told me to wait.

After a few weeks, I talked to Bob Brault and he said, "Look, Jerry, I think we ought to operate again. I think there's a foreign object in there. I don't know what it is, maybe a suture, a sponge, something, something to cause the wound to keep draining."

I certainly didn't want to go through any more operations. I felt I'd had my share already and, besides, I was starting to feel a little stronger. But Bob talked me into it. He set one date, and I didn't show up at the hospital. I was plain scared. Then he set a new date, and this time I showed up. The operation lasted six and a half hours.

Bob found in my intestine, in that area, four splinters varying in length from two and a half to four and a half inches, each about an eighth of an inch in diameter. They were lodged in a muscle-and-scar-tissue area in the lower left quadrant of the abdomen. The slivers had been in there for twelve years. When I was seventeen, I stepped on a plank of wood and the plank flew into my groin. I was operated on then, too, to have the splinters removed, but the doctor must have missed a few.

Brault and his assistants removed the splinters, resected the small intestine and the large intestine and gave me four transfusions during the operation. Ten days later, I was playing golf. I still had to have two more operations, one to fix the colostomy and one to fix a hernia near the breast bone, but everything was beautiful. If it hadn't been for Bob Brault, I wouldn't be playing professional football. I'd be doing something else, like lying in the ground.

Anyway, we had a fine dinner tonight and we had a long talk about our occupations and about life in general. Really, despite all the operations, my life's always been easy. I've never had to fight for anything. I've always been able to do almost anything I wanted to do without great effort, almost naturally. And, maybe because of this, I don't have any definite feeling of achievement. I don't have any great enthusiasm about anything I've accomplished. My life seems a little empty.

Doc Brault was telling me about some of the rewards of his profession. Just last week he was operating on a man, open-heart surgery, and the man's heart stopped in the middle of the surgery, the middle of the operation. The man died right on the table. And somehow Doc revived him and got his heart going again, and now the man is a healthy human being again. It must be tremendous to know you've accomplished something like that.

I went back to the dorm after dinner and called my wife out in Idaho and talked to her for a while, and then I got in bed, and I began thinking about our first exhibition game, against the College All-Stars, and about my particular problem, a 300-pound giant with the unlikely name of Bubba Smith.

THE GREEN BAY PACKERS' EXHIBITION SCHEDULE

DATE	OPPONENT	SITE
August 4	College All-Stars	Chicago
August 12	Pittsburgh Steelers	Green Bay
August 18	Chicago Bears	Milwaukee
August 28	Dallas Cowboys	Dallas
September 2	Cleveland Browns	Cleveland
September 9	New York Giants	Green Bay

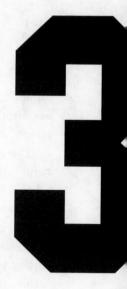

MOCK WARFARE

JULY 31

We start our exhibition season Friday against the College All-Stars, and they're supposed to have the biggest, fastest, and meanest team in the history of the College All-Stars. I suppose I've drawn the biggest and meanest of them all. Bubba Smith, the All-American from Michigan State, is going to be playing defensive tackle opposite me. He's listed at 6'8" and 287 pounds, but I've heard that a month ago Bubba weighed 325 pounds.

I've been watching movies of Bubba in the Senior Bowl game last season, and he looks like he's going to be a handful. I knew he was strong, but I didn't realize he was so fast, so quick off the ball. If he's got a weakness, it's that he doesn't seem to use his hands too well. I'll try to take advantage of that. If a man doesn't use his hands well, you can generally pop him, just drive right into him and push him back. But if he uses his hands well, he can grab you and throw you when you try to pop him, and he'll go right by you.

The Chicago Tribune's doing its best trying to sell tickets for the All-Star game. They're running big ads saying: COME SEE BUBBA SMITH HIT BART STARR. I know that if Bart gets hit Friday night, somebody else is going to get hit a lot harder, and that somebody's me.

I've got to stay between Bubba and Bart, or Coach Lombardi's going to be very, very unhappy with me.

AUGUST 1

Vince is still driving us to get in better shape, pushing us, cussing us, but now that we practice only once a day, it almost seems easy.

Paul Hornung called Max McGee today. Paul's not going to play this year—the doctors told him that if he played, he'd be risking permanent injury to his neck—but he's helping coach the New Orleans Saints. He told Max that the Saints had to do fifteen up-downs the other day, and the whole team damn near mutinied. Nobody trains the way we do.

AUGUST 2

Coach Lombardi lectured today about the importance of the special teams—the punting, punt-return, kickoff-return, and kick-off teams. He said he wanted absolute perfection from every man. We spent a full day last week working on the special teams, making certain that each man knew his assignment exactly. Phil Bengtson is in overall charge of the special units, but his assistant, Dave "Hawg" Hanner, the defensive line coach, handles the personnel. Hawg's responsible for seeing that new men replace injured men, and he's responsible for the teams being ready on the sidelines when they're needed. We try to instill pride in the men on the special teams. Vince always says that a few key plays decide each football game, and you never know when a key play is going to come up.

AUGUST 3

We flew to Chicago today for the All-Star game tomorrow, minus Jim Grabowski, our regular fullback. Jim's on riot duty with the National Guard in Milwaukee, and I don't think they'll let him go just for a football game.

The temperature was around 80 degrees this afternoon, and we had a hot, stuffy bus ride from the airport to the Drake Hotel. The hotel stuck Don Chandler and me in a closet; Henry Jordan and Bart Starr have a three-bedroom suite. Typical. I knew I should have grown up to be a quarterback—or at least to room with one. Chandler and I wandered around a bit, bought some clothes, ate dinner, then got in the bus to go out to Soldier Field for a workout.

Our practice session was beautiful. By the time we reached the stadium, it was raining and thundering and lightning. We all put on sweat pants and rain jackets, instead of our uniforms, and when we left the locker room and hustled out to the field, the lights were off. A groundskeeper came over and said, "Mr. Lombardi, the weather's too bad to use the field. Your team's got to get off."

The groundskeeper shouldn't have said that. Mr. Lombardi told him he could go straight to hell in a hurry. Vince said he'd damn well better get the lights turned on immediately. A couple of other groundskeepers showed up, trying to protect the field, and one of them said they might summon the police to keep us off the field.

"Hell," said Max McGee, "they'd better bring a whole squadron if they expect to keep Vince off the field."

Vince won, of course. The lights were turned on, and we ran out on the field in the rain and thunder and everything. We had a short drill, maybe thirty, thirty-five minutes, mostly throwing the ball around to get a little loose, and then Coach Lombardi gave us a little talk. He reminded us that we are the world champion Green Bay Packers, and that everyone who wears a Green Bay uniform should act like a world champion, on the field and off.

AUGUST 4

Jim Grabowski surprised us and showed up this afternoon. He got to the hotel around 2 P.M., still wearing his Army fatigues, and the doorman told him he had to enter through the rear door. He'd been staying up all night in Milwaukee, tramping around the streets, catching a little sleep in a pup tent. He looked bleary-eyed.

We had our pregame meal at 4:30, four hours before game time, the way we always do. We had a choice of steaks or ham and eggs and a little tea or a little coffee. We're allowed one pat of butter a man. We eat a lot of honey for energy.

The team bus was supposed to leave the hotel for the stadium at 6:20, but almost everybody was on board by 6:05. We operate on Lombardi time, which is about fifteen minutes ahead of all other clocks. If you're only ten minutes ahead of schedule, you're the last one there, and if you're only five minutes ahead of schedule, you're late. Dave Robinson got on the bus tonight at 6:15 and all the coaches glared at him like he was really late. So did all the players. Vince has us even thinking in Lombardi time.

When we got to the stadium, the crowd was starting to gather, and as we climbed out of our bus people began yelling at us, things like, "Bubba Smith's gonna eat you up," and, "You're old," and,

"You stink," nice things like that. We're not too popular in Chicago.

I went in the dressing room, took a nervous trip to the john, then stopped and chatted with Ray Wietecha, the offensive-line coach, and Hawg Hanner. Hawg played opposite me for seven years in practice, and he knows me better than I know myself. He just reminded me of a few basic things, like keep the man away from you on pass protection, nothing startling, just basic to keep me thinking. I got a B_{12} shot from Dr. Eugene Brusky, our team doctor, then swallowed a couple of dextrose pills and ate a couple of Hershey bars, anything to try to get a little extra energy, anything short of straight pep pills, benzedrine or dexedrine. There used to be a lot of pep pills all over the locker room—everybody was gulping them—but they disappeared about five, six years ago. I guess the league was afraid somebody might have an accident with pep pills, so they just vanished completely.

Everybody was nervous and sweating. Without saying it out loud, we all knew it would be terribly humiliating to lose to the College All-Stars. I remembered how nervous I was back in 1958, when I was playing for the All-Stars in this game. We were playing Detroit, and we kept telling ourselves that the Lions put their pants on one leg at a time, just like us, and I guess we were dumb enough to believe it. We beat the Lions, and it was a tremendous thrill, a tremendous introduction to professional football. I don't get thrilled so easily anymore, but I still get nervous.

"It seems like I get more nervous every year," I said to Bart Starr, and he said, "Me, too." Then I said the same thing to Coach Lombardi, about getting more nervous instead of less, and he said, "The more you've got to lose, the more nervous you are about losing it."

Coach himself looked nervous as hell. He walked over to Bob Jeter and said, "You ready to go, Herbie?" Willie Wood and I heard him, so I turned to Willie and said, "Well, Bart, let's go, let's have a great night."

I kept running back and forth between the john and Hanner, asking Hawg the time. I asked him at 7 o'clock and at 7:14 and at 7:18 and at 7:21 and at 7:23 and he gave me the right answer every time. He knows what it's like waiting for a game to start.

Bob Skoronski, the offensive captain, and Willie Davis, the defensive captain, and Coach Lombardi each said a few words—they stressed to the rookies the importance of the special teams—and then we said the Lord's Prayer and went out on the field. On the sidelines, right before the kickoff, I looked up Ray Nitschke and went through my regular ritual with him. He pounded me three times with his fists on my shoulder pads, then smacked me once on the side of the helmet. They weren't just love pats; Ray usually gives me about as vicious a blow as I'll get the whole game. He loosens me up, knocks out some of my butterflies. The rest of the butterflies disappear with the first real contact.

The game got started, and we went three or four plays with the ball, nothing much happening, and I was moving Bubba Smith pretty good. But on the next play, a pass play, he broke through me, to my inside, fast as hell, and got to Bart and threw Bart for a ten-yard loss. I was embarrassed first, and then surprised; I didn't know what I'd done wrong. Bubba was lying on top of Bart and he was saying, "All night, old man, all night long, Big Bubba's gonna be right here on top of you."

Bubba didn't get through to Bart again. He had a little trouble using his hands, and, once I adjusted to his speed, I handled him all right. His quickness, for such a big man, impressed me more than anything else. We won the game, 27–0, but it's hard to say how good we looked. It wasn't much of a contest. Jim Grabowski was our leading rusher, and I suspect we're not going to miss Jimmy Taylor too much.

At one point during the game I was supposed to block on the All-Stars' middle linebacker, and when I hit him, I was surprised by his strength. I expected to knock him down or at least make him give ground, but he stood firm. I didn't know who he was at the time. I just thought to myself, "That kid's strong. I'll have to come in a little lower, a little stronger next time." Later Gilly bumped into him, and when we were standing on the sidelines, talking back and forth about plays that we thought would work, Gilly said to me, "Boy, that Flanigan's stronger'n hell, isn't he?"

"That our kid playing middle linebacker?" I said. I didn't realize the middle linebacker was Jim Flanigan, our rookie from Pittsburgh.

"Yeah," Gilly said. "He's strong."

We had a couple of pretty good collisions during the game. Ben Wilson, our new fullback, got hit hard one time, and he got up kind of wobbly-legged and weak-kneed and wandered back to the huddle, and somebody said, "You all right, Ben?" He said, "Yep," turned around and promptly fell on his back. Passed out. He didn't know where he was or anything, but he was all right later. Another time, Max McGee got hit on the side of his head by a young linebacker, and he staggered over to me and hung on to my jersey for dear life. He laid his head on my shoulder, looked up at me and kept saying, "I knock out, I knock out." His bell had been rung, as we say, so we ushered him off the field. Other than that, we escaped with just minor cuts, scrapes and bruises. I had a little blood running down my forehead, just so I wouldn't forget Bubba.

After the game, we went back to the hotel, picked up our two kids from the All-Star squad, Flanigan and Bob Hyland, and had our buffet dinner, which is a Lombardi tradition after exhibition games. We loosened up, and most of us drank a few beers. Tommy Joe Crutcher called over a waitress and said to her, real slow, "Ma'am, I sure would like to have a pitcher a' ol' buttermilk." It took him about eight minutes to get out the whole sentence. You should have seen that big, tough linebacker sipping his buttermilk.

AUGUST 6

We got back from Chicago yesterday afternoon, all tired out, then had today off. Max and Zeke and Donny and I played golf again, and I started thinking again about our team, about what holds us all together. You could hardly find two guys more different than Zeke and Max. Max is wild, flip, irreverent, uninhibited, always talking about broads, a care-free bachelor. And Zeke is sort of serious, very polite, friendly, hard-working, a real family man. Of course, Zeke has a sense of humor, too, and I suppose there's another side to Max, though he hides it well. Yet they get along perfectly.

Chandler and I are different types, too. Donny's generally quiet, conservative, a brooder sometimes. He keeps an awful lot tied up inside himself. On the other hand, I like to make a little noise. I like to take a chance. I'm more outgoing. I hate to think there might be a party going on somewhere and I'm not at it. Still, we get along fine. There's a sort of mutual respect agreement on the team. Everybody's allowed to have his own feelings, his own preferences, his own way of life, and everybody accepts everybody else's way. Nobody judges anybody else.

I'm not so sure it's a good idea, though, to have Max and Zeke rooming together. They got into our knickers again today, took away a little more of our cash.

AUGUST 7

We started today with a general team meeting, and Lombardi wasn't in too bad a mood. He told us that the College All-Star team was the strongest one he'd ever seen and that some of our offensive linemen looked a little surprised by the strength of the All-Stars. I think he was staring at me.

Then—standard operating procedure—we broke into separate units, the offense and the defense, to watch the films of the All-Star game. Phil Bengtson presided over the defensive meeting, and Vince ran the offensive meeting. The advantages of splitting up are pretty obvious. The defense watches films only of the other team with the ball—either the team we've just played or the team we're about to play. The offense watches films only of us with the ball—or of the defensive team we're about to play. Even when we're not watching movies, we split up into separate groups—usually after a brief general meeting—because the offense and the defense have to discuss different interests, different problems, different strategy.

We spend a large part of our professional lives studying movies, and you can't overemphasize the importance of the movies, or their complexity. In the offensive meeting, for instance, Coach Lombardi will run a play over and over, maybe twenty times, examining each man, explaining what went right, what went wrong, what we might have done instead in the same situation. Usually, we work with sideline movies, but sometimes we see end-zone movies, too. We've also got special reels—one reel showing nothing but goal-line plays, another showing nothing but sweeps, a third showing nothing but off-tackle plays.

It takes years to learn exactly what to watch for in the movies—how to look for your own weaknesses, how to look for your opponent's weaknesses. The rookies and the second- and third-year men have to depend a great deal upon the coaches' comments and upon advice from veterans; their eyes aren't trained to follow the fast action on the screen. It took me four or five years before I felt that I really knew what I was seeing, before

I felt confident enough to suggest alternate plays and alternate blocking patterns.

Lombardi spotted one thing in the movies today that he didn't like at all. "I must be a lousy teacher," he said. "For nine years, I've been trying to teach you guys to block with your face, with your forehead, not to put your head down and block with your shoulder. For nine years, I've been telling you that there's no place in this league for a shoulder block. But every year you guys have to learn it for yourselves. I must be a lousy teacher."

AUGUST 8

Before we worked out today, Coach had a few more comments about the All-Star game, and he wasn't in such a good mood. First, he said that the halfbacks were absolutely useless. Then he said that the blocking by our flankers was an absolute disgrace. In fact, he said, the blocking by everybody was a disgrace. Usually, we get graded for our blocking, and Vince reads the grades out loud at a meeting. Today he said he was so embarrassed by our blocking grades that he couldn't even read them out loud. Instead, he wrote them down on little slips of paper and folded up the slips, put our names on them and handed them out.

I got a 54 for blocks on running plays and a 67 for blocks on passing plays. A passing grade is supposed to be 65 percent on runs and 85 percent on passes, so obviously Vince thought my blocking was miserable. But I checked around and I found out that my grades were about average for the game.

The coaches can make the grades come out to almost anything they want. The grading has to be pretty subjective, but even though we all know that the grades aren't very accurate, they do accomplish their purpose. For instance, if Gillingham gets 75 percent on the runs and 90 percent on the passes, and I get 65 percent on the runs and 80 percent on the passes, my pride's going to be hurt, and I'm going to block a lot harder the next week.

Actually, it's the coaches' comments that have more effect than the grades themselves. Every time you're in a game, an exhibition or a regular-season game, you're aware of Tuesday afternoon at the movies. You know that camera is up there taking down every move you make, every single mistake, and if you miss a block, even in the middle of an important game, your first thought normally is, "How's that going to look in the movies?"

AUGUST 9

Coach Lombardi gave us one of his periodic lectures today on life and football. "Winning is not a sometime thing here," he said. "It is an all-the-time thing. You don't win once in a while, you don't do things right once in a while, you do them right all the time.

"There is no room for second place here. There's only one place here, and that's first place. I've finished second twice in my time here, and I don't ever want to finish second again. There's a second-place bowl game, and it's a hinky-dinky football game, held in a hinky-dinky town, played by hinky-dinky football players. That's all second-place is: Hinky-dinky."

Vince has got to be the only person I've ever met who could use a word like "hinky-dinky," talking to football players, and get away with it.

He reminded us, for maybe the hundredth time, that professional football is not a nice game. "Some of our offensive linemen," he said, "are too nice sometimes. This is a violent sport. That's why the crowds love it, that's why people love it, because it's a violent sport, a body-contact sport. We're a little too nice. We've got to get a little meaner."

Then he made his regular speech about outside interests. "I want every minute of your day to be devoted to football," he said. "This is the only thing you're here for." He looked straight at me, with my bow-and-arrow factory and my diving business, and straight at Fuzzy, with his restaurants, and he was dying to say something. But he can't be as strict as he used to about outside interests, now that he's got so many of them himself.

After dinner, Coach was still steaming, and when a few guys got up to leave, he said, "What the hell is going on here? Sit down. Let's have some singing." Everybody was kind of down, kind of beat. Then a couple of us veterans got up and sang, and then we had the rookies sing, and then all the veterans, and then just the veterans over thirty, and Max got up and said, "How 'bout the veterans over thirty-five?"

So Max and Zeke sang by themselves, and then all the coaches sang, and then the trainers, and finally we all sang together, making a horrible racket, and the whole atmosphere changed, the whole mood of depression lifted. We were a team again.

AUGUST 10

Hawg Hanner put on his usual show this morning waking everyone up. He's the regular 7 o'clock wake-up man. He is one of the strongest people I've ever seen—he once played a full game twelve days after he had an appendectomy—just a big Arkansas farm boy. He's used to getting up early in the morning, and he's always jovial. When I get up, I'm in a world of trouble. It takes me about five minutes before I walk properly. I look like a mechanical man. My ankles creak and crack and I walk kind of stiff-legged.

Hawg came through the dorm today full of cheer. "Up,

Stumpy," he yelled to Fuzzy Thurston, who does resemble a stump. "Come on, Stumpy, get yourself up." Then he hollered to Doug Hart, "Douglas, get yourself up, boy, lift yourself up out of that bed." And he snuck right up to the side of my bed and stage-whispered, "Santa Claus is coming, Jerry, hurry up now, out of bed, Santa Claus is coming." He had a big chaw of tobacco in his cheek, and a big smile on his face, and I couldn't hardly get mad at him.

But I was dead tired all day long, and we had a big workout. We're missing Bob Long, who hurt his knee Monday and had to have an operation today. Bob Hyland, the big rookie from Boston College, is working out at offensive tackle, but Coach has told the press that he can play any offensive line position, so I suppose I'll have to keep an eye on him.

We're playing Pittsburgh Saturday night, and tonight, for the third time this week, we looked at movies of last year's exhibition game against the Steelers. I came into the meeting room worn out, and headed straight for the one big easy chair in the back of the room. It's always mine, if I want it; when I don't use it, Jim Grabowski takes it.

Coach Wietecha was running the projector, and as soon as he started the film, I was so tired I fell asleep. Chandler poked me a few times, but I kept dozing off. Finally, Wietecha turned off the projector, and Bob Schnelker, the end coach, got up to the blackboard and began diagramming some special goal-line moves for the receivers, which had nothing to do with me, and I fell back to sleep.

I don't sleep very often during the movies. Whenever there's something I feel I don't know, I'm very attentive. I study the man I'm going to be playing opposite. I study his feet, his hands, everything about him, looking for any weakness or any signal that'll tell me what he's going to do. But I had already seen this movie twice before, and, besides, the Steeler I was going to be facing, a 280-pound tackle named Ken Kortas, wasn't even playing in the movie. He was just a substitute last year.

So I couldn't stay awake. And I suppose the fact that Coach Lombardi wasn't in the meeting room made it a little easier for me to get my beauty rest.

AUGUST 11

We cut three rookies this week, and now we're down to fifty-four men, fourteen more than we can carry during the season. It's always a bad scene, when a man gets cut. Pat Peppler, our personnel manager, usually has to do the dirty work. He'll tell a guy to come see him and to bring along his play book. When you're told to bring along your play book, you're in trouble. You can forget it. Once in a while, the guys kid a little, "Go see the old man and bring along your play book," but we don't joke too much about it. Getting cut from the Packers is a very serious, and expensive, thing.

When you cut a man, you ask waivers on him, and if no other National Football League team claims him, you can put the man on your taxi squad. Members of the taxi squad don't count on the official roster and they can't play in games, but they practice with you. If you put a man on waivers and another NFL team claims him, you can withdraw him from the waiver list. But you can only withdraw him once. The second time a man is claimed, he's gone.

We're in a strange situation. We have a lot of excellent prospects, and there are many we'd like to put on waivers and pass through and keep on our taxi squad. But we put nine or ten men on the waiver list the other day, and everyone was claimed. We pulled all of them off except three. The next time we put those guys on the list and they get claimed, we lose them. We'll probably end up with just four or five on the taxi squad.

We traded Kent Nix to Pittsburgh last week for a future draft choice. Kent's a quarterback from Texas Christian University, a fine boy who played on our taxi squad last year. This year, with Bart and Zeke backed up by Don Horn, our rookie quarterback, Kent just became expendable. I saw Lombardi saying good-bye to him. He went up and shook Kent's hand and wished him well, and then, after Kent took off, Vince sort of hung his head for a while. It bothers him to lose one of his boys.

When a reporter asked Bill Austin, the Pittsburgh head coach, why he picked up Nix, Bill, who used to be our offensive-line coach, said, "Well, you know damn good and well that he's been properly trained, that he's got a great mental approach to the game." Most of our players fall into that category. We've all been disciplined and indoctrinated and brainwashed.

AUGUST 12

I tried to take it easy today before the game with Pittsburgh, but I had to spend a couple of hours this morning with my income-tax man, an attorney who's been working on my deal with Kraft Foods. If the response to the portrait program is anything like the Kraft people expect, I could make more than a hundred thousand dollars from it this year. My attorney and I are trying to figure out how I should take the income.

We also discussed a chain of steak houses here in Wisconsin that Willie Davis and I are investigating. Some people approached Willie and me about investing in the operation and promoting it. They gave us brochures, outlining their plans for franchises, and my attorney's going to look over the brochure and check out some of the people in the organization. I'm not sure whether I want to get involved in the restaurant business right now.

Donny Chandler and I spent most of the afternoon just lying around the room, listening to music and trying to sleep. I drove over to the stadium at 6 o'clock, two hours before game time, and Ron Kostelnik was already fully dressed, ready for the game. Each player has his own ritual, and this is Ron's: Two hours before a game, he's dressed and taped, and he lies down and tries to sleep.

Pretty soon, the rest of the guys began running in and out of the training room, grabbing handfuls of vitamin pills and wheat-germ pills and dextrose pills and salt pills. I guess Jacqueline Susann would have a ball in our training room.

I lay down on a table and had Bud Jorgensen, who's been a Green Bay trainer for about forty years, tape my ankles. That's one of my superstitions. Only Bud tapes me, never anybody else. We were kidding each other—I always accuse him of keeping a bottle hidden in the training room—and I happened to look over at the next table and Max McGee was sitting there with his foot up. I could see his high sock, a green sock with gold piping; it comes up to the knee and it has a stirrup that goes under the foot. Max had the stirrup off, the sock pulled up to his knee, and the doc was getting ready to give him a shot of novocaine.

I was a little surprised. Max's been playing in the NFL for twelve years, and it's kind of unusual that he'd be taking novocaine for an exhibition game. You save that for big games. But Max had a bruised heel and some problems with his ankle, so he decided to get a shot. When the doc stuck in the needle, Max's face grew a little red, and he clenched his teeth, and I looked just over his head and saw a rookie named Stan Kemp standing there staring. As the needle went into Max's ankle, Kemp kept getting paler and paler, and his baby face kept getting younger and younger, and at the same time Max kept getting darker and darker, and his face kept getting older and older. It was a strange contrast. I found out later that Stan Kemp was in the third grade the year Max started playing professional football. (Incidentally, when Donny Chandler started playing for the New York Giants in 1956, Tommy Brown, who plays regular safety for us now, was the visiting team's clubhouse boy for the Washington Redskins; Tommy used to clean Donny's cleats.)

Max is an amazing athlete. He's got so much ability it's unbelievable, more than anybody I've ever known, and he's never, in twelve years, used all his ability. He's operated on about a quarter of it, really. One of the reasons that he's such a great clutch performer—he scored two touchdowns in the Super Bowl last year, at the age of thirty-four—is that he has all of this excess natural ability. When the circumstances call for it, he can reach down and come up with the big play. He's a rare athlete. Show him any sport—from golf to Ping Pong to pool—and he'll excel at it.

After I got into my uniform, I looked at the program for the game and saw a list of the 1966 All-Pro Packers, eight of us. Six of the eight made all three major All-Pro teams, Associated Press, United Press, and Newspaper Enterprises Association. I made only the AP and UP teams; I missed the NEA team, which is chosen by a vote of all the players in the NFL.

I felt badly about not being on the NEA team, and I think I know why I didn't make it. I have a habit of letting down against a weak team. I just couldn't get excited, for example, about playing Atlanta last year. Their coach, Norb Hecker, is a good friend of mine, and so is Johnny Symank, their defensive-backfield coach; in fact, Symank's wife had been visiting my wife the week before the game. We beat Atlanta, 56–3, and I didn't do a thing. When the Atlanta players voted for the All-Pro team, they left me out.

I began thinking to myself, I really better play well against

Ken Kortas, the Pittsburgh tackle, if I want to make the NEA All-Pro team this year. I've got to impress him. I've got to get his vote. I've got to knock him on his ass. That's the best way to impress a guy in this game. I really wanted to have a good game, partly for Kortas and partly for Bill Austin, my old coach, the guy I almost punched during my contract fight in 1963.

Bill and I were actually close friends. When he was here, one of my pregame rituals was to walk up to him about five minutes before we went on the field and to say, "Bill, any words of wisdom?" He'd always say, "Keep your head up, move your feet, and be alert." So tonight, before the game, I passed Austin on the field and I said, "Any words of wisdom?" And he said, "Keep your head down, don't move your feet, and don't be alert."

I must have been overeager, because I didn't have a good game. I looked terrible in the opening series. We opened with a 42-trap, a running play through the middle. I'm supposed to pull out from right guard, cut across the field and trap the right end. I missed the guy completely. Later on, I got caught offside, a real dumb-ass play; I can count the penalties I've had in ten years on one hand.

We played sloppy, but we still won 31–20. I'd just as soon forget the game, but I won't forget one play. I blocked the middle linebacker, kept him out of the play, and when the play was over, he started to fall. As he did, he grabbed my shoulder pads, swung me around and threw me to the ground. No reason at all. I got up and looked him in the eye, and he was grinning and giggling like a damn fool. I don't know his name, but he was number 50. We play the Steelers again in December, and it's an easy number to remember.

Bart Starr raised his voice tonight, which is very, very rare. The only time he ever raised his voice to me in a game was five years ago, and then he said, "C'mon, Jerry, let's go." After that game, he apologized, "Gee, I didn't mean to holler at you." But tonight Steve Wright, our reserve tackle, was blocking Lloyd Voss, the Steelers' defensive end, and on one play Voss got through to Bart late, just after Bart had released a pass, and slammed an open hand into Bart's face, hitting him in the mouth, not vicious, but hard. When we got back to the huddle, Bart looked at Steve very sternly and said, "Steve Wright, you ought to be ashamed of yourself, letting Lloyd Voss in here. I'll tell you one thing. If I see that guy in here once more tonight, I'm not going to kick him in the can. I'm going to kick you in the can, right in front of 52,000 people." For Bart that was very strong talk. Lloyd Voss never got through again.

There usually isn't too much talk in the huddle. Bart calls all the plays himself—I can't remember Vince ever sending in a play with a substitute—and he just doesn't have any time for discussion. Once in a while, when we need long yardage on third down, Bart'll ask the receivers if they've got a maneuver they think'll work, if they've set up any particular pattern. He'll listen to a suggestion from a veteran receiver, from Boyd Dowler or Carroll Dale or Max McGee. The rest of us, if we've got something to tell Bart, we generally wait and tell him on the sidelines, when the other team's got the ball.

Kent Nix got into the ball game tonight for Pittsburgh, when we were leading 24–13, and on his first play from scrimmage, he threw a 72-yard touchdown pass. I was glad to see him do it. I wouldn't have been so happy if it had been a league game, but it was just an exhibition and we were winning, anyway. I think Kent'll be playing a lot for the Steelers this year.

We had our usual buffet after the game, and I invited a few friends over for the meal, three or four of them, which reminded me of the first buffet we had, back in 1959, Lombardi's first year as head coach. We played an exhibition game in Portland, Oregon, and my relatives came in from Idaho and from Seattle, a total of sixteen of them, and none of them had ever seen me play professional football before. I was a little leery about bringing all the aunts and uncles to the buffet. I went up to Vince and I said, "Coach, I've got a lot of my relatives here and—" Before I could finish, he said, "Well, bring 'em all in. Bring 'em all in." And he took them all and led them up to the head of the buffet line and filled their plates and sat down at a table. Some brewing company had donated half a dozen bottles of champagne, and, naturally, the veterans had confiscated the champagne. Coach Lombardi went over and took back a couple of bottles, popped the corks and poured champagne for my folks and all my aunts and uncles. He made them feel like a million dollars, and, as for me, suddenly I was no longer bothered by how hard he had been driving us all through training camp.

AUGUST 13

Before the offense watched the movies tonight of the Pittsburgh game, Vince gave us a little lecture. He started off with a few words of praise, then got himself worked up. Coach said we blocked well and hustled well, but we made five big mistakes. We gave the ball away three times on fumbles, twice on interceptions. "We had two fumbles between the center and the quarterback," he said, "and that's really a dumb play. That's worse than high school. There's no place around here for fumblers and bumblers and stumblers. If you fumble, forget it. You're going to be gone." Travis Williams, the rookie halfback, looked a little nervous. He fumbled once against the Steelers. He's got a world of speed, but he has trouble holding on to the ball.

Lombardi told Donny Anderson to stop trying to jump over the line of scrimmage or he'd get killed, and he yelled at the defense for jumping offside on a fourth-and-four play. "That's just plain stupidity," he said. "Out-and-out ignorance."

We're trying to put a new look in our offense, trying to use the extra speed we've got this year. We're using a back in motion and some pitchout plays, which tend to draw the defense offside. But they can confuse the offensive line, too. The time I was offside last night, I heard footsteps behind me and I jumped. "If we don't have the intelligence and poise and maturity to go with this motion offense," Vince said, "then we'll just stop it and go back to what the hell we've always done. We've made a living here by not making mistakes. We're a team that's noted for not making mistakes." His voice went up a few decibels. "And we will not make mistakes." I believe he means it.

Then we watched the Pittsburgh movie, and I think I would've rather seen a good Western. I especially didn't enjoy the opening scene. The movie began with that 42-trap play, the one in which I missed the Steeler right end. I thought it was a pretty terrible way to start a movie, but, apparently, Vince didn't agree with me. He liked that scene so much he showed it to us nineteen times, and nineteen times I saw myself miss that block. The next time we run a 42-trap, I suspect I'll block a little better.

AUGUST 14

We had a light workout this morning, and both ZaSu Pitts and Ron Kostelnik—we call him "The Culligan Man," or just "Culligan," because he's always searching for water—brought their little sons to the locker room. The boys are both around three or four years old, but they're certainly different types. Ronnie Pitts is an extrovert, full of pep, jumping around, and Mike Kostelnik is very shy and quiet. They were standing around while we got dressed, and Jim Weatherwax, our big reserve tackle from Los

Angeles, went over to Ronnie Pitts and said, "Come on over here and say hello to Mike Kostelnik." Ronnie bounced over and stuck out his hand to shake hands, but little Mike sort of shrunk away. He didn't know what was going on. And Elijah said, "See, Kos, your kid won't shake hands with mine. You're prejudicing him at a real early age."

Vince gave us the afternoon off, and the regular fearless foursome went off to play golf again. I started off horribly, 5–7–7, and after that, even though I drove all the way to a 319-yard green and just missed my putt for an eagle, I wasn't scoring well.

My short game, in particular, was atrocious, and on the back nine, Zeke gave me a few lessons with the pitching wedge. We were playing for cash—the match can easily run $25, $30 a man—and it's pretty competitive. But still Zeke wanted to help me improve my game, even if it might cost him money. It did cost him money, as a matter of fact. Chandler and I got hot on the last few holes and made back a little of the money we've been contributing to Zeke and Max.

After the golf match, we went over to the Century Bowling Alley for some cold pop, and there were about a dozen of the guys there, mostly veterans and a couple of rookies, including Don Horn, the quarterback from San Diego State. He's a little hard to figure out. He's a bachelor, drives a Jaguar, dresses flashy, seems like a cocky kid, not in the Bart Starr–Zeke Bratkowski quiet, unassuming mold. But the other day he walked up to one of the veterans and said he'd heard that some of the veterans thought he was cocky and he didn't want them to get that idea. He's starting to come around.

When we entered the Century, Horn asked Max to be his partner in a pool game. On most teams, from what I hear, a rookie would just get chased away from the table. But we don't haze our rookies; we don't try to treat them badly. Maybe we just figure that all of us get treated badly enough by Lombardi. Anyway, Max agreed to take Horn as his partner, and they played a game together, and lost, and then we went back to the dorm for dinner and for our first meeting on the Chicago Bears, who'll be our opponents this Friday in Milwaukee.

Lombardi spent forty minutes tonight telling the whole offense about the Chicago defenses, mostly their special defenses against our passing plays. He kept talking about the Sarah and the Mabel and the Frank, all defensive-backfield maneuvers, and I couldn't give a care less. In the offensive line, we're just concerned with those linemen up against us, and we don't care what the defensive backs are doing. We don't care if they run to the john in the middle of a play.

The fans get excited about code words like Sarah and Mabel, but we don't pay much attention to them, not even to the defensive line's code. They use signal words, like Indiana, when they want the defensive tackles to come inside, or Ohio, when they want them to go outside, but there's a million things to do up there on the line without worrying about what the defense is saying. They're calling their signals at the same time you're calling your offensive plays, and you've got to listen to your quarterback. You can't listen for Indiana or Ohio or Mabel or Frank or anything like that.

If you pick up any tips at all, you pick them up from the man in front of you. The defensive left tackle, in my case. Maybe his right foot is back two or three inches if he's going to charge to the right, to the inside. Or if he wants to go to the outside, he may bring his right foot up a little bit. He really doesn't have much choice; he can only charge inside or outside. Once in a while, when you've got a long count, say a three or a four—which means the ball will be centered on the third or fourth "hut" from the quarterback—the tackle'll lean on two, on the second "hut," showing you which way he's going to go. But, still, even if you know which way he's going, the big job is to stop the man.

I was reading George Plimpton's book tonight, *Paper Lion*, and he wrote about the friction between Detroit's offensive and defensive units, the rivalries within the team, something which we make a conscious effort to avoid. It's very, very easy for the offense to get mad at the defense, and vice versa. When Dan Currie played with us, he used to get very emotional during a game, and he'd come off the field cussing the offense. But to minimize the friction—and we do minimize it—Lombardi deliberately makes us think of ourselves as a unit, as a group of forty men, not as an offense and a defense.

AUGUST 15

I've got a big kid by the name of Frank Cornish playing against me this week. He's about 6'6", maybe 285 pounds. He was a rookie last year, didn't play too much, kind of a humpty. He didn't move too well laterally, and I popped him a few times, put my head right in his chest and I bounced him around a little. I was able to pop him and move away from him without too much difficulty. You can't do that against the great tackles, like Merlin Olsen of the Rams or Alex Karras of the Lions; they've got so much agility and speed they'll slip past you.

Right now, I'm planning to play Cornish the same way I did last year, popping him, blocking aggressively, but I may have to adjust in the game. Most men improve quite a bit when they're playing regularly. Cornish may have picked up some new moves. He may be quicker. I like to think every man I'm going to play against is terrific. It makes me play harder. Besides, I hate to say anything unkind about an oponent, not because I'm such a nice guy, but because I don't want to upset him. I don't want to give him any extra incentive against me. Our whole team feels this way; the worst thing we'll generally say about an opponent is that he's a fine football player. We always say so-and-so is very tough. We always say so-and-so is a real competitor. We always sweet-talk our opponents—usually to death.

Tonight we got the list of plays we'll be running against the Bears. We've got a total of about sixty or seventy-five running plays, and an equal number of passing plays. But for each game, the coaches pick out twenty-five or thirty plays that they think will work well against the particular defenses the opposition uses.

For example, one of our favorite plays is our 49, our sweep to the right. In the huddle, Bart'll call, "Red right, 49 on two." The color indicates the position of our running backs; we have red, brown, and blue formations, and in the red formation the running backs are split, one behind each tackle. "Right" indicates the strong side, the side on which our tight end will line up. "Forty-nine" means that the "four" back, the running back on the left, will take the ball into the "nine" hole, the area outside the right end. "On two" means that the ball will be snapped the second time Bart says "hut." On this play, I pull out to my right and go after the left cornerback.

If Bart comes up to the line of scrimmage and sees the defense set up to stop a 49, he'll call an "automatic"—also known as an "audible"—a signal to change the play. Before he says "hut," he always calls out two numbers, first a single-digit number, then a double-digit number. If the single-digit number is the same as the snap signal—"two," in this case—that means he's calling an auto-matic; the double-digit number that follows is the new play. In this case, if he comes up to the line of scrimmage and says, "Two-46-hut-hut," I know that the 49 is off, that the new play is a 46, the four back into the six hole, between the left tackle, and the left end, and that, instead of pulling to my right, I have to pull to my left. Then I can either work a double-team with the fullback on the right linebacker or, if I see that the fullback is going to force the linebacker outside, I can cut up through the six hole and block the middle linebacker.

I realize it sounds complicated—it even looks complicated on paper—but after a while it all comes very easily, very naturally. Vince likes to make certain that we do the right thing naturally, that we don't stop to think, that we just react automatically.

We got more than just our plays tonight. We got a lot of hell, too. We'd had a pretty miserable practice this morning. No one felt like wearing pads; everybody looked dead. The Bears like to blitz, to shoot their linebackers, so we had a long blitz drill, practicing our passing attack against blitzing and red-dogging linebackers. The drill is mostly for our offensive backs, getting them to move around to pick up the charging linebackers, so the linemen generally sort of play brother-in-law. The offensive linemen take it a little easy. You don't go 100 percent. You just kind of practice your steps a bit, keep your head up and your feet moving. And the defensive linemen don't really try to get to the quarterback. If they've got you beat, they move back in front of you, so that you don't look too bad. The coaches were taking movies of us today, and we didn't know it. Lombardi saw the movies this afternoon and reviewed them for us tonight. He panned the whole show.

"We are not going to have half-assed performances around here," he said. "You all looked like a bunch of cows. You're out of your mind if you think you can win like that." He really got on Lee Roy Caffey for loafing when he was blitzing. "Lee Roy," he said, "if you cheat on the practice field, you'll cheat in the game. If you cheat in the game, you'll cheat the rest of your life. I'll not have it." Then he cussed Marvin Fleming up one side and down the other and said he was going to give Marvin one more chance and that if he didn't produce, he was going to trade for a new tight end. Vince is a little hard on Marvin sometimes.

AUGUST 16

More than anything else, I suppose, Lombardi is a psychologist. Maybe a child psychologist. Today he kept telling Bob Hyland, the big rookie, how great he is. "Fantastic, Hyland, fantastic," he kept saying.

Hyland has come in for a lot of praise from the old man—and only from the old man. Actually, he's made a couple of blocks that were sort of medium, semi-good, and Coach has told him that they're great. Lombardi has a habit of praising the young people when they do anything at all. He was that way with Gillingham last season—everything Gilly did was fantastic—but now he's riding Gilly every day, chewing him, chewing him, chewing him. The courtship is over, the romance is gone, and Gilly's got to work his ass to the ground. The strange thing, and maybe it isn't strange at all, is that Gilly is twice the ballplayer this year that he was last year. He's taken Fuzzy's job away for good.

Vince has always chewed Fuzzy and me pretty hard, and once we stopped and figured out why. First, Vince was an offensive coach before he was a head coach, so he's tougher on the offense. Second, he played the line himself, so he's tougher on linemen. Third, he was a guard, so he's tougher on guards. And fourth, from my own point of view, he was a right guard, so he's tougher on me than on anybody.

In 1959, his first year, he drove me unmercifully during the two-a-days. He called me an old cow one afternoon and said that I was the worst guard he'd ever seen. I'd been working hard, killing myself, and he took all the air out of me. I'd lost seven or eight pounds that day, and when I got into the locker room, I was too drained to take my pads off. I just sat in front of my locker, my helmet off, my head down, wondering what I was doing playing football, being as bad as I was, getting cussed like I was. Vince came in and walked over to me, put his hand on the back of my head, mussed my hair and said, "Son, one of these days you're going to be the greatest guard in the league." He is a beautiful psychologist. I was ready to go back out to practice for another four hours.

Coach is working some of his psychology on us right now. We were all up for the College All-Star game, really high, physically, mentally, and emotionally. I think Vince is pushing us extra hard now, trying to wear us down, trying to take away our fine edge. He knows you can only hold that edge for a certain length of time. He hasn't been telling us lately what a great team we can be. My suspicion is that he wants to whip us down and keep us down for a few weeks, then bring us back up just before the start of the season.

I'm pushing myself to get ready for the opening of the season. I'm constantly asking Ron Kostelnik, who plays opposite me, "Can you read me? Can you tell what I'm going to do?" I'm striving to keep my stance exactly the same, whether it's a running play coming up or a passing play, whether I'm pulling left or pulling right. I've got a right-handed stance, with my right foot back a bit, and, because of this, I sometimes lose a little speed going to my left. But I don't want to compensate by moving up my right foot, or the tackle'll know which way I'm going. I also concentrate on keeping the same amount of weight on my hands whether it's a running play or a pass. I can't be leaning backwards, giving the tackle a key, indicating a passing play.

The defensive men can pick up little things. When Bill George was playing for the Bears, he used to be amazingly quick off the ball against us, always anticipating the snap, and we finally figured out the problem. Our center, Jim Ringo, would keep his hands slightly loose on the ball, and then, just before the snap, his hands would tighten up. George was reading Ringo's hands and moving when the fingers tightened. Once we caught on, we stopped George pretty quick. Ringo would squeeze the ball one count early, and George would jump offside. After a few penalties, George stopped trying to read Ringo's hands.

You often try to fake men into reading the play wrong. Every once in a while, when I think the defensive man is watching my head, I'll use a head fake. If the play's going to the left, I'll make a quick motion to the right with my head, and the defensive man'll move that way, thinking the play's going in that direction, and then I'll just stand up and shield him. It's a cute little maneuver that saves you a little work, but it doesn't always succeed. I tried it against Pittsburgh the other night and Kortas beat me to the inside. I was a little lazy.

Experience, of course, is a tremendous edge in this game. For instance, on a 42-trap, four back through the two hole, just to the left of the center, I have to pull out and trap the right end. A rookie would just think to himself, Pull, trap right end. But suppose I was up against a guy like Doug Atkins, who used to be with the Bears. I knew that Doug had a funny way of dropping his left shoulder into a trap block and twisting his body, trying to go under a trap. So on a 42 I'd automatically think, Pull, trap Atkins, use inside-out position, get low to meet his left shoulder, go like hell.

Our whole running game is built around Coach Lombardi's theory of running to daylight. Except on special plays, you don't have any predetermined place to take the man you're blocking. You just take him where he wants to go. If he wants to go inside, I'll drive him inside, and the back runs outside. If he wants to go outside, I'll drive him outside, and the back runs inside. If he doesn't want to go either direction, I'll just stand there and meet him, put my head in his chest and keep my feet moving, and when he reaches for the ballcarrier, as he inevitably must do, I push him backwards as hard as I can. It's a simple game, really.

AUGUST 17

We took two chartered buses today from Green Bay to Milwaukee, after our morning workout, and on the way down, while we were playing cards, I happened to rub the scars on my forehead. I'd forgotten all about them. I got the scars originally about a month ago, from that first nutcracker drill, from bumping up against Ron Kostelnik and Bob Brown, and once the head is skinned, it becomes more susceptible to getting skinned again. I took another chunk out of it just two days ago, and I know I'm going to have to live with it all season. Once the season's over, and I stop wearing a helmet, it'll heal up in about three or four days. But during the season, we wear our helmets at least three days a week, usually Sunday, Wednesday, and Thursday, so the wound never gets a chance to heal fully.

I hate my helmet. I've always hated it, I guess. You'd imagine that a person would become accustomed to wearing a helmet after eighteen years of football, but I've never really learned to live with it. After every offensive play of every game I play, I immediately undo the chin strap to my helmet. I used to take off my helmet between plays whenever I got really tired. It seemed to be the only way I could breathe. I'm sure it was all in my head, not in my lungs, but I still take the helmet off at every opportunity, for a time-out or a measurement or anything.

I'm not going to throw away my helmet, though, because it's a good weapon, probably the best weapon I've got. When I get mad at somebody—maybe the defensive tackle's been clubbing me with his forearm—I use my helmet on him. I hit him with the helmet high on his chest, then slide up into his chin. Of course, I'll hit him with a forearm too, if I think that'll be effective.

It seems that the longer you play the less equipment you wear. I stopped wearing rib pads in college, but my rookie year in Green Bay I wore knee pads, thigh pads, and hip pads. During the next few years, I threw away the hip pads and changed to smaller knee and thigh pads, and then I started slimming down the size of my shoulder pads. I don't use my shoulders that much, anyway; at least I shouldn't use them much on a block. You hit with your head first and then sort of slide off on your shoulders. About five, six years ago, I found a beautiful pair of light shoulder pads—discarded by some halfback, I think—and I wore them for three or four years till Dad Braisher, the equipment man, gave them away to a high school team. He was ashamed of them, but I was furious. I had to find a new pair, a stiff pair, and it took me a long time to break them in so that they didn't choke my size-19 neck.

AUGUST 18

I had a busy, profitable morning. I got up around a quarter to ten after a good night's sleep, ate breakfast, then visited the local RCA-Victor distributor, who gave me a color-TV set because I'd made a commercial for him. I also picked up a color-TV set for Don Chandler, a stereo set for Ron Kostelnik, and stereotape recorders for Max McGee and Donny Anderson, all at bargain prices. When I got back to the hotel I chatted with the local Lincoln-Mercury dealer, who gave me a real fine price on my Lincoln last year because I'd made a commercial for him, and we talked about another commercial. Then I went over to McNeil-Moore's clothing store and picked out part of the $500 wardrobe that they're giving me to wear on my weekly TV show. Finally, I hustled up eight tickets to the game for the sales manager of my archery company to give out to a few of our customers. About three o'clock I lay down and rested for an hour.

The game itself was less rewarding. Frank Cornish was strong, awfully strong, and he was ready for me. I think he remembered the way I popped him last year and he wanted to get even. He pushed me around quite a bit. The whole Chicago defense was rough, and we didn't score a touchdown until halfway through the last quarter. Up till then, my roommate was our total offense. Don kicked three field goals in four tries, one of them from 45 yards out, and Ron Kostelnik made an end-zone tackle, so that we were ahead 11–0 when we finally did get a touchdown. The game ended 18–0, and I was happy to get out alive. We never did get our running attack going; we gained only 65 yards rushing all night.

Coach Lombardi, naturally, had an appropriate comment after the game. "We stunk up the joint on offense," he said.

AUGUST 19

Right near the end of the game last night, Lionel Aldridge, a quiet, sort of dignified guy—surprisingly, he gets so emotional before every game that he gets sick to his stomach—who plays defensive end for us, hurt his ankle and limped off the field. I walked over to Lionel and said, "You all right, kid?" He said, "Yeah, I think so. It's in the ankle. I don't think there's anything wrong, but I can feel something moving around in there." He didn't seem to be in much pain. He stood on the sidelines and watched the last few minutes of the game.

This morning we found out that Lionel has a broken leg, just above the ankle. He's going to be in a cast for six weeks, and big

Bob Brown, a shy boy with a high, squeaky laugh, as though he isn't used to laughing, is going to take Lionel's place in the defensive line. Bob's strong, maybe the strongest individual on the club, but Lionel's absence has got to hurt us.

AUGUST 20

I've been thinking about the way I feel about my teammates, and I've found something that expresses it. It's from *The Madman*, by Kahlil Gibran, who wrote *The Prophet*, and it's called "My Friend":

> My friend, I am not what I seem. Seeming is but a garment I wear. . . . The "I" in me, my friend, dwells in the house of silence . . . my words are naught but thy own thoughts in sound and my deeds thy own hopes in action.
>
> When thou sayest, "The wind bloweth eastward," I say, "Aye, it doth blow eastward;" for I would not have thee know that my mind doth not dwell upon the wind, but upon the sea. . . .
>
> When it is day with thee, my friend, it is night with me; yet even then I speak of the noontide that dances upon the hills and of the purple shadow that steals its way across the valley. . . .
>
> When thou ascendest to thy Heaven, I descend to my Hell—even then thou callest to me across the unbridgeable gulf, "My companion, my comrade," and I call back to thee, "My comrade, my companion"—for I would not have thee see my Hell. . . .
>
> My friend, thou are not my friend, but how shall I make thee understand? My path is not thy path, yet together we walk, hand in hand.

I may be missing Gibran's point, or part of it, but somewhere, mixed in all those words, is what I feel about our team. We're all different. We all have our own interests, our own preferences, and yet we all go down the same road, hand in hand. Maybe, ultimately, we're not really friends, but what I mean is that no individual on this club will go directly against another individual's feelings, no matter what his own opinion is. No one ever gets into an absolutely contrary position. At the worst, if someone disagrees with someone else, he'll just say, "Well, whatever you say . . ."

We're all moving in one direction, and that direction is the world championship, the third straight world championship. There's no friction, no division into cliques. Certainly we have different groups—the swingers, the family men, the extremely religious young men—but everyone respects everyone else's feelings. Carroll Dale, our flanker, probably hasn't had a beer in ten years. He's like Bart; he's practically a saint. But he doesn't climb up on a soap box and try to change anyone else. He just says, "No, I'd rather not have a beer." He has no holier-than-thou attitude. I guess it all comes down to consideration, or maybe it's what Coach Lombardi last year called love, the love we have on our team.

AUGUST 21

When Coach Lombardi informed us one day last week that come Monday we were going to start the big push, everybody almost fell out of their chairs. We thought we'd been killing ourselves up till then. But Vince wasn't kidding. Today we started the big push.

We've been having trouble offensively with the timing between the backs and the line. We've been a little ragged. With Jim Grabowski and Ben Wilson alternating at fullback, we just haven't been marching to the same music all the time. So this morning we started with basics again. We started running the 36 play, which is an off-tackle play that Jimmy Taylor used to run extremely well. It's a simple play, all zone blocking, all one-on-one blocking on the left side of the line. The halfback will block on the linebacker, and the fullback will cut either inside the linebacker or outside, depending on the direction of the block, just run for daylight. We ran that same play fifty times this morning.

Lombardi ran us and ran us and ran us. He chewed everybody, even Lionel Aldridge, who was working out on the weight machines just two days after his broken leg was put in a cast. Vince takes injuries as personal insults. He had us wearing pads, which is very unusual for a Monday. Travis Williams, the rookie from Arizona State who has run the 100 in 9.3 seconds, was really struggling. He's nervous and he's pressing too hard. He fumbled the ball two or three times today, and finally Coach told him to pick up the ball and carry it with him everywhere he goes. "Take it to the showers, take it to meals, take it to meetings," Vince shouted. "And maybe you'll learn how to hold onto the damned thing."

AUGUST 22

The first of a series of two articles by Vince Lombardi came out in *Look* magazine yesterday, touching off a small storm. Vince wrote about the board of directors of the Packers not being properly appreciative, not giving him a vote of congratulations for winning the Super Bowl, and about the wives of the players not being properly appreciative, either. He told how he gave the wives mink stoles when we won the title in 1961, and all of them wrote

thank-you notes. He gave them color-TV sets when we won the title in 1962, and most of them sent notes. Then he gave them silver
tea sets when we won the title last year, and only three or four of
them responded.

Coach also mentioned some of the players' grades for one
game, and Ray Nitschke, who had a bad grade, was fuming. "I
thought we didn't publish grades around here," he kept grum-
bling. There was something in the article to the effect that Vince
whaled into one of his players a couple of years ago. He did, too.
During our scoring slump in 1965, he swung at big Steve Wright,
and he kind of pushed Kenny Bowman around, and he threw Carroll Dale around, and he was wild-eyed. But he wasn't trying to
hurt anybody. He was just trying to build a fire under all of us. The
newspapers printed excerpts from the article, and they made it
look like Vince was beating people on the head and frothing at the
mouth. Newspaper reporters seem to have a habit of looking for
sensationalism, of distorting and stretching the truth. Of course,
there are exceptions, but sometimes I'm afraid they're few and far
between.

Lombardi tried to laugh off the article in practice today by
making joking references to the wives and to the board of directors, but the situation seemed pretty tense. Then tonight, after dinner, Fuzzy stood up and started singing his favorite song, "He's got
the whole world, in his hands," with some new lyrics: "He's got the
greatest wives, in his hands; he's got the board of directors, in his
hands; we've got a two-fisted coach, on our hands."

Everybody broke up, and the situation eased—until another
article comes out in two weeks. What surprised me more than any
specific statement in the article was simply that Coach Lombardi
had said anything. It just isn't like him to cause any controversy.
I mentioned to Forrest Gregg that the article heightened my

growing suspicion that, at the end of the season, Vince is going to retire. "It sort of looks like it more and more," Forrest agreed.

If I live to be a million, I won't be able to figure Lombardi out.

AUGUST 23

"I'd love to be a Packer . . . I worked, I sweat, I died . . . I want to be a Packer, a Packer I want to be. . . ."

Twenty rookies, twenty young men who have survived some six weeks under Lombardi, chanted these words tonight as the finale of the annual rookie show. The faces of the rookies were awfully revealing. Some were starry-eyed. Some looked like they were going to cry. A few seemed embarrassed by the emotions the others were showing. Yet you could tell that the simple words meant something to all of them, that all of them desperately hope to become part of this club. And you knew that no more than half a dozen of them could possibly succeed.

The show didn't have a scene quite so funny as last year when Donny Anderson and Jim Grabowski, the high-priced bonus boys, showed up on stage with dollar bills pasted all over them, but the rookies managed to have a lot of fun. They picked on everyone. They held a mock interview with Max, right after he caught two touchdown passes in the Super Bowl game last January, and the rookie playing Max said, "Hell, I just hope I score as well tonight as I did this afternoon." They asked "Max" how he felt trying out for the team again at the age of thirty-five, and he said, "Practice isn't too bad, but the weekends are killing me."

They awarded Pat Peppler, the personnel man, a hatchet with a sticker saying, WE VISITED THE GREEN BAY PACKERS, and they gave Marvin Fleming the outstanding blocking award, a bit of irony which cut deeper than a hatchet. They named Zeke "Bowler of the Century," a tribute to the long hours he had put in at the Century Bowling Alley. A group of rookies portrayed the coaching staff, and big Leon Crenshaw, playing Lombardi, asked his staff whether a certain rookie should play offense or defense. All the assistants agreed that the rookie should play offense. "Good," said Lombardi-Crenshaw. "He'll play defense."

It was a lovely evening, filled with the kind of humor that perhaps only a bunch of football players could fully appreciate. Afterward, I had sort of a warm feeling about all the rookies, all the kids who were struggling so hard, against such heavy odds, to win a place on this team. I sympathized with all of them.

Dick Arndt, the boy from Idaho, is looking better on defense; the injury to Aldridge has given him a new lease on life, and Coach is noticing him more. Crenshaw's down to 278 pounds, spread over a 6'6'' frame, and he doesn't look like he has an ounce of fat left; he's worked so hard. Hyland, who's kind of quiet and shy, is starting to look better; his singing, however, is atrocious. Dave Dunaway, a flanker who's been staring at his shoes ever since he reached camp, is starting to raise his eyes and look at people; he doesn't hustle the way he should, and I suspect he'll soon be gone. Jim Flanigan, the linebacker, has been a little complacent, wasting a lot of the ability he obviously has; on the other hand, Claudis James—"Jiminy Cricket"—has the most beautiful attitude in the world. So does Stan Kemp, the baby-faced kid, but I'm afraid he doesn't have the physical equipment; he wrote the lyrics to "I Want to Be a Packer," and he wants it badly, but I don't think he has a chance.

I just can't figure out a big kid named Tom Cichowski. He's already making plans for what he's going to do here during the season, and what he's going to do after the season, and I know he's got only two chances to make this club; slim and none. I can't understand how he's lasted this long. But I could be wrong. I felt the same way seven years ago about Ron Kostelnik; I honestly thought he was hopeless, but "The Rhino" developed, worked and worked and worked and made himself a fine ballplayer. The other day, Cichowski was up singing, and Willie Wood, who's our rookie adviser, shouted, "Sing up a bit, we can't hear you," and Cichowski growled, "If you guys would shut up and quit talking, you could hear me." He's quieted down a little now. For a while, we kept asking him how he spelled his name, and he'd say, "Chicken on a cow, and a cow on a ski, and that's how you spell Chickowski."

AUGUST 24

Travis Williams dropped the ball again today in practice, and Coach told him he had to start carrying it everywhere again. I think Vince is just about running out of patience with Travis. His speed is so impressive that a lot of us are hoping he'll learn to hold the ball and make the club. Henry Jordan gave him a little lecture today. "You just think of that ball as a loaf of bread," Henry said, "and it's my bread. Every time you drop that ball, you're taking bread off my table." And Zeke gave Travis a football with a handle made of tape. The kid accepted the needling good-naturedly, but you can tell from looking at him how scared he is. He's got a wife and two kids, and a third on the way, and while we're in training camp he's earning only $70 a week. That's what everybody gets, and it doesn't go very far.

Vince is letting up a little to get us ready for the Dallas exhibition, not driving us so hard on the field, but he's still riding us in meetings about being too nice, too polite. At the same time, he keeps telling us to play hard, clean football. The whole situation reminds me of *The Taming of the Shrew*. Petruchio beats on Kate to the point where he says something like, "See that beautiful woman," and she says, "Yes, that's a beautiful woman," and he says, "No, that's an old man," and she says, "Yes, that's an old man," and he says, "No, that's a beautiful woman," and she goes along with whatever he says. Vince tells us to hate, and we say, "Yes, we hate," and then he tells us we have to play clean, and we say, "Yes, we'll play clean," and we accept everything, all the contradictions. Everything that Vince Lombardi says is so, is so.

AUGUST 25

My neck is killing me. Every week I go up against these 280- or 290-pound tackles, and every week I get shorter and shorter. I jammed a vertebra or something against the Bears, and my neck keeps aching like a bitch. I think I'll live, but I'm not over-confident.

I phoned my mother today—she and my father are coming to the game in Dallas—and I made the mistake of telling her how my neck is hurting. "Do you have to put your head into those other players and butt them all the time?" she said.

"Yes, Mom," I said. "It's the best way to do it. If I don't do it that way, they're liable to get away from me."

"Well, you cut that out," she said. "You stop doing that. You had that chipped vertebra once before. You just stop doing that."

"If I do, I think the coach'll get kinda upset. He likes me to do it the right way."

"Well, you tell him to watch out," my mother said. "You tell him I'm going to get him. Don't you be doing that butting anymore."

I guess she's just like all mothers. She's gone through a lot with me. I hit myself in the face with an ax when I was about five and left a scar in my chin. I backed into a lathe in high school and tore a chunk out of my backside—and played in a football game the same night. When I was seventeen, I accidentally knocked over a shotgun and put two rounds of buckshot in my side. Then I had the splinters in my groin, and a broken ankle, and God knows how many broken ribs, and a detached retina, and a chipped vertebra that left me with a long scar on the back of my neck. You'd think that by now Mom would have learned to stop worrying about me.

AUGUST 26

We play Dallas Monday night, and it should be a helluva game. The Cowboys have had all year to brood about their loss to us in the NFL championship game last December, and they've got a great deal of incentive going for them, probably more than we have. They've got a lot more to prove. But the game's going to be on national television, and we always seem to play well for a large audience. We're big hams. Maybe it's because we play our home games in such a small town.

I wish the season were here. We ought to make the Super Bowl again. We really ought to. I think this may be the best team we've ever had. Vince has been beating us and beating us and beating us, and we still keep winning.

I don't know how we can lose.

AUGUST 27

When we left Green Bay this morning, the temperature was about 40 degrees and it was raining. When we flew into Dallas around noon, the temperature was 94 degrees and the sun was beating down. We checked into the hotel, then went right over to the Cotton Bowl for a little workout.

After the practice session, Fuzzy Thurston and I shared a cab back to the hotel, and as we got into the cab we were talking about football. The cab driver, a young fellow, looked at us and said, "You Green Bay Packers?"

I said, "Yes, we are."

Fuzzy said, "That's right, Mac."

"What's your names?" the driver said. "What's your names?"

"You mean," said Fuzzy, using our favorite line, "you don't recognize the two greatest guards in the history of the National Football League?"

"Yeah, I know you," said the driver, "but what's your names?"

I wanted to needle Fuzzy, so I said, "You mean you've never heard of Kramer and Gillingham?"

The driver turned around. "Oh, yeah, sure," he said. "Sure, I heard of that Gillingham."

Fuzzy and I laughed and laughed. It kept us going all day.

I managed to spend a little time with my folks. Dad's been helping run the diving business in New Orleans, but I think he and my mom aren't too happy in Louisiana. They miss Sand Point. It's a little town of about 5,000 people, but it's got just about everything a guy could want. The lake's got the biggest rainbow trout in the world. There's a good ski trail only six miles away, and there's a nice little golf course. It's a great place to grow up. Mom was telling me how hot it is down in Louisiana, and I suspect they'll be going back to Idaho soon.

At the hotel tonight I bumped into Dick Arndt, talking in the lobby with another big young boy, about 6'4".

"Hi, Jerry," the fellow said. "You don't remember me, do you?"

I didn't know who he was from Adam.

Finally, he said, "My name's Jerry Ahlin, I used to be your paper boy in Boise."

"You're kidding me," I said.

"No," he said. "I even remember your address—2225 Cherry Lane. I'm trying out for the Cowboys now. I'm a linebacker."

You know you're getting old when your paper boy becomes a pro linebacker.

AUGUST 28

Tommy Joe Crutcher was scrambling around for tickets this morning. He comes from McKinney, only about thirty miles outside Dallas, and he went up to Tom Miller, who's our assistant general manager, and said, "Tom, I've gotta get me twenty tickets." When Miller pulled out a thick wad of extra tickets he'd picked up from the Cowboys, Tommy Joe said he didn't want all twenty seats together. "Give me nineteen off the front," he said, "and one off the back."

"What is it, Tommy Joe?" one of the guys hollered. "You got a wicked city woman stashed away here?"

Tommy Joe's a bachelor—one of our few eligibles, because we don't count Max, who is single but, after a couple of marriages, not especially eligible—and he's always kidding and taking kidding about his dates. Once he told us he had a new girl friend named Will Rogers. "Why do you call her Will Rogers?" somebody asked. And Tommy Joe said, " 'cause she never met a man she didn't like." And then, of course, the big country boy blushed.

The temperature was 93 degrees at game time tonight, and it had to be at least 100 on the floor of the Cotton Bowl. Most of the guys had good cases of nerves before the game. Gilly was so tense he got sick to his stomach. The heat and humidity almost killed me the first half of the game. I was soaking wet. In the locker room at half-time everybody felt sick.

But it was a beautiful football game, from our point of view. Our defense was absolutely superb. Bart pulled a rib muscle in the first quarter, and Zeke came in off the bench and did an excellent job. My roomie kicked two more field goals and we won the game 20–3, surprisingly easy, without any difficulty. Maybe the Cowboys were too high emotionally, too eager, too worked up. They couldn't get their offense moving at all.

I don't think I had one of my better games, but it's hard to tell. Coach Lombardi's got me so psyched out now, as he has everyone else, that unless I play a perfect game, without a single fault, I'm disappointed in myself. I got caught offside again, a stupid, mental error, an asinine thing to do.

My man tonight was Jethro Pugh, 6'6'' and 260 pounds, one of the smaller tackles I've seen this season. I really didn't expect much of Jethro—he was a substitute last year—but he surprised me. He was much, much quicker than I had anticipated, really exceptionally quick. He gave me quite a bit of difficulty the first two or three passing plays, but then I got my head up and started feeling serious and everything came along pretty well. He didn't give me too much trouble on the running plays.

The plane ride back from Dallas, in our chartered 727, was thoroughly enjoyable. We drank a few beers, and we sang, and the time passed very quickly. When you lose, you think you're never going to land.

AUGUST 29

After supper tonight I was lying on my bed, dreading the movies, dreading the screaming and the hollering from Coach Lombardi, and Kenny Bowman came in and lay down on the other bed opposite me.

"Man, I can hear him now," Kenny said. "You know what would be wonderful? If he just came into the meeting tonight and said, 'We're not going to look at the Dallas movies. We don't have time. We've got to get ready for Cleveland Saturday.' "

"I'd kiss him if he did that," I said.

"Me, too," said Kenny.

"He's going to be terrible," I said. "He'll be shouting, 'You stupid —— you crazy —— what in the hell are you thinking about?' "

Kenny looked sad. "I suppose," he said, "we'll be in that meeting too damn long to get out in time to see *The Fugitive*."

Very reluctantly, we got up and went to the meeting, and, as we expected, Vince was upset. He got on me a little and on Gilly, and then he really got on Donny Anderson. Donny just isn't quite with it yet. There's a little something lacking. We have to get better effort out of him. I don't know whether he's paying too much attention to the girls or what, but he seems to be suffering at football. He's trying to follow in Paul Hornung's footsteps—we called Paul "Golden Boy," and when Donny joined us last year, we started calling him "Old Yeller"—but Paul could go out at night and do anything in the world and the next day he'd come back and bust his ass on the football field. If I go out and have more than one beer the night before a game, it affects my mind the next day. I just don't play as well. I have to take care of myself and get a lot of rest. Maybe Donny's this way, too, but he'll have to find it out on his own. Coach told him he'd better shape up and start running his plays a little better and getting a little more out of them.

Vince got on Marvin Fleming, as usual, and he even got on the defense. The defense only allowed three points, but he cursed them because they didn't contain the pitchouts too well. You can't feel too bad when he gets on everybody. I guess that's why he gets on everybody.

"I'm going to tell you the facts, gentlemen," Lombardi summed up, "and the facts are these: At Green Bay, we have winners. We do not have losers. If you're a loser, mister, you're going to get your ass out of here and you're going to get your ass out of here right now. Gentlemen, we are paid to win. Gentlemen, we will win."

As we were walking out of the meeting, Lee Roy Caffey turned to me and said, "Who the hell won that game, anyhow?"

AUGUST 30

The miracle healer has worked his wonders again. The doctors removed Lionel Aldridge's cast today just twelve days after he broke his leg. Originally, he was supposed to have the cast on for at least six weeks, but he has mended early. He has been mended, I'm certain, by evil looks from Lombardi.

We started getting ready for Cleveland today, and we worked for about two hours. The Browns haven't won a preseason game yet this year, and they always have championship thoughts, so I suppose they'll be up for us, the way everybody gets up for us. This'll be Cleveland's first game at home this year, and there'll be about 85,000 screaming idiots in the stands. If anyone thinks we don't play our exhibition games as hard as our regular games, I'll tell him he's out of his head.

Bart Starr stayed completely out of the practice session. He isn't running or throwing or doing anything except resting. He's had a number of minor injuries this summer—a pulled hamstring, a jammed thumb, a torn muscle, one thing after another—and I hope we hold him out of the Cleveland game. It's hard to have an injury heal when you have the hell beat out of you one day every week.

My wife and children came home from their vacation in Idaho this evening. I spent the afternoon airing out the house and buying groceries and getting the cat out from the vet's. I even went over and got the Continental washed. There's a gas station here in Green Bay that washes the cars of all the Packers for nothing. I knew there had to be some advantage to being a professional football player.

AUGUST 31

The varying attitudes of the rookies never cease to amaze me. We're coming down to the wire now. We have fifty-two people left—we dropped two rookies Monday—and, with Long and Aldridge on the disabled list, we have to drop ten more men before the season starts. Almost none of the dozen or fifteen possible candidates thinks it's going to be him, with the exception of Travis Williams. He thinks he'll go. He fumbled again in practice today, and I guess that just about signs his death warrant.

Tom Cichowski is still a mystery to me. He continually talks about this season, about his wife coming up here, about going hunting with me, about how he's going to miss the oyster fries back home. To my way of thinking, the guy has no chance to make the club, but it just never dawns on him. The other day, we were talking about Lombardi, and he said, "Boy, I sure hope we don't lose too many during the season, 'cause if he chews us out like this when we win, I wonder what it'll be like when we lose." With Cichowski, everything is "we" and "us" and "during the season," and I just know he's not going to be here. Of course, I may be wrong. Maybe I'm the one who's going to be gone.

SEPTEMBER 1

We flew to Cleveland today, and when we checked into the hotel I ran into Jim Martin, who's a coach with Detroit. The Lions are playing the opening game of the double-header tomorrow, and Martin told me they're going to whip us in the first game of the regular season two weeks from now. I know they're waiting in the weeds for us. It's so damned difficult to repeat as champion because, automatically, everybody's out to beat you, everybody's looking to knock you off. Nobody ever lets up when they're playing against you; they're always sky-high. And if it's hard to win the title twice in a row, imagine how difficult it is to win three straight world championships. Three titles in a row. That's what our season is all about. That's what's driving us. It would be beautiful.

SEPTEMBER 2

The Browns were really laying for us tonight, and they jumped out in front by two touchdowns, 14–0. Some people thought we were in trouble, but we knew we were going to win. We go into every game we play knowing we're going to win. And we always do. We never lose a game. Sometimes, of course, the clock runs out while the other team still has more points than us, but we know that the game isn't really over, that if we kept playing we'd end up ahead. From our point of view, we haven't lost a game in years.

There were almost 85,000 people in the stands, and they kept screaming and hollering as Cleveland built up its lead, but, finally, toward the end of the first half, they began to quiet down. We wear the crowd down the same way we wear our opponents down. They come into the game high—all keyed up for the Green Bay Packers—and we just do our job and do our job and do our job and methodically grind them down, grind their enthusiasm right out of them. Finally, they just say, "Aw, hell, I knew we couldn't beat them."

At the half, we were just a point behind the Browns, 14–13. And then, with Zeke running the team and Ben Wilson showing a lot of heart at fullback, and my roomie kicking his third field goal in three attempts, we moved out in front, 30–14. By the time Cleveland scored its last touchdown to cut the final margin to 30–21, not more than 25,000 people were left in the stands. The rest had just crept away in the night.

It was a good feeling to quiet down that big crowd, and afterward, in the bus going to the airport, Forrest Gregg and I began remembering our game against Baltimore in 1958, when the Colts whipped us 56–0, and, with a minute to go, with us moving the ball, all of the 57,000 fans were still in their seats and all of them kept chanting, "Hold 'em, hold 'em," not wanting us to get a single point. You hear the crowd. You really do.

This was one of the most physically bruising games I've been in for a long time. Cleveland had a kid named Walter Johnson facing me, about 270 pounds and extremely strong, a straight-ahead guy, nothing fancy about him. I didn't have to worry too much about his moves, but I really had to pop him to slow him down. He didn't give me as much trouble as Jethro Pugh—he didn't have Pugh's quickness—but he was a lot more violent. Once Johnson slapped Gilly across the head, and Gilly came back to the huddle and said, "That 71's a lot of football player."

Earlier in the week, we had watched movies of our game with Cleveland last year, and the same kid played opposite me, and he didn't show much. I chewed him up. I did almost anything I wanted with him. I pass-blocked him beautifully. I drove him. I took him inside. I took him outside. So I went into the game figuring I was going to whup up on him again, and I came out of the game with a black eye and a bruised hip, a sore knee and a jammed neck. I got the black eye on a pass play. I pulled out to block on the outside linebacker, and he stuck his fingers through the cage and got my eye.

We had a strange incident during the plane ride home. Ray

Nitschke and I sat down to play cards, and Marvin Fleming wandered over and said something I couldn't quite hear, and Ray said, "Shut up and sit down." Ray's always talking loud, and he never means anything by it. But all of a sudden, Marvin took offense and snapped, "Don't tell me to shut up." And Ray got hot, because Marvin was hot, and he said, "Shut your mouth."

"You get up and shut my mouth," Marvin said. "Don't tell me what to do. I'm no dog."

"I'm gonna get up and shut your mouth," said Ray.

I sort of stepped in between them and said, "Cool it," and they both calmed down, and Marvin walked away.

Later, Marvin came back and sat down, and Ray said, "Marvin, I'm sorry. I apologize. I didn't mean anything by yelling at you."

"Oh, man, I know that," Marvin said. "I'm just upset. I've got a bad stomach and I'm up tight."

Within a couple of minutes, they were about ready to hug each other. It had been a long time since I'd seen a flare-up between teammates on this club.

Ray's an interesting guy. Actually, he's two interesting guys, two completely different guys, on the field and off. He loves to hit people, he loves body contact, yet out of uniform he's quite gentle, quite sensitive, almost professorial. We played together on the College All-Star team in 1958, and one day, kiddingly, I made a vague reference to his intelligence. I just said something like, "You genius," and he got so angry he wanted to punch me. I had to talk fast to calm him down.

He can be absolutely murderous during practice. He seems incapable of letting up, even against his own teammates. He's always grabbing people, hitting people, throwing elbows. I've lost my head with him more than I have with anybody else. I don't feel there's any reason for him to hit me in the head with a forearm during dummy scrimmages. He did it just the other day. We were running through plays, sort of going through the motions, and my assignment was to block the middle linebacker. I moved out and positioned myself in front of Ray, not intending to hit him or take him down, and he was wearing a forearm pad which wasn't too thick, and he brought his padded forearm all the way back and then lifted it right into my face. He really stung me. I don't think I even had my chin strap on. I didn't say a word to Ray, but I was steaming. I went back to the huddle and told Zeke to call the same play again, and I went out and hit Ray and pushed him and drove him to the ground. He got the message. He didn't even know he'd been hitting me so hard; he just gets carried away on the field.

His first few years on the Packers, Ray was something of a wild man. He drank a little and fought a little and carried on a little. But then, about five or six years ago, he got married and he turned into a monk, no drinking, no carousing, no nothing. He and his wife, Jackie, adopted two little boys, and Ray, who had a pretty rough childhood himself, lives for those boys. I think he's the most devoted father I've ever seen. He built his older boy a treehouse in their backyard, and the only thing it doesn't have is color television, I'm pretty sure it does have black-and-white. His boy said he wanted to go fishing last year, so Ray, who's one of the very few Packers who doesn't take an off-season job—he's turned down dozens of offers—took the youngster to Florida for a month.

A few years ago, after Ray had given up all his wildness, Dan Currie, who also liked to party, walked up to Nitschke one day and said, "Hey, Ray, what's it like, not drinking?"

And Ray looked at him and said, "It's quiet, man. Real quiet."

SEPTEMBER 3

Donny Anderson looked a lot better in the Cleveland game, so maybe Lombardi's lectures last week have already had some impact. Obviously, Vince wanted to get him mad. "You're going to be doing the punting," Coach told Anderson the other day, "and if that's all you want to be around here, a punter, that's all right with me. You can be the most expensive punter in the league, and maybe you can run back a few kickoffs."

Lombardi also needled the rest of us to work on Andy. "I'll tell you this, gentlemen," he said. "If I were playing and I had an individual or two on my ball club who was messing with my $25,000 bonus, endangering my chances to play in the Super Bowl, I'd damn sure let him know in a hurry that I expected 100 percent effort out of him." Vince didn't mention Donny by name, but we all knew who he meant.

I'd been goading Donny a bit myself, even before the coach's comments. "Donny, you better lay off the girls before the games," I told him. "You better get yourself some rest. You better give those girls some rest, too." I was laughing and grinning when I said it, but underneath the kidding tone, I wanted to let Donny know that we're expecting a lot out of him. We want him to carry his share of the load. He's got all the natural talent in the world, and we need him.

SEPTEMBER 4

"When the hell are you going to start running, anyhow?" Vince asked Lionel Aldridge at the meeting tonight. "When're you going to stop loafing?" Lionel's leg's been out of the cast for four or five days now, and it hasn't even been three weeks since he broke it, and Lombardi wants him to start running. Vince means it, too. Bob Long is trotting already, less than a month after his knee operation, and Coach thinks it's time for Lionel to be running, too. Lombardi has got to have the highest threshold of pain in the world; none of our injuries hurts him at all.

SEPTEMBER 5

Dick Arndt came up to me this morning at breakfast and told me he'd been traded to Pittsburgh. He said he wanted to thank me for all the help I'd given him. Dick's a nice kid, and he worked like hell trying to make this club. The only thing he needed really was to be a little meaner, a little more aggressive. I felt that perhaps I'd let him down, that I hadn't worked with him or helped him quite as much as I should have. "You don't have to worry, Dick," I told him. "You're going to play a lot of pro football." We talked about the possibility of Bill Austin building a football dynasty in Pittsburgh, and we talked about the possible end of a dynasty here, the end of a reign. There's more and more speculation every day about Lombardi retiring at the end of the season.

Dick wasn't the only victim today. We cut six other rookies, including Stan Kemp, the kid who wrote "I want to be a Packer," and a fullback named Jim Mankins, a good fellow who played the harmonica all the time. Mankins had his wife and family up here in Green Bay. It's a terrible thing: Momma's up here getting acquainted with the other wives, going to games with them, making friends, and suddenly it's all over. We also dropped Dave Dunaway, who was a high draft choice, but the word is around that he has a $100,000, three-year, no-cut contract and that nobody wants to pick up the bundle. If no other team claims him, he'll be on the cab team, the taxi squad. He'll get his full salary and he'll be the most expensive taxi player we've had in a long time.

I saw that my old old friend Dan Currie was cut by the Rams, and I started thinking back to my socializing days, my old habit of running out every Monday afternoon and getting a little bombed with Currie and Bill Quinlan and Ron Kramer and a few others. "I don't mind you going out," my wife, Barbara, used to say, "but do you have to go out with Quinlan and Currie?" They really liked to party. Now, with them gone, I've gotten away from socializing.

The cuts brought us down to forty-three active men, only three over the limit, and reminded me of my rookie year. I didn't have a chance then. The team had five veteran guards in camp, and they were only going to keep three. My College All-Star coach John Sandusky, who had played with Green Bay the previous year, told me, "You'll play in the NFL, but not with Green Bay. You won't make that club."

So I had kind of a lackadaisical attitude, just having fun, enjoying myself, waiting to get cut, until one day Scooter McLean, our head coach, called me into his office and said, "Jerry, what in hell's wrong with you? You've got size and speed, but one play you look great and the next play you look like you're out to lunch." I told him that I didn't expect to make the team, that I was just relaxing until he traded me. That week Scooter promoted me to the first team and started me in an exhibition. I got up against a guy who didn't have too many moves on the pass rush, and I was big and strong, so I had a good game. Two veteran guards were cut the next day, and when we got back to training camp, I called my wife in Idaho and said, pretty cheerfully, "Honey, I think we've got the club made. They cut two veterans."

Jim Ringo, the team captain, happened to be standing outside the phone booth, waiting to make a call, and he heard me and he didn't talk to me all year. He hated my guts the whole season. He hated me not so much because I was gloating, but because I was happy that two of his close friends were leaving the club. He told me the whole story about three years later.

Coach Lombardi's second article came out in *Look* yesterday, and once again a few of the boys resented his comments. He said Henry Jordan tends to be satisfied and needs to be whipped, which upset Henry, and he said that when Bob Skoronski doesn't start a game, he suffers a psychological relapse. Today Ray Nitschke was calling Bob "Psycho" — "C'mon, Psycho, you'll be able to start Saturday" and Bob really seemed hurt by the whole thing. Tomorrow, I imagine, Coach Lombardi'll pat him on the head, rub his back, scratch his ears, and everybody'll feel a little better.

SEPTEMBER 6

We look like we're in pretty good shape. Bob Long's running almost at full speed now, only four weeks after his operation, and Lionel Aldridge's hobbling around, lifting weights, almost ready to run. Bart seems to have shaken his injuries, and I imagine he'll play the final exhibition game against the New York Giants Saturday.

Bart was in a playful mood tonight. He and Henry Jordan room together and tonight, after dinner, Bart got back to the room first and hid behind the door. When Henry came shuffling in, Bart leaped out and hollered, "BOO!" Henry almost fell over backwards.

Bart's usually quiet and calm. He's got so much character, so much willpower. He's about as complete a person as I've ever known. He admires Lombardi tremendously, and the affection is mutual. When Vince bawls Bart out in a meeting, it's always about the receiver he didn't see, or the play he didn't call, never about not putting out enough. I really think the only reason Vince ever criticizes Bart is just to show the rest of the club that he's impartial, that he'll even yell at his favorite.

Bart was telling me tonight about his father-in-law, who lives down South somewhere, owns about seventy acres of land and has maybe eight or ten head of cattle, and likes to think he's a big rancher, watching over his herd. Boyd Dowler and Max and I were sitting with Bart, and I mentioned how beautiful I find a herd of white-faced heifers grazing in a meadow.

"Yeah," said Boyd. "Can't you just see them in a high meadow, mountains rising above them on both sides, and a beautiful little stream winding down into the meadow?"

"That's certainly beautiful," said Bart.

"I can't imagine anything lovelier," I said.

Max looked a little disappointed in us. "Hell," he said. "I can't think of anything prettier than a herd of broadies sitting at a bar grazing on Martinis."

SEPTEMBER 7

A couple of NFL officials came into camp today and gave us a test on the new rule changes. Coach gave us a little talk before we took the exam.

"It's a tough test," he said, "and I don't expect you to get all twenty answers right. I just took it and I missed two questions myself."

"Don't worry, Coach," Max hollered out. "They'll change those two rules."

Max and Willie Davis each got seventeen questions right, and they shared first prize, a dozen golf balls. I think Max cheated; he was out of golf balls.

We've been studying movies of the Giants, and it's kind of hard to take them seriously. We almost laughed out loud at some of their mistakes. They looked a little ragged, to say the least. They simply are not a good football team. I hate to say that, because, inevitably, this is the kind of team that beats you, or gives you a helluva game. But their backs sure do funny things on defense; they have trouble staying out of each other's way.

I'll be up against a former University of Idaho ballplayer, Jim

Moran. When he was a freshman six or seven years ago I helped coach the team in spring football. He's about 6'5'' now, about 275 pounds, and I think he's the Giants' best defensive lineman. He's quick and fairly agile.

A few years ago, when Jim was on the Giant taxi squad, he told me he wished he'd be traded to Green Bay. And Roger Brown, who was traded today by the Lions to the Rams, once told Bart that he wished he could come to Green Bay. A lot of football players do, for the extra money we win, for the organization, for the attitude. Everything here is first-class, now that the grass drills are over.

SEPTEMBER 8

Three more men have got to go by Monday, and the situation is tense. It's gotten to the point now where we have to cut real good football players. Claudis James, a flanker from down South, has been looking very good, ever since Coach Lombardi told him that if he dropped one more pass, he was going to send his butt home. Claudis is a colored boy from Mississippi, and he says the one place he doesn't want to go is home. Travis Williams has been holding the ball better, and he may survive. Leon Crenshaw, holding his weight at a trim 278, is in a strong position because of the injury to Lionel. Two veteran defensive backs, Doug Hart and Dave Hathcock, are in danger; they're competing with a rookie, John Rowser, and I know Vince'll keep only two out of the three as reserves. Doug's one of my closest friends, and I'd hate to see him go. Hyland, Flanigan, and Horn look like they've made the club, even though Lombardi's been riding Horn hard lately. He's a night person, likes girls, likes bars, likes moving around a little, and today when he called the wrong play in practice, Lombardi screamed, "Horn, what in the hell you been doing every night?

Don't you study at all? What in the hell do you do every night?" Coach Lombardi knows exactly what Don Horn's been doing every night. He knows everything that happens in this town.

If Cichowski makes this team, I'm going to be one of the most surprised men in the world.

SEPTEMBER 9

We weren't too high for the game tonight—the Giants didn't exactly inspire us—but there was a noticeable intensity, a sense of concentration. We wanted to do everything right, partly because it was our last exhibition game and partly because we knew the game was going back to New York on television. I heard a few of the guys comment that a lot of New York sportswriters would be watching the game, and we wanted to impress them.

I wasn't nervous, but during the day, I did a good deal of thinking about the game. I had noticed in the movies that Moran, who's had several knee operations, protects his knees, that when anyone gets around his knees, he stops and backs off a bit. So I decided that if he gave me trouble, if he rushed me too hard, trying to overpower me, I'd throw a cross-body block at his knees. We're friends, but this is a rough game.

I had also noticed that he puts his head down on a pass rush and butts you and then tries to go to either side. Sometimes he slaps you with one hand, like a right cross to the side of the head, then tries to go the opposite direction. And I'd noticed a couple of occasions in the movies when he brought his right foot up parallel to his left and then, invariably, made an outside move, to his left. I wanted to remember all of this for the game.

The first or second play we had the ball, Moran and I had a little conversation, which is rare on the field, even among college friends. He just said, "What you doing, Kramer?" And I said,

"How you doing?" Then, three or four plays later, someone moved offside and Jim, reacting to the movement, charged in and slammed me in the head with a forearm. I hadn't moved out of my stance, and he got in a pretty good lick. He said, "I'm sorry, Jerry, I didn't mean to hit you that hard. But I had to move." I said, "That's OK, kid, that's beautiful, I know you had to move."

I forgot all about cutting down his knees, and, at half-time, when we passed each other coming from the locker rooms, we chatted about our wives and our families. Still, I played a good game against him. He never got to the passer, and he never got to the ballcarrier until the man had gained at least three or four yards.

We won the game 31–14, without any sweat, and we had one really beautiful play, a 46-power play that was just gorgeous. Elijah Pitts was carrying the ball through the six hole, between the left end and the left tackle. Jim Grabowski, at fullback, was supposed to take the outside linebacker out; our tight end, Marv Fleming, and our left tackle, Bob Skoronski, were supposed to double-team the end (which is why we call it a "power" play); Gilly was supposed to take the left tackle inside; and I was supposed to pull out and either help Grabo with the outside linebacker or cut up through the hole and get the middle linebacker. When I came over, Grabo had erased the outside linebacker and somebody else had wiped out the middle linebacker, so I went straight up the hole and took out the safety. Elijah sprinted ten yards to the end zone without even being touched.

One little incident demonstrated the importance of studying the movies carefully. On pure passing situations—on third down with ten yards to go, for instance—the Giants often use what we call a tackle-end twist. The end, instead of rushing his normal way, will cut inside the tackle's rush, and the tackle, of course, will come outside. They reverse positions, trying to confuse the offensive line. About four years ago, Forrest Gregg noticed that whenever the Giants did this, Jim Katcavage, their left end, would put his right hand down on the ground, instead of his left hand. For at least four years, Katcavage has had this absurd habit, and, apparently, no one on the Giant coaching staff has ever warned him about it.

On a second-and-nine situation in the first half tonight I came up to the line of scrimmage and looked over and, sure enough, the Kat had his right hand down. Forrest, playing next to me, didn't notice it. I said, "Forrest, be awake, baby." Then Forrest looked up and saw what I meant. We stopped the Kat and Moran without much trouble, but maybe Katcavage caught my little comment. In the second half, they used a tackle-end twist again, and the Kat had his left hand down. I wasn't in the game then, but Forrest told me about it.

One other beautiful thing: I was on the kickoff return team tonight, for the first time this year, and when the Giants kicked off to start the second half, I was supposed to block No. 83, the man just to the right of the kicker. I dropped back to block him toward the sidelines, and he came at me, then hesitated. I squared away, ready to hit him, and moved up within four yards of him. Suddenly, he leaped up in the air, about four feet off the ground, and screamed, "EEYOW!" Then he kind of drop-kicked me. His cleats tore my jersey and brushed my helmet.

"What in the hell is this?" I asked myself. Lombardi had been teasing during the week about a Giant defensive tackle named Moto or something, saying that he was a Sumo wrestler. I said to myself, "That's got to be this guy." I was going to get him on the next kickoff, but he eased up and didn't jump. I felt a little frustrated. I was in the perfect mood to hit somebody.

SEPTEMBER 10

I never got to sleep last night. As soon as the game ended and we had the usual buffet dinner, Doug Hart and I climbed into my Continental and I drove about 225 miles due north to go bear hunting. We were going after black bear, with bows and arrows.

I was all hopped up, the adrenalin flowing the way it always does for several hours after a game, and along the way, almost automatically, I began thinking about Alex Karras, the defensive left tackle of the Detroit Lions. As far as I'm concerned, the two toughest tackles in the league are Karras and Merlin Olsen of the Rams, and I never, never say that either one is better than the other, because I don't want to get either of them angry. Playing against Karras is like playing a chess game. If you try to pop him, he'll beat you like a stepchild. You've got to be thinking all the time. You've got to be thinking about the move he beat you with two years ago. You've got to remember that everything with him is a countermove. I thought about him for 100 miles.

Obviously, I spend a lot of time thinking about defensive tackles. Football is a team game, but especially for the linemen and the receivers, there's a dramatic, and important, individual game within the game. To help your team succeed as a team, you have to succeed as an individual; you have to win your own match-ups. In my position, sooner or later I've got to block almost every man on the opposing team—every lineman and every back. But 75 percent of the time I've got to block the defensive left tackle. Naturally, he dominates my thoughts and consumes most of my energy.

Professional defensive tackles can be divided into the strong ones and the quick ones. This simple division works as long as you remember one thing: The quick ones are strong, too. If there's a weakling playing on the defensive line in the National Football

League I haven't had the pleasure of meeting him. They all weigh upwards of 250 pounds, some considerably upwards, and even though several of them have paunches that you'd notice in the dressing room, they've all got muscles that you notice on the field. They can all hurt you.

When I analyze a tackle I'm facing and my first thought is of his strength, and my second thought is also of his strength, then, in a real sense, I'm criticizing him. I'm telling myself that he isn't fast. This doesn't mean that he can't give you trouble. Anybody's going to beat you at least two or three times in a game—even if he doesn't have great quickness—and if he happens to beat you at critical moments, you've wasted the whole game. (And you almost never know in advance when a critical play's coming up.) The strong guys pound, pound, pound. They're ramming their helmets into you all the time, and if they catch you the slightest off-balance, they'll knock you right on your can—and they'll run over you. Normally, they won't cause too much damage because no matter how strong a tackle is he just uses up too much time running over an offensive guard. The crucial first two or three seconds of a play have passed, and if the play is perfectly executed he's too late to stop it. Unhappily, from my point of view, the perfectly executed play is rare, rarer than you'd think, considering all the planning and practice that goes into every play.

By now, of course, my thought process before each play is automatic, almost subconscious. First I think about my spacing, how far I should be from the center. I'll vary the distance. If the center has to cut my man off, I'll line up closer to him to make his job easier. But if I'm going to pull to my left, I'll make certain that I don't edge closer to the center because I don't want to tip the direction I'm going. Then I think about my stance. I don't want to vary my stance at all; I don't want to give the tackle any hint of the direction or nature of the play.

On rushing plays, my blocking is aggressive. I've got an assignment and I get off the ball as fast as I can and try to carry out my assignment. It's relatively simple. Pass blocking is a stiffer test. You seldom lash out on a pass block; you receive the blow. It's mainly a negative block; it's a countermove. The tackle moves, you move. It's dangerous to commit yourself.

Suppose I'm up against the typical defensive tackle, which means, in our league, that he's a pretty good tackle. Usually, his first move will be to hit you with his helmet—boom! He's got his forearms moving and he's reaching up with his hands to try to throw you, probably by the shoulder pads. It's sort of a one-two punch— hit you low and throw you high—without any real time lag between the two moves. You have to meet him with your head or give him a little jab with your left hand or with both hands—it's illegal, but you do it a lot—and sometimes you'll go down fast and cut out his legs. If you cut him down, you're gambling. He's liable to get up quickly and if the pass play isn't exactly on rhythm—one, two, three, throw—he'll be in the quarterback's face before the pass is released. You use the cutoff mostly as a change of pace, and once you and your man both hit the ground, you try to keep scrambling on all fours, try to keep your body under his feet so that he can't get up. Logically, you don't want to do the same thing every time. Occasionally—almost never against a Karras or an Olsen—on a pass block, I'll come off the ball real quick and pop the guy and take the initiative away from him. Or, if I want to be real cute and risky, I'll take sort of a half step to the outside, fake the man that way, then stand up and try to shield him.

Against the great tackles you can't relax for a second. They beat you with their quickness and their intelligence. They won't go directly at you more than one time out of twenty. They go around you. They go inside. They go outside. Then it's a matter of agility against agility, knowledge against knowledge. To an extent, quickness is learned; it's partly natural, but it also comes with experience and understanding. There's nobody quicker than Alex Karras, but the year after he was suspended from pro football for a season—for betting on his own team—he wasn't quite so quick. He had to get his timing back.

By the time we got to the hunting camp in Upper Wisconsin this morning, I had stopped thinking about tackles. We ate a big breakfast about 4:30 A.M., picked up our guides and our dogs, then set off into the woods.

We hunted for more than four hours, and we didn't even see a bear. Maybe it was just as well. Before we left, Max warned us not to go. "Don't forget," he said, "the score so far this year is: Bears 3, People 0."

SEPTEMBER 11

Tom Cichowski was sitting in the dressing room this morning, in his sweat clothes, all ready to go out on the practice field, and somebody walked over and told him he had been cut. The kid had to get out of his sweat clothes, change back into his street clothes, pack up his gear and go tell his wife, who had just arrived in town last week, that he had been cut. I really felt sorry for him. I never expected him to make the team, but I had to feel sorry for him.

Leon Crenshaw got the bad news, too, which surprised me. I imagine he'll be back in camp with us next year. He's planning to play in the Continental League this season and he wants to go through all our punishment again next year.

We lost one veteran. Lombardi traded Dave Hathcock to the New York Giants for a future draft choice. The survivors breathed deeply for the first time in weeks. Travis Williams was more relaxed than I'd ever seen him, laughing, feeling good. Claudis James had a big smile on his face, showing his gold teeth. We've got seven rookies on the roster: Williams, James, Hyland, Horn, Flanigan, Rowser, and Dick Capp, who can play either tight end or linebacker.

We've also got two rookies on the taxi squad: Jay Bachman, a boy from Cincinnati who can play both center and guard, and Dave Dunaway, whose big, no-cut contract frightened away all the other teams. When Lionel Aldridge, who was running today, and Bob Long return to active duty, the men they replace will probably join the cab team.

We watched the movies of the Giant game, and on the opening kickoff Tom Cichowski slipped past his blocker and really hit the ballcarrier. "Way to go, Cichowski," Lombardi yelled. "Way to go. Attaboy." Nobody said a word, and Lombardi suddenly realized that Cichowski was no longer around to hear his praise.

Personally, I found the movie thoroughly enjoyable. I had my best game of the exhibition season. I didn't make one mental error, and my man did no damage. I really had a beautiful game.

"Gentlemen," said Lombardi, after the movie, "we have our team now. We have the men we're going with, the men who have a chance to bring Green Bay a third consecutive world championship. Gentlemen, no team in the history of the National Football League has ever won three straight world championships. If you succeed, you will never forget this year for the rest of your lives. Gentlemen, this is the beginning of the big push."

Training camp is closed. We're human beings again.

THE GREEN BAY PACKERS' NFL SCHEDULE

DATE	OPPONENT	SITE
September 17	Detroit Lions	Green Bay
September 24	Chicago Bears	Green Bay
October 1	Atlanta Falcons	Milwaukee
October 8	Detroit Lions	Detroit
October 15	Minnesota Vikings	Milwaukee
October 22	New York Giants	New York
October 30	St. Louis Cardinals	St. Louis
November 5	Baltimore Colts	Baltimore
November 12	Cleveland Browns	Milwaukee
November 19	San Francisco 49ers	Green Bay
November 26	Chicago Bears	Chicago
December 3	Minnesota Vikings	Minneapolis
December 9	Los Angeles Rams	Los Angeles
December 17	Pittsburgh Steelers	Green Bay

ARMED COMBAT

For the first time in history, the National Football League this year is divided into four divisions, Central, Coastal, Century, and Capitol. We're in the Central Division, along with Minnesota, Detroit and Chicago, three teams that suffered through losing seasons in 1966. Chicago and Detroit are rebuilding this year; Minnesota has traded its star quarterback, Fran Tarkenton, to New York. We should have no trouble winning our division.

The whole setup's kind of confusing, but the way our schedule works, we play two games against each of the teams in our division, one game against each of the teams in the Coastal Division (Atlanta, Baltimore, Los Angeles, and San Francisco) and one game against each of the teams in the Century Division (Cleveland, St. Louis, New York, and Pittsburgh). At the end of the season, the Coastal winner plays the Central winner for the Western Conference championship, and the Century winner plays the Capitol winner for the Eastern Conference championship. Then, as usual, the East plays the West for the NFL title, and the NFL champion plays the American Football League champion in the Super Bowl. Last year, we collected $9,813 a man for winning the NFL championship game and $15,000 a man for winning the Super Bowl. We're sort of counting on that extra $25,000 a man again this year.

We're in a strange position, being in the Central Division. Each of the other three divisions has at least two strong teams in it; each of the other divisions looks like it's going to have some good competition for the championship. In a way, we're lucky that there's nobody powerful to challenge us in our own division, but, at the same time, we're in danger of getting lazy, getting complacent. I can't imagine us getting too lazy, though, as long as Lombardi is around. Even if he lost his voice, even if he couldn't scream at us, he'd manage to scare us. All he's got to do, really, is look at us. His looks can freeze you.

SEPTEMBER 13

The Lions didn't have much fire last year, much zest, but I suspect their new coach, Joe Schmidt, is going to give it to them. Joe was one of the great linebackers in the game, always battling, never quitting, and I think he's instilling this spirit in his team. We watched the films of their last exhibition game today, their 21–7 victory over St. Louis, and they looked tough. Besides, I'm sure they're looking for us. They're always looking for us. We've had some great football games in the past ten years, and some great victories, though I'll probably remember longest the game they beat us 26–14, on Thanksgiving Day, 1962, the only game we lost that year. Schmidt and Alex Karras and Roger Brown and all of them killed us that day. Every time they guessed, they guessed right, and they ripped us apart. They spent half the game in our backfield. After the game, in the bus going to the airport, Fuzzy turned to me and said, "Well, at least it wasn't a total loss. We learned a new block today." I said, "What the hell do you mean?" And Fuzzy said, "The lookout block. You know, you block, and then you yell, 'Look out, Bart.' "

SEPTEMBER 14

Alex Karras is spending a lot of time with me this week. He eats breakfast with me, goes to the john with me, brushes my teeth with me. I'm thinking about him every minute, how difficult he is to cut off on the inside, how he likes the outside on a pass rush, how he just loves to hit the quarterback.

Alex has half a dozen different, effective moves—it took him three or four years as a pro to develop them—and he uses all of them. One of his moves is a little hop and a skip to the outside. He actually hops, and it looks funny, but it works. He charges to the outside maybe 90 percent of the time, but you can't overadjust because he likes to change up and come to the inside with a real strong move, doubly hard to stop because you don't expect it.

I've got one extra weapon against Alex this year. Most teams have only one really good defensive tackle, and if you're up against him, the center can help you out on blocks. But when we were playing the Lions in the past, with Karras at one tackle and Roger Brown at the other, the center just didn't know which way to turn. Now that Detroit's traded Brown, I should be able to get some help. I may need it.

SEPTEMBER 17

Before I left the house this morning for the stadium, my oldest child, Tony, who's nine, asked me who my man'd be in the game. I told him Karras.

"What's his number?" Tony said.

I said, "Seventy-one."

"I'll watch for him," Tony said.

"It shouldn't be too tough," I said. "You'll probably see a lot of him."

I thought I was just making a little joke, but the joke was on me. I had a bad day. Alex probably figured he had a good day. I don't know yet how many times he got to the passer, how many times he rushed past me, but it seemed like every time I went to the sidelines, Vince screamed at me.

The game started off as though Detroit wasn't going to give us any special trouble. They weren't hitting particularly hard—and that's usually a reliable indication. But then a rookie named Lem Barney intercepted one of Bart's passes, turned a somersault and ran for a touchdown, and, suddenly, they got higher than a kite. They promptly tried a short kickoff, a smart, gambling, aggressive move, and I was the nearest Packer to the ball and I didn't get to it, and they recovered and moved in for a field goal, and I just wanted to quit. I wanted to walk off the field and never play football again.

Alex started beating me to the outside, and one time I knew he had me and I was so frustrated I reached out and grabbed a big handful of his jersey and just pulled him to the ground. Nobody saw it, and Alex got up calling me every name he could think of. I'm sure that he's been held by about 90 percent of the guys he plays against, but he didn't expect it from me. I was desperate.

The first half, Detroit intercepted four of Bart's passes, and at half-time they were whipping us 17–0. In the locker room Ray Wietecha, our line coach, chewed me up and down. Even though Bart starting hitting his targets in the second half, and Elijah Pitts plunged for two touchdowns, and Chandler kicked a field goal, and we managed to get a tie, 17–17, and came within a few seconds of winning the game, I still felt miserable, totally disgusted.

When I came out from the locker room, my insides all torn up, and climbed into my car, my son Tony looked at me and said, "Daddy, do you like Alex Karras? I don't mean as a football player. I mean as a person."

"Shut up," I said.

SEPTEMBER 18

My right ankle's extremely sore today, all discolored, black and blue and red, bruised, painful, everything. I guess it's going to be all right, unfortunately. For a while I was kind of hoping it was broken. Then this damned season would be over for me.

SEPTEMBER 19

When I entered the locker room this morning everybody was awfully quiet, awfully subdued. The guys kept looking at me sort of compassionately, sharing my apprehensions about a big ass-chewing in the movies. When we went into the meeting room for the movies, Gale Gillingham came over and sat down beside me, and Kenny Bowman sat directly behind me. We huddled like three lambs about to be slaughtered. It's ridiculous the way supposedly adult individuals cower and hide from one short, fat Italian.

(The other day Bob Skoronski told me that he took his kids to the Dairy Queen for ice cream cones, and just when they started licking their cones, he saw Lombardi coming. So Bob hid his ice cream cone behind his back. "I'm thirty-three years old," he said, "and I've got a family, and I've got all the responsibilities in the world, and here I am hiding an ice cream cone from the old man.")

My apprehensions were very well grounded. Vince began his lecture at 9:30, and he chewed my butt like he hadn't for two or three years. All he could talk about was what a great day Karras had and what a lousy day I had. "One man made us look like a bunch of dummies," he said. "One man tossed us around like a bunch of dolls."

On and on and on and on he went, and he really got to me. I had several different thoughts during the course of the lecture. I didn't know whether to tell him to stick it in his ear or to hit him in the mouth or to quit or to cry or to just shut up. Lombardi ran the movies over and over, and, actually, Karras got to the passer three or four times maximum. Three of them were my fault. But I got the blame for everything. We threw the ball thirty times, and he got to the passer three or four times, and I'm the lamb, I'm the reason we had such a lousy game. Vince really burned my ass.

"Hell, you didn't have that bad a day," Fuzzy said to me after the movie. "If Bart hadn't had such a bad day and if everything hadn't gone so wrong, he wouldn't have said so much."

After the screaming, hollering maniac finished up the films, he had some beautiful comments about outside interests and lack of complete dedication, lack of singleness of purpose. Lombardi began shouting, and I began thinking, I've got to go see Blaine Williams this afternoon about the Kraft deal, and I've got to go cut a few commercials for Elmtree Bakery and RCA-Victor and Pepsi and Citgo, and then I've got to tape my TV show. Maybe Vince is right.

Finally he let us out on the field, and we had our regular

Tuesday-morning touch game, the offense against the Big D. I think the D stands for dummies instead of defense; we beat them easily. Then Ray Wietecha delivered a speech about the past performances of the offensive line, what a great job the offensive line had always done, enabling Bart Starr to set all his records, and the implication was clear; Kramer ruined everything. I hated Wietecha, too.

We went back inside and got a scouting report on the Chicago Bears, our opponents this week, and afterward Donny Chandler and I were sitting in the locker room, looking at a catalogue for shoes, wholesale alligator shoes. The next thing I know, I'm ordering twenty-one pairs of shoes for the guys at about fifty dollars a whack. I don't know why I took the orders; I hope I don't get stuck. I guess I'm everybody's mark this week.

At noon I went home, and my wife was out, so I walked across the street to Henry Jordan's house to have lunch with him. Olive, Henry's wife, is a great lady; Ma Jordan feeds the hungry and shelters the homeless. But Olive started talking to me about Karras.

"How'd the meeting go, Jerry?" she said, with a smile. "Did Coach Lombardi have anything to say?"

I got upset and hollered at her, and told her to get off my back, and, of course, I got her mad at me. She didn't mean anything.

When I left Henry's, I went over to the barber, and that stupid sonuvabitch didn't have anything to do but talk in my ear about Karras for an hour and a half while he cut my hair. Then I drove downtown to see Blaine, and everywhere I went people kept saying to me, "What did Lombardi say? What happened?" This is one of the beautiful things about a small town. Everybody knows what should have happened, what I should have done; everybody had a few words of friendly advice. They're good people and they mean well, but sometimes they do get on your nerves, they do antagonize you.

Normally, I enjoy being recognized as a pro football player—
I'm a little susceptible to hero worship—but sometimes, like today, I just wish I could escape. I used to make up different
identities for myself when I was traveling during the off-season.
I'd be in a restaurant or in a cocktail lounge, and when somebody'd come up to me and ask if I were a professional football
player—I do look the part; I'm not inconspicuous, like a defensive
back—I'd tell him that I was a shoe salesman or a cab driver or a
construction worker. When Henry Jordan was playing for the
Cleveland Browns he did the same thing. He even invented a new
name for himself—Buck Johnson—so that he wouldn't get into
football conversations. You can pass for a normal human being in
a big city like Cleveland; you can't in Green Bay.

To be honest, I've got to admit there was another reason—
besides wanting to avoid football talk—that I'd pretend not to be
a pro football player. Too many times, a guy'd come up to me and
ask the obvious question and I'd say, "Yes, I'm a football player,"
and he'd say, "What's your name?" and I'd say, "Jerry Kramer,"
and he'd give me a totally blank look and mumble, "Who do you
play for?" or he'd confuse me with Ron Kramer and say, "Oh,
you're the end from Michigan." It hurt. But I guess that's the price
of playing right guard.

I taped my first TV show of the year tonight, and my two
guests were Herb Adderley and Bob Long. I always have two of
my teammates on the show, and we look at the highlights of the
previous game and we talk about their experiences and their
plans. McGee was supposed to be on tonight—I wanted him for
the first show because he's always a good talker—but he didn't
show, and I had to rush Bob Long over to the studio. Max is utterly undependable. He's Fuzzy's partner in the restaurant business and once, not long after they opened a place in Manitowoc,
Max disappeared, just vanished from the face of the earth, for al-

most two months. Nobody heard a word from him, and Fuzzy, afraid of foul play, put tracers on him, and, finally, after about seven weeks, some of Max's checks came through to the bank. They had been cashed at the Racquet Club in Miami. Fuzzy put in a call to the Racquet Club and paged McGee, and when Max came to the phone, Fuzzy said, "Max, Max, where the hell you been?" And Max said, "Hold it, Fuzz, I'm in the middle of a set. I'll call you back later."

On the show, I asked Bob Long how it felt to be substituting for Max, and Bob said that he was used to it, that when he reported to Green Bay, Coach Lombardi told him, "This Max McGee is one of the greatest ends of all time, and I just want you to watch him, and do everything he does."

"So I watched Max," Bob said, "and I tried to do everything he did. It wasn't so bad on the field, but those nights killed me."

We didn't get finished taping the show till 11:30, so I added Max's name to the list of people—Lombardi, Wietecha, Karras, Olive Jordan, my barber—I was going to have killed.

SEPTEMBER 20

All morning today I was in a foul mood. I was thinking of going to Alaska and hunting polar bears, thinking of doing anything except playing football anymore. After a brief meeting, with some more choice comments about the Detroit game, we went out for a blitz drill. They were taking movies from the tower, so we couldn't brother-in-law; we had to hit pretty hard. I was blocking Kostelnik, and I guess I got in a good lick, and Vince yelled, "Way to go, Jerry, way to go. Beautiful. That's the way to go. Attaboy." He was trying to make up to me. After the drill, he walked over to me and pounded me on the shoulder and said, "That's the way to go, Jerry." Then he lowered his voice and said, "You know, that just breaks my heart when that guy Karras beats you like that. It breaks my heart." I stood there a few seconds, thinking, and I said, "Coach, it doesn't make me feel too damned good, either." He laughed, and now we're back on speaking terms again. I guess I won't have him killed, after all.

I got home after lunch, just starting to feel a little better, and I saw the story in the newspaper: The Associated Press had named Alex Karras the NFL's Defensive Player of the Week for his outstanding performance against Green Bay. Beautiful! I'm tempted to say some things about Karras, but we're always the good guys, always the people who don't say bad things about anybody, always the nice guys. I'm tired of that nice-guy stuff, but I guess I really shouldn't say anything about that nearsighted hippopotamus.

SEPTEMBER 21

When Vince chewed me out Tuesday, one of the things he said was that I ought to give Bart my whole pay check this week for the way I got him beat up Sunday. Today was our first payday and I'd sort of forgotten what Vince said, and when I went into the locker room Bart was standing by my locker.

"Where is it?" he said.

"Where's what?" I said.

"Your pay check," he said. "I've been looking for the check all week long."

We had a big giggle, and I relaxed a little for the first time all week. Kenny Bowman's wife had a little boy yesterday, and Kenny, who's a law student during the off-season, was walking around the locker room, handing out 25-cent cigars to everybody. My first few years at Green Bay, whenever anyone had a baby they'd hand out cigars, but they'd be the two-for-a-nickel or, at best, the two-for-a-dime kind. But Kenny had real good cigars, and he's a lineman, an interior offensive lineman, naturally not one of the highest paid men of the club. Our standards of living have certainly gone up.

Hawg Hanner's wife had a baby Sunday, and Herb Adderley's wife is pregnant, and so is Travis Williams' and a few of the other wives. It's a good sign. As long as we've got pregnant wives, and all those Cadillacs and Continentals sitting in the parking lot, we're going to be a hungry football team.

SEPTEMBER 22

We've settled into our regular-season schedule, the schedule we'll follow all year: Game on Sunday, off on Monday, loosen up and hear a scouting report from head scout Wally Cruice on Tuesday, heavy workouts with pads on Wednesday and Thursday, medium workout without pads on Friday, loosen up on Saturday, meetings and movies every day from Tuesday through Friday. Today we had a goal-line drill, practicing the plays we use near the goal line. Vince was cheerful and smiling again, and he asked a few of us whether he should climb up in the tower and watch practice from there, the way he does each Friday.

Lombardi's superstitious, just like everybody else connected with our team, and he likes to do everything exactly the same when we're doing well and he likes to change his pattern when we're going badly. We looked terrible last Sunday, so he was reluctant to go back up in the tower.

"We haven't lost yet, Coach," Zeke said.

"Yeah," said Vince, "we haven't lost. I guess I'll go up." He did. He's superstitious second, and a perfectionist first.

My ankle's pretty sore. It was feeling better Tuesday and Wednesday, but now it's hurting again. I guess it'll be all right for the game.

My wife and I spent the evening tonight at the Jordans'—Olive isn't mad at me anymore—and we had a long discussion of Edgar Cayce and some of his beliefs on reincarnation. We had a relaxing evening, and it even gave me a little hope. Maybe in the next life I'll be the coach and Vince'll be playing for me.

SEPTEMBER 23

Vince gave out a few awards for the first game today, certificates for players who did something special. Forrest Gregg and Boyd Dowler got the only blocking awards, and Gravel Pitts and Donny Anderson got runs-over-20-yards awards, Tom Brown got a fumble-recovery award, and Lee Roy Caffey got a blocked-field-goal award. Then Fuzzy stood up and said, "How 'bout giving Willie Davis an award for attempting to get close to the passer?"

In his pregame speech last Sunday, Willie had said, "You got to *wont* that game. You got to *wont* it more than they do. You got to *wont* that ball. I myself, I *wont* Bradshaw. I *WONT HIM*. I *wont* to put something on him." Charlie Bradshaw was playing offensive tackle for the Lions, opposite Willie, and he gave Willie a terrible time. Willie didn't get close to Milt Plum, the Lion quarterback, all day.

At the award meeting, after Fuzzy's suggestion, somebody yelled, "Well, you got that Bradshaw, Willie. Maybe next time you can get Plum." And then everybody began shouting, mimicking Willie's voice. "I *wont* that Bradshaw. I *wont* that guy. I *WONT* HIM. I *WONT* HIM." And we all broke up laughing and went out for our final light workout before the Bear game.

We've got something to prove tomorrow. We lost some respect around the league by getting tied last Sunday, and we want to get it back.

SEPTEMBER 24

When I got to the locker room today before the game, Max and Ron Kostelnik were resting, lying down, almost completely dressed, and Tommy Joe Crutcher was playing his Ernest Tubb records on the stereo. We let Tommy Joe hear his country music till the dressing room began to fill up. Then we put on some popular stuff. When I went in to get taped, Fuzzy and Don Horn were lying on the tables, and Bud Jorgensen, our trainer, was taping Horn's knee. "What the hell you wasting all that tape for, Horn?" Fuzzy said, needling the kid. "You've been in here half an hour getting taped, and there ain't no way you're gonna get to play, unless Bart and Zeke and three other guys get hurt." Horn laughed. He's coming around. He's lost a little of his cocky attitude, and he's starting to fit the Green Bay Packer mold.

After he finished with Horn, Jorgy began taping me. Right after he got started, Jorgy put the roll of tape down for a second, and Ben Wilson reached over, grabbed it and took a couple of inches off. I got shook up. I have that superstition about nobody else using my tape. So I made Jorgy throw the roll away and start over with a fresh roll.

Dave Hanner wandered around, checking all the men on the special units, the kickoff teams, the punt teams, the extra-point teams. Hawg was mostly reminding the men on the kicking teams about Gale Sayers, about how tough he is on returns.

I checked with Gilly on our assignments, checked with Coach Wietecha, then had a little talk with myself. I wanted very much to have a good game, especially after last week.

I got the hell beat out of me in the game, somewhere in the first quarter or the second, I don't know which, I got kicked or something, and I got a slight concussion. I remember very little about the game. I have a vague recollection of half-time, of trying to get some plays straightened out. I couldn't remember the plays. I mean I could remember the real old plays, the ones we've used for six, seven years, but the new plays, the ones we put in during the last two years, I just couldn't remember. I drew a complete blank. I don't even know how long I played today. I don't have any idea, and I won't till I see the movies.

We won the ball game, 13–10, and the first time I recall looking at the scoreboard we were winning 3–0. We went ahead 10–0, and they tied it up 10–10, and then Don Chandler won the game in the last minute or so with a 46-yard field goal. It's funny the way I remember the field goal was 46 yards long.

We couldn't have looked very good. I know Bart had another bad afternoon, and I know it was a rough game. When I finally woke up a little in the second half, I saw two or three Bears carried off the field, knocked cold. After the game, I showered and shaved quickly, and Doug and Marilyn Hart and Barbara and I took off for the north country to go deer hunting. I had a terrible headache all the way up. I took three or four Emperin-codeine pills, but they didn't help much. My stomach was hurting, too.

I'm going to go to sleep now, but I still feel pretty screwed up.

SEPTEMBER 25

I woke up at 5:30 this morning to go deer hunting, and my first thought was, 53-drive, which is a new play, and I said to myself, 53-drive, get the middle linebacker, if the tackle closes, take him with you. Then I thought, 53, take the tackle all the way, and then 47-drive, drive the tackle or drive the linebacker, 46-pull, and all the new plays just came to me one after the other, snap, snap, snap.

We spent most of the day hunting, and none of us got a deer, but it was good fun. My headache wouldn't go away, but I guess I'm going to be all right.

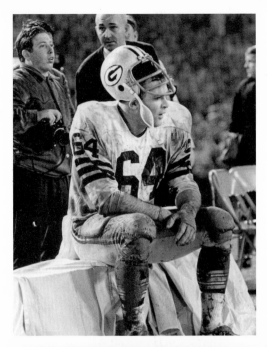

Man at work.

Many nights, we would drive by the office at one or two in the morning and the coaches were still there. Coach expected a lot of his players, but he also expected a lot of himself.

The first time I thought seriously about football, I was a sophomore in high school, in Sand Point, Idaho. In my senior yearbook it says that my ambition was to play professional football for the Los Angeles Rams.

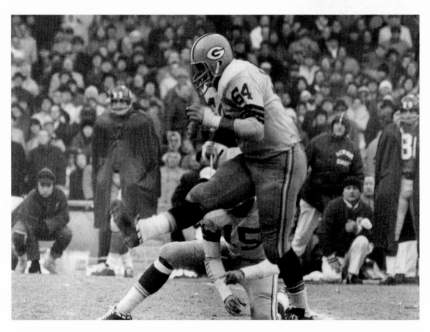

In 1962, I filled in as kicker for the injured Paul Hornung. It led to one of my most memorable days. Yankee Stadium, three field goals, one extra point. A Packer victory, 16–7, World Championship.

1961. Fuzzy Thurston and I lead Jim Taylor on a sweep to the outside.

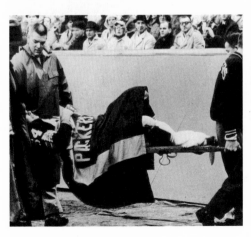

This is how the 1961 season ended for me.
A broken ankle against Minnesota.

When you're out hurt, you somehow no longer feel really a part
of the team.

The Kramer boys. Tony, Danny, and Jerry.

Packer linemen warming up before the 1963 game with the College All-Stars.

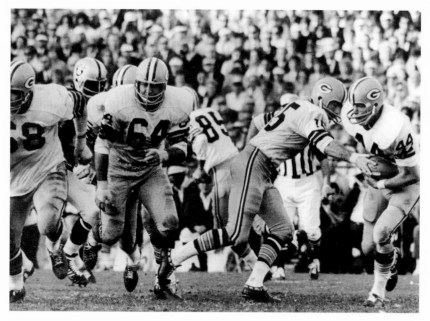

Sweep left in 1967. Gale Gillingham (no. 68) has replaced Fuzzy, and the "Golden Palomino," Donny Anderson (no. 44), has replaced the Golden Boy.

Cleveland World Championship game in 1966. Bart enjoys perfect protection.

(above) 1968. Protecting Zeke.
(right) Telegrams from the fans.

Thurston and Kramer, "the NFL's greatest," contemplate the meaning of life.

(above and right) 1967. During our two-a-day workouts, the agony was beyond belief. Grass drills, agility drills, wind sprints, everything. You wonder why you're there, how long you're going to last. No other team in pro football worked as hard as we did. Of course, no other team won so often, either.

The block against Dallas in the last fifteen seconds for the 1967 NFL Championship, our third in a row.

(above) Coach once said I have a burning incandescence in my gut.

(left) 1967 Super Bowl. Mutual admiration . . . at last.

(above) After the Super Bowl. Gerald Louis Kramer. Age thirty-one.

(right) This stairway led to the tunnel and onto the field. The top sign was Coach Lombardi's favorite.

Any man's finest hour - his greatest fulfillment to all he holds dear - is that moment when he has worked his heart out in a good cause and lies exhausted on the field of battle - VICTORIOUS

LEAVE
NO REGRETS
ON THE FIELD

SEPTEMBER 26

I woke up this morning feeling fine and went to the stadium to see the movies, and we were all sitting there waiting for the roof to fall in. We expected Coach Lombardi to start screaming and ranting and having convulsions, and once again Kenny Bowman and Gilly and I huddled together, the three sheep.

Right before the movies, Vince came over to me, patted me on the head, roughed up my hair and said, "Boy, you came out of there on one block and knocked the halfback down and went on and knocked the end down. You were just great. One of the greatest plays I've ever seen." Of course, I didn't even remember the play.

Lombardi surprised everyone by saying that we showed him the best line blocking he had seen since 1961. He said the offensive line was great, and all through the movies, he kept yelling, "Beautiful block . . . fantastic . . . great job . . . way to go." He was using a new brand of psychology.

On one play, a 42, Gilly turned to me and whispered, "Oh God, watch this. Oh, watch this. I'm really going to get chewed here." On the screen, Gilly pulled the trap, and the defensive end closed down real tight so he couldn't take him outside, and Gilly tried to take him inside and slipped and fell down. Gilly cringed, watching the play, and Lombardi shouted out, "OK, Gilly, way to try. That's a good effort. Way to try."

Gilly stared at me in disbelief. "Well, hell," he said, "if he didn't chew me for that, I ain't ever gonna get chewed out."

I saw the play that gave me the concussion. I cut down the defensive end, Ed O'Bradovich, and I rolled over on my back and, as I raised myself toward a sitting position, Dick Evey, Chicago's right tackle, started to jump over me. I came up, and his knee caught me flush between the eyes. I went down like a shot, but then I got up and went back into the huddle. I played a few more plays in the second quarter, then sat out the whole second half. The moment it happened, I knew I had a concussion. I knew I was in a world of trouble. Physically, I felt all right, but I knew I couldn't think straight. Four or five years ago, against the Los Angeles Rams, I played most of a game with a concussion. Forrest Gregg told me what to do on every play. He said, "Block the tackle," or, "Pull and block the end," and I actually played fairly well. I did what I was supposed to. Between college and the pros, I've had four or five concussions now, and I suppose I'm getting used to them.

After the movie, Coach said he was disappointed with the way we were filling out our player reports. After every game, we have to fill out reports on the opposing personnel, their ability to diagnose plays, their quickness, their lateral movement, everything. We grade them excellent, above average, average, below average, and poor. When someone becomes available and Lombardi thinks about trading for him, he goes through these reports and gets a lot of valuable information. It's a good bank for him.

"Everybody we're going to play this year," said Lombardi, "has read all this stuff in the papers about who's going to beat the Green Bay Packers, who can do it, who can beat them, can anybody beat them. So everybody says, 'By gosh, we can, we can do it.' This is the price of winning. This is the price of the last two championships. You're paying for it now because everybody in the league wants to beat you. They're giving it their maximum supreme effort. There's no loafing, no halfway, against the Green Bay Packers. My father told me when I decided to quit law school and go into coaching that there'd be a hell of a lot of days like Sunday, days when you wished you'd stayed in the locker room. But I fooled my father. We've won a hell of a lot more than we've lost. OK. Let's go."

Then we ran out for calisthenics. On Tuesdays, instead of lining up in rows, we form a big circle, and one man gets in the middle and leads the exercises. Fuzzy always starts off the session and I finish it, and in between we call upon the men who've played outstanding games. We called upon Jim Grabowski first today. Jim gained 111 yards rushing against the Bears, the most any Packer has gained in two years. Donny Anderson and Elijah Pitts, who both had good running days, took turns in the middle, and so did Ray Nitschke, who played a helluva game, and Jim Weatherwax, who played the whole game at defensive end. After the calisthenics we played our usual touch game, and I threw a couple of touchdown passes—in the touch games, I play tailback on offense and free safety on defense—and the offensive line beat the defensive line again.

We finished up early, and several of the boys took time for long sauna baths, to sweat out Sunday and Monday nights.

SEPTEMBER 27

We watched movies of the Atlanta Falcons today, saw them lose to Baltimore and to San Francisco, then went out and had a big work day, practicing for about an hour and a half in 40-degree weather. Winter has descended upon us a little early.

My folks came in from Louisiana this morning. My father and my partner in the diving business, Urban Henry, had a personality conflict, and my folks didn't enjoy living in Louisiana, so I guess they're going to go home to Idaho. I think it'll be good for my father to get home. He and I played nine shivering holes of golf this afternoon, and we didn't score well, but we had fun.

We all went over to Blaine Williams' house for a dinner party, and afterward we watched my show, then watched the *Kraft Music Hall*, which carried a commercial for the portraits we're distributing. The Kraft people tell us that the portraits should start moving well real soon.

SEPTEMBER 28

I brought half a dozen green berets to the locker room today. Each of the berets has a gold tassel on top, and each bears the words: World Champion Green Bay Packers. Blaine Williams and I are promoting them. We're going to have them made up in the colors of all the teams in the NFL and try to sell them around the country. Everybody on our team wanted one—for nothing, of course—so I guess I'll have to supply them. We'll have to chalk it off to public relations.

All my businesses seem to be flourishing. The archery company is starting to gross about $50,000 or $60,000 each month, the diving company's coming along, and my TV show has been getting good reaction. My only competition, really, is *The Vince Lombardi Show*. We're both syndicated around the state, and he does have a few more stations, but I know my show is better. With my personality and my good looks, Vince just doesn't have a chance.

I read an article today about Bubba Smith, called "The Human Side of Bubba Smith," which interested me and irritated me at the same time. As if he were anything but human. The image that some people have of the professional football player—the monster, the subhuman type—really burns me. The story about Bubba said, "You don't feed him, you oil him." There are a lot of sportswriters I'd like to oil.

SEPTEMBER 29

The atmosphere at practice this morning was strange. It was one of carefree frivolity, everybody laughing and kidding, everybody goofing off, even during the workout. About halfway through practice Lombardi turned to the defense and said, "Come on, defense, give us a picture over there. You're acting. You're jumping around. We've got the hokies this week, huh? We've got a bunch of patsies, and you're gonna fool around, just laugh around and have a good time, huh? Well, you're a bunch of fools, every one of you, a bunch of damned fools."

I think Vince had a right to be upset. The defensive team was getting a little cocky, and Willie Davis was mouthing off a little bit. "Come on, offense," he'd say. "We're gonna build up your confidence." It was nothing serious, but they certainly weren't concentrating on their assignments. They were trying to have some fun, for a change.

SEPTEMBER 30

We took our chartered buses down to Milwaukee this morning and went to County Stadium for a brief workout. Coach Lombardi had several bitter words for us.

"I don't know what I can tell you," he said. "I've never had to talk to a team like this. I never had to holler at them before a game. They were always ready. But you people aren't ready. You've got a lackadaisical attitude. You're just gonna go out there tomorrow and get the hell kicked out of you. I tell you, it's gonna be a hell of a game. Those Falcons aren't going to lie down for you."

We want to believe Vince, we want to get ourselves up for the game, but we just can't. When you're going to play a game on Sunday, you have to start getting mentally ready on Tuesday. You have to work up a good hatred, a strong desire, and you can't just do it on Friday and Saturday. It's too late by then. We're having trouble every week getting up. We thought the Lions would be easy; they'd even lost an exhibition game to Denver. We thought the

Bears would be easy; they'd lost their opener to Pittsburgh. And now Atlanta hasn't won a game, and we beat them last year, 56–3, and there just doesn't seem to be any way in the world Vince can convince us we're in trouble.

After Vince's lecture, we posed for our official team picture. Tommy Joe Crutcher and Jim Grabowski were both off at National Guard drills. They thought they'd be absent from the picture, but Tommy Joe showed up at the last minute, wearing his Air Force blues and saluting everybody in sight. Tommy Joe's a medic, and he actually goes around giving shots to people, which is something he never did before in his life, except maybe to cattle. Grabo didn't make it, so Dave Dunaway, from the cab squad, put on Grabo's jersey and took his place in the team picture. Later on, they'll superimpose Grabo's head on Dunaway's, and it'll look like he was there for the picture. I suppose Dunaway's the highest-paid stand-in in the whole world.

Tonight my wife and I had dinner with two of our best friends, Johnny Symank, the defensive-backfield coach of Atlanta, and his wife. Normally, I wouldn't even think of fraternizing with somebody from the other team the night before a game, but, somehow, with the Falcons, it seemed all right. I talked to their head coach tonight, Norb Hecker, another good friend of mine, and he invited me to Atlanta during the off-season to play golf with him. How can I get excited about the game?

OCTOBER 1

I had a little trouble waking up this morning, so I missed our first devotional service of the year. I just barely did get up in time for breakfast.

We started the devotional services last year, for the benefit of the Protestant boys on the team who can't attend church services when we're on the road. Four and a half hours before game time, half an hour before breakfast, we get together and read from the Bible and say a few prayers and sometimes have a little discussion, led by Bart Starr or Carroll Dale. We've got about twenty guys who usually go, and I felt a little bad about missing the service today.

Vince got upset at breakfast. We have a choice of ordering ham and eggs or steak, but most of the guys seem to take whichever appears first. If a man's ordered ham and eggs but the waitress comes around with a steak, he'll take the steak. And vice versa. Of course, there's always a few guys who really want steak or really want ham and eggs, and they're left at the end without the meal they ordered. Lombardi doesn't know what to do about it, but I guess it isn't his major problem.

Right after breakfast, we had our usual meetings, the offensive in one room and the defense in another. We found out at the meeting that Lionel Aldridge and Bob Long had been reactivated for the game, and that Dick Capp and Claudis James had been placed on waivers. If nobody claims them, I imagine they'll both be playing on our taxi team.

When we got to the stadium and got into the locker room, no one seemed too enthused about the game. Everybody seemed to feel it was one of those situations where you have to show up, you have to play, and you have to win. If you lose, you look like a dummy. We showed up, we played, and we won, 23–0, but it was a real mediocre effort.

Bart Starr got hurt in the first quarter, racked up on a blitz. Bob Riggle, the Atlanta safety, and Tom Nobis, their middle linebacker, both blitzed, and Riggle hit Bart first, jarring him, and then Nobis slammed him. Bart got hit in the armpit, and his right arm went numb. The safety blitz was a perfect example of the gambling attitude teams have when they play us. A safety blitz is an absolute gamble. If the quarterback gets away from it and gets off a good long pass, it's a sure six points. But the Falcons were willing to gamble against us, willing to try anything to score an upset. They were blitzing their safety and their halfbacks and their linebackers and everybody else. I think Norb Hecker, their coach, was ready to blitz one time.

Zeke replaced Bart and did his usual good job. He threw two touchdown passes to Carroll Dale, and he called a fine game. He's got to be the best second-string quarterback in the NFL, and he never gripes about playing second-string. Ben Wilson picked up a lot of yardage, and Lionel Aldridge, only six weeks after he broke his leg, played an excellent game at defensive end.

Bart's had such a frustrating season. He's had nine passes intercepted; most years he doesn't give up that many interceptions all season. Until today, I didn't realize quite how frustrated Bart was, how intense he was. When he came out of the game, he stood next to me on the sidelines and started kicking the ground. He told me how much he wanted to get back in. He was just so disappointed about being hurt. When Zeke threw his first touchdown pass, Bart was the first one to shake his hand, the first to congratulate him, but still, all during the game, he was terribly unhappy. Tears actually came to his eyes on the sidelines. I'd never realized how dedicated he is, how much he wants to win, how much he wants to excel.

After the game, I drove home to Green Bay, ate a light meal and went right to bed. I intend to get a lot of sleep this coming week. We play the Lions in Detroit next Sunday, and I want to be fully rested for my friend Alex Karras.

OCTOBER 3

Coach Lombardi seemed more disturbed than angry during our meeting this morning. He said there's a general lack of enthusiasm on the club, a lack of desire, something he can't quite put his finger on. He said that sometimes he would rather lose and have everybody play a perfect game than win and have everybody look sloppy. My immediate reaction is to say that's crazy, that's ridiculous, he couldn't really mean that, but, somehow, I suspect he does, at least in theory. His desire for perfection is immense, and he's been very unhappy with our habit of doing only as much as we have to do to win.

Then Vince talked about Bart. He told us that Bart's been playing with injuries ever since the season began, and as he spoke, he got very emotional. "I don't know if you guys know it or not," Lombardi said, "but this guy's been hurt and he's been in pain, and he's been playing hurt, and he's been—" And Vince couldn't finish the sentence. He got all choked up and misty-eyed, and he looked like he was going to start crying, and he just motioned to another coach to turn the lights off and start the projector. He was sort of quiet while we suffered through the movies of the Atlanta game.

After the movies, we played our regular touch game, and I intercepted four passes, an all-time Tuesday morning record. The guys awarded me the game ball, and I just hope this is an omen of the game to come. There's been a lot of stuff in the papers about Alex Karras and how great he is. I guess it's been a while since the writers could find anything to zing Green Bay, and Alex's been giving them a mouthful. I'd like to give him a mouthful—of my shoe.

OCTOBER 4

Everybody is on me about Alex Karras, the newspapers, my coaches, my teammates. Lee Roy Caffey offered me a few subtle hints today, and Willie Davis came over and sat by my locker and chatted with me, and Henry Jordan told me what he'd do to handle Alex. Coach Lombardi drove me extra hard, trying to be helpful, and Tommy McCormick, our backfield coach, who hadn't said two words to me all year, came over and told me about the letters he's been getting with advice for me. I wish everyone would leave me alone.

I think about Alex all the time, morning, noon, and night, even when I'm watching television. I think about the way he's built, stocky, like a bowling ball, and I think about his strength. He's been a wrestler and a weightlifter, so he's got tremendous power in his arms and his upper body. But most of my thoughts are vicious. A Milwaukee sportswriter, who's a complete ass, had an article this morning in which Alex was talking about how he plays better against a good team and about how much he's looking forward to playing against the Green Bay Packers again. I'm looking forward to killing him.

OCTOBER 5

We're going to get our first indication Sunday of what kind of a team we've really got this year. This is the first time we've taken an opponent seriously, the first time we've realized we're in for a football game, the first time we've faced up to a challenge. Right after the Atlanta game, Lee Roy Caffey said that part of the reason we looked so bad was that we were all looking beyond Atlanta to the Lions, and I'm sure he was right. If we're not up this week, we'll never be.

We had a long workout today, polishing our game plan, and the game plan comes down to one thing: Pass protection, pass protection, pass protection. Vince kept stressing the pass rush of Detroit's defensive tackles, Karras in particular, and how we're going to stop it. We're working on draws and screens and on running in-side, between their tackles, and from a personal point of view, I couldn't be happier. It's just what I'd do if I were calling the plays. I'd try running plays right up the middle to keep their defensive tackles aware of our ground game, and then, on passing situations, I'd use a lot of draws and screens so that they can't mount an all-out pass rush. In other words, I'd keep them guessing. Lombardi's thinking exactly the way I am, so I guess he really is a very great coach.

OCTOBER 6

Dave Hanner gave me a few tips this morning, mostly on pass protection, and he reminded me that I had played a particularly good game against Alex in 1965. So after practice Kenny Bow-man, the center, and I stayed at the stadium and went over the 1965 films.

I think I've got a pretty good idea now of what Alex is going to do Sunday, and I've got a much more positive attitude about how I'm going to block him. If I did screw up in the first game — and I'm not convinced that I did — my main problem was an un-certain approach to the game. I thought I'd make my moves and let Alex react and then I'd counter-react, and I'd be quick enough and strong enough to handle him. I did handle him, to a certain extent, but not well enough. Now I'm going to try to anticipate his move, which is to the outside 90 or 95 percent of the time. He likes to come in, hesitate for a moment, then give you a quick move to the outside, push you to the inside and rush for the quarterback. I'm going to anticipate him Sunday. I'm going to attack him, to get in front of him and stop him.

Bart hasn't healed yet, and Zeke's definitely going to be our quarterback Sunday. Today, at the end of practice, Bart and Zeke were talking together, and Bart said, "By the way, I've got a great book for you to read when we get to Detroit tomorrow."

Zeke perked up and said, "Yeah? What is it?"

And Bart said, "Well, the name of the book is *Quarterbacking*, and it's written by a guy named Starr."

Zeke broke up laughing.

OCTOBER 7

After a brief workout in Green Bay this morning, we flew to Detroit and checked in at our hotel. I was in a real hurry to get to the hotel, because I'd heard that when the Lions played us in Green Bay, Alex Karras won a lot of money playing cards the day before the game. I figure this is my week. I won big today, a good sign for tomorrow. I think we're all going to be ready to play.

OCTOBER 8

Just for a little extra insurance, I made sure that Chandler woke me up this morning in time to go to the devotional service. I figured a few prayers certainly wouldn't hurt me any against Karras. (Hank Gremminger, who was with us a few years ago, used to eat fish on Friday, even though he was a Protestant, just in case.) Carroll Dale read from the Bible, and then Bart gave a little sermon saying that if a man doesn't use his ability to the fullest, he's cheating on God. The theme of the sermon, of course, came from the Book of Vincent, and Bart did a very nice job.

I think most of the guys on the team are fairly religious. There may be a few atheists, but they keep their feelings quiet, I guess, because Coach Lombardi is so religious. Personally, I enjoy the chance to pray before a game. I have two special prayers of my own: "Don't let me make a fool of myself" and "Don't let anyone get hurt." I rarely pray for victory, but if we're in a big game, I sometimes say, "I don't like to ask You this, Lord, but . . ."

We don't have too many religious discussions on the team, but I remember Max McGee once arguing with Hornung. "You run around every night, Paul," Max said, "and then you go to church on Sunday. You're really a hypocrite."

"Max," said Paul, "you go to church with the hope that if you go enough, it'll help you eventually. Maybe some day you'll overcome your weaknesses."

Max wouldn't accept Paul's answer, and they argued back and forth and, finally, they called over Bill Curry, a deeply religious young man who used to play with us, and presented their cases to him. Bill listened very carefully, then said, "This isn't something between you and me, Paul, or between you and me, Max. This is something between both of you and—"

McGee interrupted. "Oh, no," he said. "Don't bring that Lombardi into this."

After the service this morning, Don and I went back to our room to watch cartoons for a while. I guess we've seen all the cartoons ever made. There isn't much else to watch on television Sunday mornings.

By the time we reached the locker room, I'd worked up a feeling of pure hatred. For three weeks, I'd been hearing about nothing but Alex Karras, and I wanted to destroy him. By the time the game was over, I also wanted to destroy my old University of Idaho teammate, Wayne Walker. Wayne is my friend off the field, a nice, sweet guy, but on the field, he is a miserable sonuvabitch. He has got to be one of the most obnoxious players in football. In one game about six, seven years ago, I blocked him a few times successfully and knocked him on his butt. Then we punted. I was held up at the line of scrimmage, and when I saw one of our men down the punt, I turned to go off the field. I was completely re-laxed. Wayne Walker slammed me from the blind side. I went down, and he stood over me, laughing. "Guess I got you back, didn't I?" he said.

I couldn't stand up. My knee was killing me.

"I didn't mean to hurt you," Wayne said. He reached over and helped me up and then helped me off the field to my bench. That's the only time an opposing player ever helped me off the field—af-ter he'd blind-sided me.

Today, on one play, we ran a screen to the left. Our center was blocking on Wayne, who was at right linebacker, and I was just try-ing to go around him, and Wayne came up and hit me right in the head with a forearm and really rattled my cage. I would have mur-dered him if I could have gotten to him, but the referee stepped between us before I could hit him. "Cut it out," the referee said. And Wayne said, "That's my buddy, that's my buddy, we're only kidding." I looked for him the rest of the game, and if I'd reached my buddy I guarantee I would have given him my best shot. I wanted to break his neck.

Detroit jumped off in front of us again, 10–0, on a couple of deflected passes that were intercepted by their defensive ends. The first one set up a field goal by Walker, and the second was car-ried into the end zone by one of their big dummies. But we never panicked. We never hesitated. We knew we were going to win the game, that it was just a matter of time. As I've said before, we've never been defeated; we just run out of time once in a while.

We didn't run out of time today. We bounced back with one touchdown in the second quarter and then Chandler kicked a pair of field goals to put us in front 13–10 early in the fourth quarter, and then Dave Robinson deflected one of their passes and Ray Nitschke intercepted it. Even though he pulled a muscle on the play, Nitschke ran 20 yards for a touchdown. A few minutes later, Zeke threw his second touchdown pass, and we wrapped up the game. They scored in the closing minutes to make the final margin 27–17.

I don't think Karras got through me to the quarterback once all day. I'd like to say this was because I had a great day, but I'd be lying. I had a good day. But, actually, from a sheer technical standpoint, I didn't play much better than I'd played against Alex in Green Bay. I was ready today, mentally and physically. I was more aggressive. I had help from Bowman on the inside, so I concentrated on stopping Alex's outside charge. But the big difference between this game and the first one wasn't me. The difference was partly our game plan and mostly Zeke.

The game plan worked beautifully. We ran very well to the inside, forcing the Lions to keep looking for the run. Zeke called a fine game, but, more important, he got rid of the ball quicker than Bart had three weeks ago. Right after the first Detroit game, I'd suspected that I hadn't played so badly as some people thought. What happened today confirmed my suspicion. When you've been playing for a long time for a good team, you subconsciously get a little lazy on your pass blocks. You hold your man off for exactly the amount of time it takes your quarterback to get his pass off, and then you let up. The first time we played the Lions, Bart wasn't getting the ball off on time, probably because of his injuries. He was holding the ball a second or two seconds too long, and, as a result, I looked lousy. Today, Zeke was releasing the ball right on schedule, and I looked great. The sportswriters all think I demolished Alex today, and I'm not about to correct them. He got the credit last time; I'll take it today.

We're leading our division comfortably now, with a record of three victories and one tie; the Lions are a distant second with one victory, two defeats and a tie. I don't think I'll be hearing about Alex Karras again for a while.

OCTOBER 9

I let go today. I enjoyed myself completely. I drank a few beers and played a little cards, a lovely day off. I'd put a great deal of time and mental effort into the Detroit game, so I felt I'd earned a day of relaxation. I'm not a very well-disciplined person anyway, and for me to regiment myself for any length of time is difficult.

OCTOBER 10

"Gentlemen," Coach Lombardi said this morning, "today we start the big push." I think I've heard that line before.

Vince had a few nice words for everybody. He said we did a truly remarkable job. But he seemed to be a little confused about our tendency to let down when we have an easy game and to play extremely hard when we have a difficult game. "Well, I guess it's all right," he said. "As long as you keep winning the big ones, that's what we want. But, I don't know, it isn't really all right, because if you're going to let down, you're going to look like hell sometimes. Hell, I don't know what to say." That was a very rare admission for him.

Fuzzy Thurston was one of my guests when I taped my TV show tonight, and I asked him how it felt to be a substitute after so many years as a regular. "Not being a starting guard is kind of hard," Fuzzy said, "but after ten years, I think I can adjust to it. And if anything happens to you or Gilly, I'll be ready."

"You were certainly ready for the Bears when I got hurt," I said. "You played a fine football game."

"Yeah," said Fuzzy. "I was ready. I was the guy who kicked you in the head."

OCTOBER 11

Vince came up next to me during practice today, slapped me on the back, and said, "How you feeling?"

"Great, Coach, great," I said. What the hell can you say?

"That's good," he said, with that big grin of his. "Makes you want to play this game a few more years, doesn't it?"

"Sure does," I said. I'm full of clever remarks.

I've been talking about quitting and retiring for God knows how long, and it was such an effort to get ready to play this year, but the way Lombardi acts, you get all confused. He screams at you, hollers at you, makes life unbearable until you're about ready to quit, and then he starts being real nice to you and makes your life enjoyable for a while.

I've been wondering about his retiring, too. The talk has sort of quieted down, but just the other day, waiting for the plane to Detroit, I turned to his wife, Marie, and said, "Coach is never going to retire, is he?"

"The heck he's not," she said. Obviously, she's had some household talks with him about it, and her feelings in the matter are pretty clear.

We started serious preparations for the Minnesota Vikings today, and I've been warned about a big rookie named Alan Page. He played for Notre Dame last year, and he's about 6'5", maybe 270 pounds, and he looks real tough in the movies. I guess I've got my hands full again. I thought after the Lions I'd have a medium week, but that's out. I've got another miserable week.

The alligator shoes Chandler and I had ordered came in from

the manufacturer today, about $1,200 worth, and when we handed them out to the guys and tried to collect the money, some of them started complaining, "These don't fit. Send them back." I got disgusted. I told them all to stick it in their ear. They can send them back themselves if they want to. That's what happens when you try to do something for somebody.

After the workout, I stopped in at Blaine Williams' office. We're a little concerned about the portraits. They're not moving as well as they should. Kraft told us that we should be set up to fill 20,000 orders a day, and we've been receiving only fifty to a hundred. Blaine went to Chicago the other day to talk to the Kraft people, to see if we could get another shot of advertising on the Kraft Music Hall. He told me today that we'd get a couple of more shots, that the Kraft people said we were premature in our thinking and our worrying. So I'm going to quit worrying about it.

OCTOBER 12

Coach said this morning that our timing is coming along, that our halfbacks are starting to hit the holes a little better. He said the whole program is beginning to escalate, that we're moving toward our peak. We sure haven't reached our peak yet, but I guess things are moving slowly in that direction. "If things start going right, I'll really be a genius," Lombardi said. "Everybody'll say we took it easy the first four games, we didn't rush anything, we didn't hurt ourselves, and I really must be a genius. . . ."

The meeting room was very quiet, until Willie Davis boomed out, "OR . . ." He didn't say anything else, but we all got a giggle out of the implication: "Or if things don't pick up, you'll be a dummy." That's the way the football world works, I guess.

We're having trouble again getting up for the game, but we really shouldn't. Minnesota always gives us a rough time. In fact, they were the last team to beat us; they won, 20–17, in the middle of last season. Since then, we've gone seventeen games without a defeat—two playoff games, six exhibitions, and nine regular-season games. For some strange reason, the Vikings always seem to think they're capable of beating us. They have no trouble at all getting up for us. But it's hard for us to get too worried about them. So far this season they haven't won a game.

OCTOBER 13

It was raining hard this morning, too hard for us to go out to practice at the usual time. So, instead of having one meeting before practice and another afterward, we had our two meetings right in a row, at the beginning. "Don't worry," Lombardi said. "We'll be able to work out after the meetings." I don't think any of us were really too worried about not being able to practice.

We all began kidding about how Lombardi controls the weather, at least in this part of the world, and by the time we finished our meetings, the rain had let up and the field was halfway usable. Vince looked up at the sky, like he was looking at one of his assistants, and said, "See, I told you it would clear up." I think he's starting to believe he controls the weather.

Max McGee didn't get to play against Detroit last Sunday—one of the first games he'd sat out completely in a long time—and he was feeling pretty low, pretty dejected. So today Lombardi was cussing Bob Long, riding his tail, kind of making up to Max by being rough on Flakey. "C'mon, Long, c'mon," Vince screamed. "Let's see you block. Let's see you hit somebody." About three plays after Lombardi chewed him out, Flakey went out to block Bob Jeter on a sweep. Jete started to step around him, and Flakey moved in front of him and pushed him. Jete pushed him back, and Long threw a forearm, and then Jete threw a forearm and cut

Flakey's mouth, two or three stitches' worth. Flakey promptly began swinging. Somebody broke it up, but things were kind of hairy for a while. We hadn't had anything like that on the practice field in a few years, and afterward Flakey was going around with a fat lip, and Jete felt bad about the whole thing, because it wasn't his idea in the first place.

Our workouts, obviously, can get violent. There's never any tackling, not even on Wednesdays and Thursdays, when we wear pads, but there's a lot of contact in the line, a lot of forearms flying and elbows swinging. Generally, when we're working on running plays we concentrate mostly on getting position, coming off the ball fast and moving to the right spot, and we just shield the defensive man; we don't cut him down or really clobber him. But in blitz drills, with the linebackers charging through to get to the quarterback, the contact is fiercer and more dangerous. It's not at all uncommon to have someone bleeding during a blitz drill.

The violence of the sessions varies, often, with Lombardi's mood. If he's angry, if he's been chewing the offense, telling us that we're big cows, we're going to take it out on the defense. The reverse is true, too. If he's been hollering at the defense, calling them lazy and stupid, they're going to hit us a lot harder. The tone of Vince's voice in the prepractice meeting lets us know how badly we're going to get beat up.

Most of the scrimmages are controlled, or semicontrolled—we don't want to injure teammates—but a couple of guys don't know what control means. Nitschke, as I've mentioned, can be a wild man any day. Bob Brown is just as exuberant. With Brown, it's a little more understandable; he's a reserve, and the best chance he has to prove himself is in practice. When he gets too excited, when he's hitting us with too much enthusiasm, we'll say, "OK, Bob, you win the game watch. You get the game watch today." Our sarcasm works. He lets up for a while, then slips back into his violent habits.

Don Chandler and I held our regular Friday kicking contest today. I haven't been needed as a place-kicker since 1963, but just in case Donny should get hurt, Vince likes me to keep practicing. I kick three days a week — Wednesday, Thursday, and Friday — and I enjoy it. I especially enjoy it Wednesdays and Thursdays, because if I weren't kicking, I'd have to be running plays for the defense. On Fridays, Chandler and I compete, and the loser has to buy the winner a chili lunch. We started kicking from the 20-yard line today and worked back to the 50, kicking three times from each five-yard stripe. He made sixteen out of twenty-one, and I made seventeen and beat him, which doesn't happen too often. He wins four times out of five, but every time he does, I needle him about the 1962 championship game, when I kicked three field goals for the Packers and he kicked none for the Giants, and we won the game 16–7.

As I was walking off the field today, grinning after beating Chandler, Lombardi yelled to me, "I can see you when you're forty-five. You'll still be out here kicking. You'll be trying to make the team as a kicker."

Not me. I don't want to be a football player much longer.

OCTOBER 14

On the bus going down to Milwaukee this morning we started talking about a player on another team, and one of our men said, "Boy, that guy's got a lot of guts. He has no fear."

And I had a sudden thought: He's either got a lot of guts or he's just plain stupid. Sometimes I wonder if they're not the same thing, which scares me a little, because I don't have any fear either, except maybe of Lombardi.

We loosened up at County Stadium this afternoon, then played a little poker back at the hotel. I went out to dinner with Nitschke and Zeke and Bart and Chandler and Davis and Jordan and Adderley, and on the way back to the hotel, a few of us started talking about the money we'd won playing poker. I said that I had a little money stuck away for a rainy day, just a few dollars that I hadn't bothered putting in the bank. We got into a discussion of how the guys hide money from their wives, and somebody said that whenever he needed money of his own he just wrote out a check and told his wife he'd lost the money playing poker. And another guy said that he and his wife maintained separate checking accounts. "Hell, I can't do anything like that," said Nitschke. "I can't fool my wife at all. I just get red in the face. Jackie reads me better than I can read those linemen."

OCTOBER 15

Everything was pretty calm this morning. Nobody was excited about the game or about anything else. There seemed no reason to get excited. A few of my friends came in from Idaho, and we started talking about the possibility of an upset, and I told them that this would be a perfect day for it. But I couldn't really believe it myself, and no one else could, either. We were all feeling cocky, and I felt like I was going to have a real good game.

In the locker room, just before the game started, we decided that our opening play would be a draw-left. On a draw-left, I had to block my man to the outside. But I'd been watching the Minnesota tackle, Alan Page, in the movies, and I'd noticed that he likes to rush to the inside, which makes it almost impossible to take him to the outside. I told Ray Wietecha that on the opening play, I'd like to make a switch in the blocking. I suggested that the center block Page and I'd pull out and get the middle linebacker. Wietecha said no, so I was a little leery about the first play.

On the first play, I got off the ball fast, the kid took a beautiful block to the outside and we gained about three yards. It looked like it wasn't going to be too tough. After a sweep, which lost a few yards, we tried a pass play, and I stopped the kid cold without too much of a problem. Three plays later, on another pass play, the kid caught me and drove me about five yards backwards. It was raining and the turf was a little sloppy, and my cleats wouldn't hold. Still, I wasn't worried; I was just feeling the kid out, to see how strong he was. We ran a few plays, and I handled him pretty well, and then Zeke called another pass play. I popped the kid, and he moved to the outside, and I popped him again, and then he slipped away from me. I was thinking to myself, "Hurry up and throw the ball, Zeke, hurry up, dammit, throw the ball," and I fell to my knees. Just then, Kenny Bowman and Zeke and another guy all fell on my right ankle.

I felt a sharp, cutting pain. I've been told that I've got a high threshold of pain, but this really stung. My first thought was, "Maybe it's broken. Here we go again." I hopped off the field, afraid that I might be seriously injured. I wasn't. The trainer put an ice pack on the ankle immediately and froze it, numbed it, and I began limping round on it, getting the circulation back. In the dressing room at half-time the doctor examined the ankle, told me it was just a slight sprain, and gave me a shot of novocaine. I gulped a few codeine pills, too.

I spent the entire second half standing on the sidelines, feeling frustrated. At least when I got my head kicked against the Bears, I felt like I'd accomplished something. I didn't do a thing today. I kept bouncing around the bench, trying to look spry. Two or three times, I told the coach that I was ready, that I could do the job, but he turned down my offers. I got a little paranoid. Gilly had shifted to my spot, and Fuzzy had moved in at left guard, and Fuzzy had played a good game against the Bears, and I started thinking that maybe they weren't interested in my services. Maybe they didn't need me.

A few times, I tried to offer some advice to Gilly—we do a lot of talking among the offensive linemen on the sidelines, more than most teams do, discussing which plays will work, which men we can move, offering our suggestions to Bart—but all of a sudden I felt like an outsider. The uniforms on the field were a horrible mess, covered with mud, water, and sweat, and the guys were wearing them like a red badge of courage. I was jealous; I wished I could get back in there.

The game itself didn't cheer me up any. We looked miserable. We had no running game at all, and even though Zeke played pretty well, filling in for Bart again, we could never really get moving. We went into the last quarter, holding a 7–0 lead, but then the Vikings scored ten points and beat us, 10–7. They hadn't won a game all year, and we hadn't lost one, and they beat us. They beat us at our own game, too, solid, conservative, unspectacular football.

We had one last chance for victory when we got the ball, deep in our own territory, with only ten or fifteen seconds left in the game. Zeke completed two passes, which carried us just about to midfield when the clock ran out. I came walking off the field next to Forrest Gregg, and Trees was sort of talking to himself, mumbling. "Damn, damn, ten more seconds, if we just had ten more seconds, we could've beat 'em."

He meant it. He really believed it. That's how brainwashed we are. We can't believe defeat.

OCTOBER 16

My ankle's sore, but it didn't stop me from going hunting today with Barbara and the Chandlers. Don had two or three shots at deer, but none of us had any hits. I guess we just can't score this week.

OCTOBER 17

Coach Lombardi really seemed strange this morning, confused and frustrated and almost powerless. There was no tongue-lashing, no whiplashing, no screaming and hollering, none of the things which are so characteristic of him. He said that he had looked at the films of the game and that things weren't all that bad, that there were nine good blocks and one bad block out of each ten, that it wasn't a breakdown of the whole team.

Then he held a meeting of the older guys, the fourteen men who had been on the team at least seven years, at least since our first NFL championship in 1961. He called us all in a room and gave us a private little talk. "Frankly, I'm worried," he said. "I just don't know what the hell to do." He said that it was going to be up to us, the veterans, to bring the new boys along, to get something out of them and help him. He kind of put the horse on our shoulders and told us to carry it. It was a whole new approach for Lombardi, and we really didn't know quite what to think. He's always known exactly what to do with a season, when to get us up and when to drive us down.

I'm beginning to suspect that he wants to keep us down till we get close to playoff time, till the games really count. We're certainly low. We're certainly not mentally or physically ready. I'm wondering whether this isn't by design, and I think everybody's wondering the same thing, trying to figure Vince out. Maybe he's trying to double-psych us or something.

Bart was one of the guests on my TV show tonight and he said that he's starting to feel fine. "Most of the things that have been bothering me have cleared up," Bart said, "and if this shoulder just comes around, I'll be in great shape."

We watched the highlights of the Minnesota game—I suggested they be called the lowlights this week—and then Bart and

I chatted, and he told me a nice story on himself, a story that he loves to tell. He said that he came home one afternoon and barged into the house and yelled at one of his children and spanked another one and then snapped at his wife, Cherry, for not getting some letters out in the mail.

Finally, Cherry said to him, "What's wrong with you? I've never seen you so edgy."

"I've got a jillion things to do," Bart shouted at her. "A jillion things. And I've got to go to a banquet over in Appleton tonight."

"What kind of a banquet?" Cherry said.

And Bart, still in a foul mood, said, "I'm receiving a nice-guy award."

"You're putting me on," said Cherry.

OCTOBER 18

Vince was not confused this morning. He was fuming. He came into the locker room with his bulldog look on his face, the look we call "Gameface," and other things less printable. First, he called Fuzzy into his office and gave Fuzzy a talking-to. Fuzzy filled in for me against the Vikings, and he didn't have a good game. He had lots of trouble with his man, Paul Dickson. It's difficult to sit on the bench week after week and then finally get in there to play and be expected to do a great job.

"What is it, Fuzzy?" Coach said. "What's the matter? What's wrong with your attitude? Aren't you happy? You think you ought to be playing?"

And Fuzzy, who told me about the conversation later, said, "You know, Coach, I've played ten years and I'd like to be playing all the time, I'd very definitely like to play. But if I can't play, I'm going to do my best to help, to be ready when you need me."

There wasn't too much Fuzzy could say. I think Vince was being too hard on him. Fuzzy's got more determination than anybody in the world; he always wants to win, even when he isn't playing. He sits next to Gilly in the movies and talks to him on the sidelines, offering him advice, giving the kid all the benefit of his experience.

After he talked to Fuzzy, Vince came out of his office and faced the whole team and started screaming and cussing and carrying on. "I want to tell you this," he said. "I had another look at those movies, and they stink." He kept pointing at guys and saying, "You didn't run," and, "You didn't block," and, "You didn't do a damn thing," and, "You stink," and it was the Lombardi of old. He told the offense that we were going to stay late and watch the end-zone movies so that we could see exactly how bad we were. And he let us know in no uncertain terms that he would run guys out of the league, trade them, get rid of them, put them all on waivers, do anything he had to do, but he wasn't going to be part of a losing team.

He picked up a chair and waved it at Marv Fleming's head and said, "I get so damned mad at Marvin Fleming I'd like to beat him on the head." For a moment, I thought he was going to drop the chair on Marvin. The day before, in the veterans' meeting, he had asked us to try to help Marvin, to encourage him, and now he was holding a chair over Marvin's head. Marvin had a severed Achilles tendon during the off-season and he's lucky to be walking and playing football at all. He's slowed down. He really has.

Coach shook everyone up, and I believe this is what we need, this is what it takes to get us going. We're so damned complacent, we're so damned used to winning, we figure we can win without really trying. We've got to be whipped. We've got to be cussed. I think that's the only way Lombardi'll have any success with us.

We had a helluva practice today, the best we've had in weeks.

OCTOBER 19

I've been getting a lot of phone calls from sportswriters this week, asking what's wrong with the Green Bay Packers, what's wrong with the offensive line, is the team getting old, questions like that. The writers remind me of a bunch of vultures circling around, hoping the carcass won't turn over and get back up on its feet. I've been trying to evade the questions as much as possible. I've been talking about how hard it is for us to get up for games in our division. But the questions are getting to me, especially after the loss to Minnesota, and now I'm beginning to have my own questions, my own doubts.

I'm pretty certain that we don't have any real problems, but I'm not absolutely certain. A little doubt's creeping into my mind. I'm starting to question my own ability, my teammates' ability. I'm wondering, most of all, how good a team we've really got. I think a lot of the other guys are asking themselves the same questions. No one's saying anything out loud, but I can feel it, I can sense it.

On the practice field this morning, I heard Bart yelling to Bud Jorgensen, the trainer, asking him for a No. 3 pill, an Emperin-codeine compound. I asked Bart if it was for his head or his shoulder, and he said he was taking it for his shoulder. He told me he's been getting quite a bit of pain in his shoulder, and he has to take one or two pills a day to get through practice. But he's coming along. He's not throwing real hard or real sharp yet, but at least he's throwing and he's throwing long. There's a good chance that he'll play Sunday in New York against the Giants.

We had another excellent practice today. I think the carcass is going to get up this week.

OCTOBER 20

Right after calisthenics this morning, I watched the defense going through its starting drill. About fifteen linemen and line-backers were down in three-point stances, in a long line, and Hawg Hanner was standing about ten yards in front of them. When he moved the football he was holding, they all moved. I kept looking at Ray Nitschke. He's got a very bad leg, still nursing the pull he suffered against the Lions, and he can't get down in the three-point stance. He kind of bent over at the waist and leaned forward and hobbled down the field a few yards.

I had a good glimpse of Ray's leg in the locker room. He's got a torn muscle and internal hemorrhaging, and the back of the leg, from the middle of the calf to the middle of the thigh, is a bright purple, with an olive border and splatches of yellow and blue. It is one of the most Godawful things I've seen in a long time, and I can't imagine him playing a game. But by the end of practice to-day, he was moving pretty well, putting more and more pressure on the leg, and I know he's going to try to play Sunday.

During the workout, when the offensive line was running a few plays, Coach Lombardi came over to us and said, "Look, I'm thinking about starting Bart. Do you think you can protect him? You think you can keep those people away from him? We can't let anybody get close to him."

Naturally we all said yes. What else could we say?

OCTOBER 21

I got up at 7:30 this morning and rushed over to the dentist to have him replace a porcelain cap on one of my teeth. I chewed it off, I guess. I'm always chewing and grinding my teeth, especially when I'm in a nervous situation, and we've had a lot of them lately.

We had a pretty spirited little workout this morning, and then Coach Lombardi delivered a short speech. He told us we were going to the biggest city in the world, his home town, and he warned us about all the evils of the big city. Everybody was high as a kite, jumping around and kicking up their heels. Everybody was wearing their new alligator shoes. They wanted to impress the city slickers.

We had a good 727 flight to New York, playing cards all the way, but when we got to the airport, one of our chartered buses had broken down. Vince let a few of us take taxis and we rode in style to the Waldorf-Astoria, the real big time, and checked in, and I had a bed about the size of an army cot. Chandler phoned downstairs and had us moved to a larger room with larger beds. Then Don and I went out for a walk. We wandered over to Abercrombie & Fitch so that I could see their guns. I saw one I'd like to add to my collection. It was on sale for $2,950.

About 5 o'clock we stopped back at the hotel, and in the lobby I ran into a classmate of mine from the University of Idaho. He had called me long-distance earlier in the week, had told me he was now a doctor in New York and had asked me to get him a pair of tickets for the Giant game. "I've got a girl friend here," he had said, "and I'm really in love with her. It's the real thing. Will you phone her and tell her that you're working on the two tickets for me? I'll reimburse you for the call. It'd impress her a lot."

"Hell," I'd said, "I don't want to call the girl."

And he'd said, "Come on. It'd be a big favor."

So I'd made the call for him, and I'd arranged to get him two tickets.

Today, in the lobby, he invited Donny and me to join him and his girl friend for a drink, so we sat in the lounge for a few minutes and sipped sodas while they drank. We left them sitting there, and I told him I'd leave two tickets at the box office in his name.

He seemed pretty happy to see me again, and I guess his girl friend was impressed.

Then Chandler and I, Bob Skoronski and his brother, and Ray Nitschke and Carroll Dale went to dinner at Kenny's Steak Pub, right near the Waldorf, and while we were eating a few of the Giants came in—Joe Morrison, Earl Morrall, and Jim Katcavage. Kat came over and said, "Hi," and I said, "Hi," but we were both kind of reserved. We kept looking at each other, knowing that tomorrow we'd be trying to destroy each other. After dinner, Don and I went back to the hotel and watched the Giants' coach, Allie Sherman, on his TV show. Naturally, I found Sherman's show much inferior to mine, so I went to sleep early, feeling pretty good.

OCTOBER 22

Bill Quinlan, our old teammate, came roaming around the hotel this morning, searching for tickets for the game. Bill, who was a great socializer but not very good at carrying money, kept saying, "Got to have three tickets. Cash deal. Cash deal. Cash on the line." He rushed up to Coach Lombardi and said, "Coach, Coach, I was on some television show the other day called 'What Is Vince Lombardi Really Like?' and I told them what a great guy you were. I did a helluva job for you, Coach. I really did. I got to have three tickets."

Coach Lombardi couldn't help grinning and, finally, he gave Tom Miller, the assistant general manager, three tickets for Bill. "Here they are, Bill," said Miller. "Three on the 50-yard line, for $15." Quinlan reached into his wallet and pulled out a $5 bill and a couple of singles, then turned to me. "Hey, Jerry," he said, "lend me $10." So I ended up buying two of his tickets for him. Quinlan hasn't changed at all.

On our way to the bus, Chandler, who'd paid the incidentals

on our hotel bill, said to me, "I didn't know you'd signed anything at the restaurant."

"I didn't," I said.

"There was a $17 restaurant bill," Don said.

"What was that for?" I asked.

"I don't know," he said, "but it had your name signed to it."

I got a little bit nervous about my old friend from Idaho, and to make things worse, as we were going into Yankee Stadium, I found I'd lost the two tickets I'd bought for him. So I bought two more from Fuzzy, who had a few extras, and left them at the ticket window. That made $20 I'd put out for tickets, plus a $17 restaurant bill, plus $10 for the phone call to the girl in New York, and I hadn't seen a dime back. If I don't get some money in the mail from my classmate this week, I'm going to check him out through the university.

As soon as we settled into the locker room, Coach Lombardi came over to me and nudged me and said, "Why don't you take some of the younger boys out and show them around Yankee Stadium?" We hadn't played in New York in five years, so I walked around with Anderson and Grabo and Crutcher and a few of the rookies, showing them The House that Ruth Built, the plaques of Ruth and Gehrig and DiMaggio. I'm not much of a baseball fan myself, but the first time I came into Yankee Stadium, in 1959, I was really impressed. The place had so much history; so many great athletes had played in it. Andy and Grabo have been exposed to the big city, so they didn't seem too impressed, but Tommy Joe kept gaping at everything. "Boy," he said, "this here place would sure hold a lot of hay."

Right before the game, Bob Skoronski gave an emotional little speech to the team. Ski talked about his home town in Connecticut, and said that he wanted us all to look good in front of his friends. He said that he's tired of hearing about how old our offensive line is, how we're too old to win anymore, that all the talk makes him sick. And that's my feelings exactly. For the first time in a long time, I'd built up a real hate for our opponents. The New York writers had helped me with all their talk about the old offensive line. I was just filled with hate, the perfect attitude for a good game.

I looked around the locker room, and I saw Bart taking his codeine, and I saw Herb Adderley, who had a torn muscle in his right biceps, getting a shot of novocaine, and I saw Ray Nitschke getting his leg taped from his ankle to his hip. We looked like a lost army getting ready for battle.

Early in the game, we had the feeling we could do anything we wanted to do against the Giants. But even though we kept picking up good running yardage, Bart wasn't hitting his receivers too well, and at the half the Giants were leading us 14–10.

We went into the dressing room and, as usual, I grabbed a few cups of Gatorade, which has got to be one of the greatest things ever invented for athletes. It's a drink developed in Florida. It's got everything you need in it—a solution of water, salt, and glucose—and it tastes good. We serve it between the halves and on the sidelines during a game. After I satisfied my thirst, I got together with Gilly, Fuzzy, Ski, Forrest, the whole offensive line, for about a minute, and we all agreed that none of us was having trouble with his man, that we were moving the Giants well.

Then Ray Wietecha joined us and said, "What can you do in there? What'll work?"

"What do you like?" I said. "Just name a play. Anything will go. Anywhere."

The way we always do at half-time, we picked out a few plays, and Wietecha reviewed them on the blackboard, reminded us of some basics, then went over to Coach Lombardi and the quarterbacks and told them what we'd discussed. Lombardi got the whole team together for a few seconds, told us we were playing well and sent us out for the second half.

Every play worked in the second half, everything we tried, particularly through the left side of the Giant line, through Katcavage and Jim Moran. Kat wasn't tipping his moves anymore, but Forrest and I didn't need any help. We chewed them up. We scored 38 points in the second half and crushed the Giants 48–21. We gained 249 yards rushing, the most we'd gained in five years.

Bart had a beautiful second half; in the last quarter, he threw his first touchdown pass of the season. Jim Grabowski and Elijah Pitts both ran for big yardage; Grabo gained 123 yards, and ZaSu scored three touchdowns. Nitschke and Adderley, ignoring their injuries, had great days; Herbie's biceps was twice its normal size after the game. And Dave Robinson, playing in front of his hometown friends from New Jersey, intercepted two passes. Everybody came up for the game, everybody put out his best effort, and everybody thoroughly enjoyed the victory. Late in the fourth quarter, Ray Wietecha asked me if I wanted to take a blow, to sit out a while, and I said, "Hell, no." I wanted to keep playing. I was having too much fun.

And after a lovely flight back to Green Bay, we really went out and celebrated. We had fifteen or twenty couples, the Dowlers, the Grabowskis, the Chandlers, the Starrs, the Greggs, the Nitschkes, just about half the team, and we all went out for dinner and dancing, hitting Speed's and The Office, the hot spots of Green Bay. We were all laughing and giggling and having a good time, and Pat Chandler, Don's wife, said, "This is the happiest I've seen the Packers since I arrived in Green Bay three years ago. This is much better than the Super Bowl." And she was right; we hadn't celebrated so hard in years. It was an indication that we were all a little more concerned about our football team than we wanted to let on, that, without saying anything, we were really beginning to wonder, beginning to doubt. The Giant game made us feel a lot better.

OCTOBER 25

We don't play again until Monday night in St. Louis, so we had two days off to recuperate from our victory over the Giants and from our partying. I'm still feeling the glow from the Giant game, and so are the rest of the guys. Everybody on the offensive unit watched the films today with a great deal of pleasure; for once, we don't owe our salaries to the defense.

I think our next three games, all against teams outside our own division, are going to tell a lot about our club. We play St. Louis, Baltimore, and Cleveland; St. Louis and Cleveland are tied for first place in their division, and Baltimore, leading its division, is the only undefeated team in the National Football League. All three are good, solid football teams, and I know we'll be emotionally ready. We're really going to be giving all-out efforts, and if we win all three games, then we'll be certain we've got a strong team. If we get beat, then we'll just as certainly have cause for concern.

OCTOBER 26

I've got two things to worry me against St. Louis. They've got one of the better defensive tackles, Sam Silas, and they've got an unpredictable defense. They like to blitz. They'll shoot their safety, they'll shoot a halfback and they'll shoot linebackers. And they jump around a lot, moving in and out of different defensive alignments. I imagine Bart'll be calling more automatics than he usually does, changing his plays depending on the way the Cardinals line up.

I played against Silas in an exhibition game a few years ago and I remember him well. He's hard, he's fairly quick, and he's got a few good moves. We watched the movies today of the Cardinals playing the Browns, and Gene Hickerson, the Cleveland guard, handled Silas pretty well. That won't make me overconfident. Gene's capable of handling anybody on a good day.

During our workout today, Travis Williams, the rookie, was catching punts and catching kickoffs, and as I walked past, Coach Lombardi said, "Looks pretty good, doesn't he?"

Just then, Travis fumbled a kickoff. "Should have kept my big mouth shut," Lombardi said.

"He's going to be a helluva football player," I said. "He can really move."

"No question about that," said Vince, "but what the hell can I do with him? Where can I use him?"

It's a pretty nice problem Vince has. He figures Pitts'll be around for five more years at least and Anderson should be good for eight or nine years, and that just doesn't leave too much room for another halfback. But I don't know how we can keep Travis out of the lineup for long. He's so fast.

We had a team meeting after practice today, and we invited the coaches to join us. Fuzzy ran the meeting. "Each year," said Fuzzy, "it's our custom to present an award to the assistant coach we feel has contributed the most to the team's success. We'd like to make the award this year to Assistant Coach Dave Hanner." Then Doug Hart, Steve Wright, and Allen Brown brought in a brown pig and let it loose in front of Hawg. We all had a few good laughs.

OCTOBER 27

Ron Kostelnik came up with a typical lineman's observation today. We linemen—offensive and defensive—spend an awful lot of time in our stance, crouching down and leaning on one hand. We're supposed to be looking forward, but most of the time, between plays, we're just staring at the ground. I was opposite Kos today, and we both got into our stances, and he looked up and said, "Jerry, how come only potato bugs live out here all year around?" Suddenly, I realized how much time we spend studying the ground. Kos had become quite a naturalist. I'd just been reading Thoreau, all about his love for the outdoors, and here I had a teammate who was just as interested in the birds and the bees and the bugs. I told Kos he ought to categorize his knowledge and take it up with the Potatomen's Association of Northern Wisconsin.

OCTOBER 28

Bart brought in several copies of his book, *Quarterbacking*, this morning and autographed them and handed them out to the guys. When he got his copy, Zeke turned around and yelled to me, "Hey, Jerry, I'm writing the Polish book of quarterbacking. By Zeke Bratkowski. It's going to be a half-page pamphlet."

Zeke is a funny guy. He's sort of the master of ceremonies of the sauna bath. The sauna gets a lot of use early in the week—we're not allowed to use it the last three days before a game—especially on Tuesday, when the guys are trying to sweat out Sunday and Monday nights. Zeke always stands in front of the window, pours extra water on the hot rocks and hollers, "Repent, you sinners, repent. Repent and be saved."

A lot of the guys are taking an interest in my book. I took some notes the other day, during the movies, and I happened to leave them lying around the locker room and Gilly picked them up and read them. He didn't seem to mind them, even a part where Lombardi was chewing him out. I guess most of the guys figure whatever I say, I can't be any rougher on them than Vince was in *Look*.

Max has been insisting that only a bachelor can write the full story of what it's like to be a professional football player. He says he'll give me some material that'll make the book sell like *Peyton Place*. If I don't use his material, he says, I've got to call the book *Half of It*.

Vince gave out the blocking awards today for the Giant game, and I didn't get one. I haven't gotten one yet this year—you have to receive a grade of 65 or higher on rushing blocks and 85 or higher on passing blocks—but if I ever deserved one, I deserved it for the Giant game. I'm convinced that the coaches use the blocking grades just to psych us, and I can't pay any attention to them. I'm not embarrassed by bad grades. I know what I'm supposed to do and how I'm supposed to do it, and I know when I'm succeeding and when I'm not. I know better than the coaches do.

OCTOBER 29

We flew into St. Louis today, and even though there was a little drizzle, we worked out in Busch Stadium, getting the stiffness out of our muscles. We didn't wander around town at all after the practice session, but we got a glimpse of the new Gateway Arch. You can't miss it. It's really an impressive sight. It's the tallest monument in the world, I'm told, and it cost $29 million to build. I think that's more than it cost to build the whole city of Green Bay.

Tomorrow afternoon, before the game, a fellow I know is going to take me over to the offices of the Rawlings Sporting Goods Company. I'm a fanatic for buying sports equipment—anything, guns, golf clubs, fishing rods, hunting knives—but I'm not going up there looking to buy anything. I just want to talk to the people at

Rawlings to see if they'd be interested in buying the company I own part of, the American Archery Company. We've built it up pretty nicely, but, eventually, we want to sell out and show some capital gains.

OCTOBER 30

On the opening kickoff tonight, young Travis Williams made a vicious tackle, jarring the ball loose and forcing the Cardinals into a hole deep in their own territory. Two or three plays later, Herb Adderley intercepted a St. Louis pass and ran it back for a touchdown. We were winning 7–0 before the offense ever got on the field. The rest of the first half was miserable. I couldn't get going; Silas slipped away from me a few times. At half-time, we were leading 14–10, but we hadn't frightened anyone. The Cardinals were definitely up for us.

I honestly think their safety, Larry Wilson, is the finest football player in the NFL, and he fired up their whole team. He blitzed. He shot. He red-dogged. He hurled himself through the air to make tackles. His enthusiasm was infectious.

When the Cardinals went ahead 23–17 in the last quarter, I felt we were in real danger. But then they kicked off, and Travis Williams, playing on the kickoff return team for the first time because Adderley had bruised his hand, took the ball and headed straight up the middle. I was on the front line, nearest the Cardinals. I hit one guy with a forearm and knocked him backwards, then took about four more steps toward another guy. Suddenly, I felt Travis breeze by me, zip, zip, zip, zip, like I was standing still. He went all the way for a touchdown, 93 yards, and we were back in the lead.

Even after we opened the gap to eight points, 31–23, with only a few seconds to play, Larry Wilson wouldn't quit. We were just running out the clock, and Larry, instead of staying back at his safety position, moved up like a linebacker and began leaping over people, throwing himself at the ballcarrier, trying to steal the ball. Two, three, maybe four times in a row, as the game came to its end, Larry made tackles at the line of scrimmage. It was a bewildering feeling, seeing a safety practically toe-to-toe with a defensive tackle. We don't have any blocking plan to cover a suicide situation like that. Wilson's all football player; I'm kind of glad that he's from Idaho.

One of our safeties, Tommy Brown—he used to play baseball for the Washington Senators and he's still a regular reader of the averages in *The Sporting News*—is not known as a violent tackler, like Larry Wilson, or even as a particularly rugged ballplayer. Tommy's a quiet, almost shy guy, something of a loner. But he proved his ruggedness tonight. In the first half, he hurt his shoulder and came over to the sidelines, and, naturally, the doctor told him he was OK, which is probably what the doctor would tell you if you broke your neck during a close game. About two minutes before the half ended, the doctor took Tommy into the locker room and found out that his shoulder was dislocated and popped it back into place. Tommy went out and played the whole second half. "Some people say you're not very tough," Coach Lombardi told Tommy after the game, "but I want to tell you: You're tough enough for me."

Nitschke played a tremendous game. He is having a great season, and he was all over the field tonight, making tackles. In the locker room, when the game was over, Coach Lombardi walked up to Ray and gave him a kiss. He kissed him right on the cheek. Vince better not do that too often, or he's going to ruin his reputation as the meanest coach in football.

NOVEMBER 1

I was very apprehensive about the movies today. I thought I had played extremely poorly in the first half of the St. Louis game. All day Tuesday, I felt like I had a heavy weight hanging over my head. I kept thinking about a certain play where I had looked simply lousy. I slipped and Silas beat me easily on a pass play, and Kenny Bowman had to pick him up. I was cussing and cussing myself, and when the play came up in the movies today, Coach Lombardi passed right over it. He didn't say a word. I couldn't believe it.

Vince had hardly any bad comments at all during the movies. He seemed pretty anxious just to get the films over with so that we could start thinking about Baltimore. We went out and played touch, and I was fantastic. I ran the length of the field, about 50 yards, for one touchdown and I passed for one touchdown and I knocked down two of their passes, and I just intimidated those defensive dummies completely. I think I enjoy the touch game more than any other part of the week. We put the rookies and the second-year men up on the line, and the veterans get to play the backfield. Bowman and Gregg and Skoronski and I just roam around the backfield, and we have a ball. We haven't lost a game to the defense yet this year. Those big dummies are getting pretty upset about it.

NOVEMBER 2

Coach Lombardi announced today that we were starting "our big push"—once again—then read us a letter that he'd received from Colonel Earl Blaik, who was the head coach at West Point when Vince was an assistant there. Vince has a great deal of respect for Colonel Blaik, so he read the letter very reverently.

Mostly, Blaik talked about the St. Louis quarterback, Jim Hart, and how the high trajectory of his passes cuts down the area in which a defensive man can get to the ball. It didn't really seem terribly important, since the odds are we won't be playing St. Louis again, but one part of the letter dealt with Nitschke, and when he got to that part, Vince stopped and said, "Ray, he calls you Neetzie."

"Hell," said Ray, who spent his early years in Green Bay sitting on the bench, "it took you five years to learn my name, so I don't feel bad about him misspelling it."

"I knew it," the old man said. "I even knew how to spell it. I just didn't want to use it. I didn't have any need to call on you."

Ray had no answer to that; he just grumbled a little.

We're going into the game against the Colts as three-point underdogs, which is a very rare position for us. I can't remember the last time we were underdogs in a game. I suppose Baltimore deserves to be favored—they're still undefeated—but we're not awed by them. We've beaten them the last five times we've played them.

NOVEMBER 3

I still haven't received a penny, or even a word, from my old college buddy who hit me up for the tickets in New York. I've asked my wife to check with the university to find out if he ever really studied to be a doctor and if they have an address for him. I wish I'd kept his girl's telephone number. I'd like to call her and tell her about him. She seemed awfully gullible. Come to think of it, I guess I did, too.

We're not quite so excited about playing the Colts as we might be, partly, I suppose, because we've had so little time to think about the game, and partly because we're not really in any danger of losing the championship in our own division. We know that the Colts are always a threat to score as long as Johnny Unitas is at quarterback—he's having one of his best years—and we know that the strength of their defense is in their unity, their cohesiveness, rather than in any individual stars.

I may be facing my College All-Star friend, big Bubba Smith, Sunday—either Bubba or Billy Ray Smith. Bubba's had a bad right knee most of the season and he's been favoring it, but, judging from the movies, he's gotten better and better the past three weeks. He's starting to get a little confidence in his knee and he's getting a little stronger, but if he gives me any serious trouble Sunday, I'm going to kick him in the knee or cut him down or something. Billy Ray's not as big as Bubba—in fact, he's one of the smallest defensive tackles in the league, no more than 250 pounds—and he's not as strong or as quick, but he's got a tremendous amount of desire, sort of like Larry Wilson, and he's got experience. The Colts may use him Sunday just because he does have experience in big games.

Zeke hurt himself in practice today. He started to hand off and slipped and wrenched his back pretty badly. We're lucky that Bart finally seems to be completely healthy. He's been off the pain pills for more than a week now.

NOVEMBER 4

We had a typical glamorous day on the road today. We worked out in Green Bay, flew to Baltimore, checked into our hotel, played poker for a couple of hours, ate an early dinner at the Chesapeake House, went back to the hotel, watched television and went to sleep. It certainly is exciting to be a professional football player.

The big drama of the day came when Ron Kostelnik lucked

into a big pot in the poker game. We play a crazy game we call high-low, shotgun, roll 'em with a shuck at the end—with a wild joker. You get five cards to start with, then throw away two of them. You're dealt a fourth card, and you bet. You're dealt a fifth card, and you bet. Then you draw to your hand, just like in regular draw, anywhere from zero to three cards. Then you roll your cards one at a time, except for a hole card, and you bet after each roll. At the very end, you can throw away one card, either the hole card or one of the up cards, and get a fresh card. Then, after all the betting, you declare high or low. Kostelnik stayed all the way with two pair, and a pat flush betting into him, and at the end, he shucked his hole card and drew the case card for his full house. He laughed like he knew all along it was going to happen.

NOVEMBER 5

Carroll Dale read an inspirational article during our service this morning, and then, after breakfast, we had our inevitable little meeting. Coach Lombardi said that because we had had a short week to prepare for Baltimore, things were a bit hectic and disorganized. He said he didn't think that would bother us. He thought we were a good enough team to overcome it. We all felt the same way.

It was a bloody battle. Early in the first quarter, we lost Elijah Pitts. He twisted his ankle, probably tore an Achilles tendon, and may be out the rest of the year. Two minutes later, Jim Grabowski got his knee banged up, and he had to leave the game. Except for the rookies—Travis Williams and Don Horn—we had only Ben Wilson and Donny Anderson at running backs and only Bart at quarterback. Zeke had his uniform on, but he was in terrible agony. Max had to help him out of bed this morning and had to help him tie his shoelaces. Zeke couldn't bend over. He probably should have been in the hospital, perhaps in traction, but he was in uniform, willing to play and suffer, just in case anything happened to Bart.

One incident showed me the kind of game it was. Billy Ray Smith played opposite me, but on one occasion, they were playing an odd-man line and Billy Ray was head-on on our center, Kenny Bowman. My assignment on this passing play was to check the left linebacker to see if he was going to red-dog, then go back and help the center. I took a few steps to my right and then I heard Kenny yell, "JERRY!"

I looked back to the inside. Billy Ray had gotten away from Kenny and was rushing toward Bart. I came running across, and Billy Ray, seeing that I was going to cut him off before he could get to Bart, leaped in the air, and I hit his feet and I knocked him right on his head. His nose was bleeding, his face was bruised and he looked dizzy. But he got up and the next play he was just as wild-eyed, still playing with the same reckless abandon.

I thought, "This guy won't stop at anything. I've got to really keep my head up. I've got to be alert. I don't know what this crazy guy's going to do next." You generally don't pop a guy like Billy Ray. He picks the direction he's going to go and he goes full force in that direction, and you just drive him as hard as you can, drive him into somebody else or knock him down or force him out of the play. We had a good battle all afternoon; Billy Ray played the entire game.

Late in the fourth quarter, we had a 10–0 lead, and the way our defense was playing we figured we had the game locked up. With just a little more than two minutes to go, Unitas threw a touchdown pass, but when Lou Michaels missed the extra point, our 10–6 lead looked fairly safe. I was standing on the sidelines, next to Boyd Dowler, who'd been knocked silly, and he turned to me and said, "What happened? How'd they score? They kicking off?" He didn't know what was going on, but I didn't have time to tell him because I had to get on the field with the kickoff-return team.

We expected them to try an on-side kick, a short kick. I yelled to Willie Wood, "Willie, Michaels is left-footed, and if he tries an on-side kick, it'll go to our left. Be alert over there. Tell everybody over there to be alert." Willie relayed my warning. We had five or six guys up front, ready to pounce on a short kick, and Michaels came forward and kicked it, and it wasn't even a good on-side kick. He kicked the ball too hard and, instead of simply rolling over the 50-yard line, it sailed right past our front line, right in between Tommy Joe Crutcher and Doug Hart and took a bounce to our left. Doug spun around, raced to the ball and overran it. One of the Colts, Rich Volk, broke right through our line and fell on the ball.

They got the ball on our 34-yard line, and then our defense held them to four yards in three plays. On fourth and six, Unitas faded back to pass, saw that all of his receivers were covered and decided to run. He scrambled and stumbled for seven yards, barely enough for the first down. On the next play, Unitas threw a pass to Willie Richardson for a touchdown. They beat us, 13–10.

The locker room was awfully quiet afterward. Everyone felt disgusted with the way we'd lost the game. I was near the coaches' room, and I heard Lombardi screaming, "Damned stupid high-school play like that. Damned stupid play. What in the hell were we doing? What in the hell were we waiting for?" Bob Hyland, the big rookie, was sitting with a towel over his face, like he might have been crying. Tommy Joe slouched in front of his locker and kept shaking his head. "Wouldn't have played it any different if I had to do it a thousand times," he said. "Wouldn't have tried to bat that kick down. I felt the further it went, the better chance we had of getting it." We actually felt that we'd won the ball game, that we'd outplayed them, but that they'd scored more points. Ray Nitschke kept saying, "Helluva ball game, helluva football game."

On the plane flying home to Green Bay, Tommy Joe and Fuzzy and Gilly and Max and Li'l Brother and Lee Roy and Kos and I had the card-playing seats in the back, and Bart was sitting on the arm of a chair, watching us. Coach Lombardi made his way back through the plane, the way he always does after a game, patting people on the back, roughing up their hair, talking to everybody. "What do you think, Tommy Joe?" he said.

Tommy Joe looked up and said, "I still say, Coach, that was the only way to play it."

When Lombardi turned around and began making his way forward again, Bart crouched down between Max and me and said, "You know it, Jerry, and you know it, Max, but perhaps the young guys don't: This man is one great coach. He's got a brilliant mind. He prepares us better for a football game than any other team in the National Football League. Going into the game against St. Louis, we knew exactly what we could do, what we couldn't do, how to do it. The same thing today. I've never seen a more complete book on a team than Coach Lombardi had on Baltimore. It was really a beautiful thing to see."

Bart and Max and I all agreed that Lombardi really prepares us, really pushes us toward perfection. The conversation reminded me of a late-night movie I was watching on TV a few days ago. It was a Navy movie, and the commander was a real Vince Lombardi–type character. He got killed, and one of the men on his ship commented, "He made us all a little bit better than we thought we could ever be." It sounds corny, but that's the way we feel about Lombardi.

We landed in Green Bay at 6:30 P.M., and fifteen minutes later Doug Hart, Don Chandler, Allen Brown, and I climbed aboard a chartered twin-engine Beech and took off for the north woods—

our wives had already driven up ahead of us—for the hunting grounds, for the perfect place to forget about the kind of football game we had today.

NOVEMBER 7

I went into the movies without too much fear this morning. I felt that I'd played one of my better games against Baltimore, and I didn't think Coach Lombardi would be too hard on me. He wasn't. But he said our whole offense stank. He cussed Gilly and he cussed Kenny Bowman. Kenny had some problems with pass protection. It's a tough job to center the ball and then get set for a pass block, when a man's playing right on your head, and Kenny's been having his difficulties Vince chewed Marvin Fleming unmercifully, called him stupid and lazy and everything else, and then, suddenly, he turned on Allen Brown, who's the second-string tight end behind Fleming. "Allen Brown," he said, "I don't think much of you, either, to let a big stupe like that beat you out. You must not have much gumption to let a guy like that play ahead of you." Allen hadn't even played against the Colts, and he got chewed.

I wasn't so sparkling as I have been in the touch game. I intercepted two passes, knocked one down and scored a touchdown, but I threw some bad passes. After the touch game, we got together to run a few plays, and Kenny Bowman formed a huddle for the first series. Lombardi looked at Bowman, then looked at the sidelines and said, "Hyland, get in there." Kenny looked up kind of blankly, shrugged his shoulders and tossed the football to Hyland. It looks like the rookie, Bob Hyland, is going to get a chance to be in the starting lineup, a chance to prove that he can actually play one of his many positions.

NOVEMBER 8

Bob Hyland worked out at starting center all day today, and we've been simplifying our plays for him. Normally, we have a choice of blocking assignments on every play, depending on the call by the center or the guard or the tackle, but this week we're trying to go without variations so that Bob won't have to think too much. Early in the season he was playing tackle, so he hasn't had much experience at center.

The weather's starting to turn real cold in Green Bay. The temperature's down in the thirties, and the wind's starting to whistle, and all of us are counting the number of games till we head for warmer climates. We expect a struggle in our next four or five games, but I don't think it'll be a tragedy. We're looking forward to the Western Conference playoff game with Baltimore, presumably with Baltimore, hopefully with Baltimore. We'd certainly rather play the Colts than Los Angeles or even San Francisco. We know we can beat the Colts.

The Kraft deal is going a little better these days. We're getting about two hundred to three hundred orders a day, up from fifty to one hundred. The archery company's growing, and the TV show's getting good ratings, and I heard today from my partner Urban Henry in Louisiana that the bank has extended the diving company's line of credit from $75,000 to $150,000. Urban's an ex-Packer and he's trying to persuade me to retire and move down there and start earning a living for a change. I don't know whether I'd like that honest money or not. I don't know how it'd feel.

I'm going crazy trying to collect enough tickets for the game against Cleveland Sunday. I've got to get eight for a cousin of mine and his wife and three other couples who're coming in from Missoula, Montana. Dr. Matt Davis, who operated on me for a detached retina a few years ago, wants four tickets, and I need a pair for my Uncle Bud and his wife. That makes fourteen tickets I've got to buy. I get only one free ticket each home game, for my wife; I even have to pay for my kids' tickets.

NOVEMBER 9

Lombardi offered us another one of his sayings today. "The greatest accomplishment," he said, "is not in never falling, but in rising again after you fall." In other words, it's much more difficult to get up once you've been knocked on your butt. He's driving us to get us up for the Browns. There's a newspaper clipping on the bulletin board in the locker room saying, PACKER OPPONENTS NO LONGER IN AWE. The story says that the Packers are prime targets for the Cleveland Browns this weekend; it also says that our offensive line is slowing down. I'm sick and tired of hearing everybody crying about the OLD Packers.

We've been studying the Cleveland movies, and the Browns do look pretty good. They've got a well-balanced team. Their defense is strong, with four big people up front, and so is their offense, with fine running backs in Kelly and Green and good receivers in Warfield and Collins. They should give us a good test.

Elijah Pitts is hobbling around, and I'm pretty certain he's out for the rest of the season. He's down, of course. "Jerry," he said to me, "I remember you going around on crutches in 1961, and I never thought it'd happen to me." Coach is cussing him occasionally, just for practice, I guess, just to make ZaSu feel loved. Grabowski can't run at full speed yet, and he won't play Sunday, but he should be back in action fairly soon. We've picked up a new running back—Chuck Mercein, an ex-New York Giant who'd been on the Washington taxi squad. To make room for Mercein, Lombardi put Pitts on the disabled list.

Travis Williams blew a play during practice today and he got cussed out for his concentration period. "I suppose your concentration period lasts only about fifteen seconds," Vince screamed, "and we're over that period now, are we?" It reminded me of a similar lecture I received four or five years ago. I blew a play, jumped offside, and Lombardi came up to me and stood toe-to-toe, my 6'3" and his 5'2" or 5'3" or whatever he is, and looked me in the eye. "Kramer!" he said. "The concentration period of a college student is thirty minutes, maybe less. Of a high school student, fifteen minutes, maybe less. In junior high, it's about five minutes, and in kindergarten, it's about one minute. You can't remember anything for even one minute! Where in the hell does that put you?" I didn't have much of an answer.

NOVEMBER 10

Lombardi delivered a stern lecture this morning about bow-and-arrow hunting. It seems that some fish-and-game warden caught one of the boys—I don't know who—coming out of the woods a little late, after the curfew, so all of the bow-and-arrow people caught hell, particularly me. "There's not enough thought, not enough dedication to winning," Vince said. "There's too many outside interests, too much bow hunting and all this other extracurricular what-not." I stared him in the eye, and then he went on to cuss Gilly and Ski and Gregg and even, "You too, Bart." As if he were saying, "You too, Bart, honey," you know. He doesn't often raise his voice to Bart. After the meeting, everyone was going around asking, "Who shot Cock Robin?" And I said, "I did, with my little bow and arrow." We were having used-bow sales all day.

Our line coach, Ray Wietecha, is something else sometimes. He knows his football and he's a good coach, but sometimes I get pretty perturbed with him. Today, for instance, Coach Lombardi put in a new play, a 37-rollout pass, which no one had ever heard of before. Straight out of the blue, Lombardi just made it up. When he called the play, I yelled, "What do you want the guard to do—pull?" Nobody said anything, so I said, "Ray, what do you want the guard to do? You want the guard to pull or what?" He looked past me as though he were searching for ships on the horizon, like he was all alone on the field and hadn't heard a word. I asked him again, and he still didn't answer, so I called to Lombardi, "Coach, what do you want me to do? Pull or what?"

"It's a rollout, isn't it?" Lombardi snapped. "PULL! What the hell do you think you do?"

"Well, I never heard of the damned play before," I said. "I don't know what it is."

At that point, Wietecha shouted, "Well, pull," as if he knew all along what to do. He really didn't have the slightest idea.

Marvin Fleming did something right today, and Lombardi, who'd been chewing Marvin all week, hollered, "Way to go, Marvin, way to go. That's my boy. You're my boy, Marvin." He patted Marvin on the head and sent him on his way, smiling and happy. Coach is thinking all the time. He'll cuss you early in the week and kiss you late in the week. He doesn't want you brooding going into the game.

Bob Hyland seems certain to start at center. His nickname is "Hercules," because he's so big, about 6'5" and 260. He's muscle-mad, lifting weights all the time. He gets excited easily, and he's definitely excited about starting a game for the first time. After practice today, I gave him a lift home and I said, "Look, Bob, you and I'll get together Saturday morning and go over every play we have and every possible situation. We'll talk it all over."

"I've been studying a great deal," he said. "I've been putting in a lot of extra time this week. I certainly don't want any of you guys feeling it's a burden having me in there. You don't have to worry about me missing an assignment or anything like that. It's a great honor and a privilege for me to have an opportunity to play."

He kind of surprised me; his attitude was perfect. Whenever we come up to the line of scrimmage Sunday, I'll try to remind him what to do. Just to be safe.

NOVEMBER 11

We left Green Bay early this morning, heading for Milwaukee in our chartered buses. During the ride, Dave Robinson joined us for the first time for a card game called boo-ray, and Robby paid his initiation fee. I don't know if he's going to play anymore.

We went to County Stadium to work out, and there were about 20,000 Boy Scouts in the stands watching us. We played our little lineman's game, throwing passes on the sidelines, taking turns at quarterback, right in front of the kids. Every time we'd complete a pass, they let out a tremendous roar. Fuzzy put on a great show for them, catching passes with one hand, bouncing the ball up, bobbling it around, finally grabbing it. He fell down once and dropped the ball, and 20,000 Boy Scouts hollered, "Boooooo . . ." The cheers were terrific. It's really a thrill for a lineman to hear a cheer.

I spent most of the afternoon with my cousin and his wife, Larry and Diana Riley, from Montana. We discussed some lake-front property we're thinking of buying, and then went out to dinner at my favorite Milwaukee restaurant, Frenchy's. I'm trying to cut down my weight—I'm up to about 257, 258—so all I had for dinner was two dozen *escargots*. And a lot of garlic sauce, I guess.

NOVEMBER 12

I had a lot of trouble falling asleep last night. Those *escargots* wouldn't stop crawling around. Fortunately, game time was 3 P.M. today, so I had a chance to sleep late. For once, after breakfast we could watch something on TV besides cartoons.

On the opening kickoff today, as usual, Jim Weatherwax, Bob Hyland, and I were the three Packers nearest the Browns. We have a regular kickoff play. Wax, who's in the middle, blocks the man on either the left side or the right side of the kicker. If he takes the man on my side, Hyland blocks the second man on my side, and I cut across and block the man on the other side of the kicker. Our ends take the next two men, and then our wedge comes up the middle. Wax likes to keep shifting around, first aiming at one side of the kicker, then at the other.

When we lined up today, Wax said, "I'll get No. 34," the man on my side of the kicker. I said, "OK, I've got 64." We went down the field and crossed and I got a fair block. I knocked my man down and he got up just in time to get a hand on Travis Williams. That's all he got on him—a hand. Travis went right up the middle 87 yards for a touchdown. We couldn't do anything wrong after that. Five minutes later, Bart threw a touchdown pass to Marvin Fleming; five minutes after that, Donny Anderson plunged for a touchdown; less than a minute later, Bart passed to Andy for a touchdown. After the Browns picked up their first touchdown, to make the score 28–7, Wax and Hyland and I lined up again for the kickoff, and Wax said, "Let's block the same way."

"Yeah," I said. "It didn't work too damned bad the last time."

So Wax and I criss-crossed again, and Travis charged up the middle again, and this time he went 85 yards for a touchdown. The Browns never did get another chance to kick off. With a 35–7 lead in the first period, we went on to beat Cleveland 55–7.

(We scored so many touchdowns Don Chandler seemed to spend the whole day kicking off, and after the game his wife Pat turned to him and said, "Babe, how come you were kicking off from the 40-yard line today?" Don said, "I always kick off from the 40," and Pat said, "You do? I always thought you kicked off from the 50." The team wives are beautiful. They're the greatest fans in the world and they know all about the game and they have a million of their own superstitions, but when we've got the ball the wives of the defensive players stop watching the game and start chattering, and when the other teams's got the ball the wives of the offensive players stop watching and start chattering.)

Everything, and everybody, worked for us. Ben Wilson gained 100 yards at fullback. Anderson scored four touchdowns and played his best game at halfback. Travis Williams added a long run from scrimmage to his two kickoff returns, and Chuck Mercein, in his first game as a Green Bay Packer, gained some good yardage. Even Allen Brown got into the game and caught a pass from Don Horn, the rookie quarterback. Poor Horn, who's really come along in his attitude, was about as confused as I would've been playing quarterback. I was telling him to run a 33, and Fuzzy was telling him to run a 36, and Max was telling him to throw the ball. He didn't know who to listen to or what to do, but he looked pretty good. He handled himself well.

Late in the game, after we'd already built up our 55–7 lead, they had a big boy from Oklahoma named Frank Parker playing defensive tackle. On one play, I was supposed to cut off the middle linebacker, but the middle linebacker went the wrong way, away from the play, and Parker charged across, so I cut him down. As we lay on the ground, our faces were close together. He looked at me, with sort of a smile on his face, and I smiled, too, which is very unusual during a game. "You ol' boys," he drawled, "are jus' havin' yourselves a picnic out here, ain't you?" I couldn't help but laugh. It was a beautiful remark at the end of a beautiful day.

NOVEMBER 13

Barbara and I got up early this morning and drove to a game farm for a day of shotgun hunting. Naturally, she shot the only pheasant of the day. I guess you can't win 'em all.

NOVEMBER 14

Bob Hyland was the movie star today. He was John Wayne, Paul Newman, and Rock Hudson all wrapped up in one. Everything he did was "brilliant" or "terrific" or "great," according to Coach Lombardi. Actually, Hyland played a fair game, but Vince couldn't praise him enough. Kenny Bowman's feeling a little badly, of course; it's hard to sit on the bench after being a regular for almost three seasons.

Almost predictably, Vince cussed out some of the people today worse than he does after a defeat. He cussed Gilly and Ski, and I came in for a little abuse, too. Coach acted pretty unhappy about a few things—everything except the score, I guess—but we managed to get out of the meeting alive.

In our weekly touch game the offense emerged triumphant once again over the big defensive dummies. Willie Davis is getting a bit touchy about the offense winning all the time. He's starting to play a little harder. He knocked Ken Bowman down a couple of times today. Kenny's really got enough troubles without getting hit in a touch game.

NOVEMBER 15

We started serious preparations today for the San Francisco 49ers, who have always been tough for us. They're a big, physical football team; they pound and punish you. They beat us once last year, tied us the year before, and beat us the year before that. Of course, the way we feel right now, coming off the Cleveland game, is that nobody can beat us. We're all acting a little bit satisfied with ourselves.

Our performance in the Cleveland game meant a lot to me. It showed how well we could face a real challenge—the Browns had been leading their division—and it showed how well we could bounce back from defeat, even though both our first-string running backs were out with injuries. I doubt that Jim Grabowski's knee'll be strong enough for him to play this week. I can't understand why not. Doug Hart broke his hand against the Browns, and Boyd Dowler sprained his ankle and both of them are working out, ready to play, thanks to the miracle healing of Dr. Lombardi.

Bob Hyland, after rising to total stardom yesterday, came in for some criticism today, but I've got to confess he wasn't entirely at fault. We were having starting drills, practicing getting off the ball as fast as we can. We have starting drills every day—quickness off the ball is one of the secrets of our success—and for ten years Forrest and I have raced every day to see who gets off the ball the fastest. Ski and Gilly and Marv Fleming have gotten into the spirit of the race, and we all hurry, hurry, hurry—to the point where, a good part of the time, we actually anticipate the centering of the ball by the smallest fraction of a second. We jump the gun almost imperceptibly, and this practice carries over into our games. I've had referees come up to me and say, "Boy, it looks like you're offside every time, but I know it's just 'cause you're so quick," and I've nodded politely and smiled.

After a few years of working with the offensive line, Kenny Bowman knows what we're doing, and he's learned to come off the ball almost as fast as we do, just a little behind us, not enough to cause any problems. But Hyland, naturally, doesn't realize what we're doing. He doesn't know we're cheating, so today, during starting drills, maybe we cheated an extra fraction of a second, and we were all coming off the ball three yards ahead of Hyland.

"What the hell's the matter with you today, Hyland?" Vince screamed. "Move, move! You're slow today. You're slow." Poor Hyland was wondering where all his speed had gone.

NOVEMBER 16

Forrest and I felt a little embarrassed today about Hyland getting chewed yesterday. We got together with Ski, Gilly, and Marv and we said, "Let's go on the signal today. Let's wait for the sound."

So we waited during starting drills today, and three or four plays in a row Hyland came off the ball right even with us. "Way to go, Hyland," Lombardi yelled. "Way to go. Now you're moving. Now you're running."

Lombardi reacted less happily to the team's general self-satisfaction. "That's the way, defense," he screamed. "That's the way. You win one game, and you get sloppy. Just stand up and let anybody knock you down. You're going to get knocked down Sunday, you damn fools." He reminded us that there's a $25,000 pot waiting at the end of the rainbow, and he reminded us that $25,000 is a lot of money. He whipped us, but we needed whipping. We've been too relaxed all week.

NOVEMBER 17

Don Chandler beat me at kicking field goals today, and after practice I bought his chili lunch. My cousin Larry Riley joined us, and Don had a friend visiting from Tulsa named Never Fail. He's not an Indian or anything; he's just named Never Fail. He told us that he's got an uncle named Will Fail.

After lunch, I stopped at the bank to pick up some information about an oil-well deal in Abilene, Texas. A few of the New York Giants are involved in it, and they've been trying to get me to invest. But I don't think the potential return is worth the risk. I think I'll pass up this opportunity. I just finalized a deal for $15,000 worth of lake-front property and maybe, as Coach Lombardi says, I've got too many outside interests.

NOVEMBER 18

As we came out of the dressing room after a short practice today, some of the 49ers were drifting in. I said hello to John Brodie, their quarterback, and to Dick Voris, one of their coaches who used to be with us, and to Hugh McElhenny, who now works on San Francisco telecasts. I started thinking about the first time I played against Hugh McElhenny. It was an exhibition game in 1958, and I was on the punting team, and he was returning punts for the 49ers. He'd already been a pro for seven years, and I guess I'd been hearing about him all my life. He had played for the University of Washington before he joined the 49ers, and he was a legend, one of the all-time great football players. We punted to him, and I started running down the field, supposedly to tackle him, and I found myself thinking, "How absurd for a dumb ass like me to tackle a man like Hugh McElhenny. That would really be a dumb thing to do." It seemed inconceivable, a young upstart dum-

dum from Idaho trying to knock down the king. He ran away from me, toward the other side of the field, and pretty soon, of course, I got over my humility.

I spent the afternoon at Chandler's house, watching Southern Cal play U.C.L.A., and I kept thinking about the game tomorrow. Most of the time, I thought about the man I'll be facing, Charlie Krueger, a big old boy from Texas A. & M. Charlie and I played together on the 1958 College All-Star team, and for some reason—National Guard duty or something—he reported to camp three days late. His wife didn't know he was going to be late—none of the players knew it, either—and she kept phoning from Texas and saying, "Is Charles Krueger thayuh?" She had one of those real thick Texas accents that I enjoy so much. My old teammate, Bill Forester, probably had the thickest I ever heard. When he first arrived in Green Bay, he walked into a local restaurant and told the waitress, "Ma'am, Ah'd like a stack." She brought him a stack of pancakes, and Bill shook his head and said, "No, Ma'am. Ah want a stack. S-T-E-A-K. Stack."

In 1958, Charlie Krueger's wife must have talked to everyone in the whole College All-Star training camp, asking, "Is Charles Krueger thayuh?" And when he finally arrived, we all called him, "Charles Krueger thayuh." I saw him last year at the airport in San Francisco as a matter of fact, and I greeted him, "Charles Krueger thayuh." I don't imagine I'll have that much to say to him tomorrow.

Charlie's about 6'4", about 270 pounds, exceptionally solid, exceptionally strong. When he was drafted by the 49ers ten years ago someone predicted he'd outlast three or four coaches, and he's outlasted three already. He's right below Alex Karras and Merlin Olsen, just a notch below them. He's very similar to Cleveland's Walter Johnson. They both beat on you unmercifully; they both give you headaches and neck pains. Charlie's especially tough on running plays. It's almost impossible to move him, and he almost always gets a piece of the ballcarrier. This is a week when I really have to get off the ball quick, quick, quick. I'm afraid it's going to be a long Sunday afternoon, and I'm grateful that I've been having a good season physically, that I'm still in one piece.

NOVEMBER 19

I started off the day determined to get mean and serious for the game. It's something that can't be done just on Saturday and Sunday. It has to be done starting Monday or Tuesday, has to be done gradually, building up to the game. You work up an anger, then a hatred, and the feeling gets stronger and stronger until, on Sunday, you've got your emotion so high you're ready to explode. But I had a lot of distractions this week—friends, relatives, business deals—and after the big win over Cleveland I had a natural tendency to relax. Anyway, I really tried to get going this morning. I tried to work up a good hate for the 49ers, for Charlie Krueger in particular. I have one little habit: When I want to hate an individual, I make it a point not to look at the other team before the game, not to see the man I'm going to face. I feel if I don't see him, I can hate him a little more.

This afternoon, I deliberately didn't look at the 49ers. I didn't look at Charlie Krueger. I convinced myself I hated him. I hated him for trying to make me look bad. I hated him for trying to beat me. I hated him for trying to take money out of my pocket. I hated him for trying to tackle Bart Starr. I worked up my hatred when we did our calisthenics, and I still hated him when we started back to the dressing room to put on our shoulder pads and helmets before the kickoff. I rushed through the tunnel, started up the stairs, concentrating on my hate, concentrating on getting mad, and as I reached the top step, I heard a voice behind me saying, "Is Gerald Kramer thayuh?"

It had to be Charlie. I laughed and turned around, and he stood there, laughing, too. "How you doin', Jerry?" he said. He completely ruined my train of hate.

I tried my best to get myself up again, but the game ended up as a workmanlike effort for me, not a high, emotional effort. I did a fairly good job, but I should have done a few things much better. I looked terrible on one goal-line play. It was a new play that Coach Lombardi put in on Friday, and there were three things wrong with it: First, the play shouldn't have been in. Second, Bart shouldn't have called it. And, third, I made a lousy block. I could have wiped out the first two evils with a good block, but I wasn't properly prepared for the linebacker. I didn't think he'd be in the position he was in when I met him. He stopped me and stopped Bart, and the play looked bad.

Bart got hit in the head during the second quarter, and for a while he didn't know what was happening. He sat on the bench for the whole second half, and Zeke, whose back is almost completely healed, replaced him. We won, 13–0, and on the last play of the game, to kill the clock, Zeke took the center, curled himself around the ball and just fell on the ground in a foetal position. In this situation, when a man's down but not officially stopped till he's touched, an opponent will often pin him down with a knee or an elbow, anything sharp. But this time Charlie Krueger just reached over and sort of patted Zeke, then turned around, grabbed my hand, shook it, and said, "Good luck, Jerry. Ah wish y'awl the luck in the world. Y'awl got a helluva club. Ah hope y'awl go all the way, all the best."

I've always liked Charlie, always had a high opinion of him, and I guess this confirmed my judgment. I was moved.

We went back into the dressing room after the game and said the Lord's Prayer, as we do before and after every game, whether we win or lose, simply to give thanks for people being whole, not being torn up. When we got to the end and said, "Amen," Forrest Gregg spoke up. "Now, remember," he said. "Next week it's the Chicago Bears."

Lombardi added his own comment. "Next week," he said, "we start the big push."

NOVEMBER 20

Doug Hart, Dave Robinson, and I went hunting today, but even out in the woods looking for deer I kept thinking about the game coming up. This is Bear Week. This is the oldest rivalry in the NFL. It's a grudge match and, regardless of the position of the two teams, it's always played like a title game. This week it is a title game. If we beat the Bears, we clinch the championship of the Central Division. With four games to play, our record is seven victories, two defeats and a tie; the Bears, in second place, have five victories and five defeats. If we win, we can relax a little in the last three games, regroup our forces, and give some of the rookies a chance to play. We can start preparing for the Western Conference playoff.

NOVEMBER 21

After the movies this morning, we went outside for our usual touch game, but before we could get started Ray Wietecha said, "C'mon over here. I want to go over a couple of things." He started talking about changes in our pass blocking, but before he could finish, Vince shouted, "Bring it up here. I'll explain it up here." Then he went over the blocking changes. He was so excited about Bear Week he never did let us play touch. Instead, he had us run through a few new plays.

Actually, Vince has been kind of easy on us this year. Last year he pushed us all year long, and you could see it wearing on him toward the end of the season. He says he's getting too old to beat us and push us as much as he used to. But now that we're getting close to the pot of gold, to the third straight championship, to the $25,000 bonus, you can see the gleam coming back into his eye. You can see his blood quickening.

NOVEMBER 22

Vince whipped us today. We started early and stayed late. We had a lot to cover. The Bears use about six or seven different defenses, with variations off each one. This means that maybe 250 or 280 different situations can come up. We're getting new audibles at the line of scrimmage, new pass blocking, new plays. It's a pretty hectic week, and it means a lot of study.

Our defensive people have a habit of standing by the movie tower or sitting on the bench under it when they're not actually practicing. The offensive players don't have much opportunity to rest because we interchange almost every play. For instance, if we're running a sweep and I run thirty yards downfield, another guard, Jay Bachman from the taxi squad, will jump in and run the next play for me. But the defensive men will work for fifteen minutes and then rest for fifteen minutes. For as long as I can remember, they've taken advantage of the bench. Today, Lombardi was screaming at somebody and he happened to turn around and see a few defensive men sitting on the bench. "Get off that damn bench," he hollered. "What the hell's going on out here? Where the hell do you think you are? Get that bench the hell out of here. Throw it over the wall. Burn it."

Everything seems to be moving along nicely. Everyone seems to be concentrating. We know the Bears have been playing good ball lately, and we know they're a strong club. I read an article today quoting Jack Concannon, their quarterback, and Jack seemed to be whistling in the dark a little. "We're not in awe of the Packers," he said. "They put on their pants one leg at a time, just like we do. They're not supermen." Which immediately means he's scared to death of us. This is do or die for them—no tomorrows, and all that jazz—but I think if we stick it in their ear early, we'll take them and take them good.

NOVEMBER 23

Lombardi's pulse rate quickened today. He screamed louder and longer and at more different people than he had all week. He's really gotten himself ready for a game. I wish we could suit him up.

He was jumping around this morning before we watched movies of the Bears, and he shouted, "Boy, I'm getting a Bear itch. I'm getting ready. I don't get excited very often . . ." He stopped and thought for a second or two. ". . . Maybe three or four times a day," he said. "But I'm sure as hell getting excited now. Boys, I hope you are, too."

I think we are.

NOVEMBER 24

The Bears are what I'd call, politely, an overexuberant team. Lombardi, I'm sure, had this in mind when he gave us a little talk today. "Look, boys," he said, "We've got everything here in the palms of our hands. All we've got to do is take this game Sunday, and we've got three weeks to prepare for the conference playoff.

We've got recognition going for us, and self-preservation going for us, and $25,000 going for us. This is going to be the game of your life. I want every man to play the game of his life. I want every man on the special teams, I want even the men on the taxi squad"—they're not eligible to play—"to play the game of his life. I want tough, hard, clean football. Tough, hard, CLEAN football."

We're in fairly good physical shape for the game. Lee Roy Caffey's been limping most of the week from an injury in the 49er game, and his roommate, Tommy Joe Crutcher, will probably have to take his place. Grabo's been running a little, and he may be able to get back in action. And Bart's shook off the head injury he got last week. He still can't remember what happened, which is probably just as well.

NOVEMBER 25

We worked out in Green Bay this morning before flying to Chicago, and Lombardi was even more hopped up than he'd been all week. He came up to me before practice and said, "What do you say, Jerry? What do you say?"

I said, "Let's go get 'em."

"Attaboy," said Vince, "Attaboy. That's what I like to hear. Let's go get 'em." Then he turned to the whole squad and said, "Boy, I'm really excited."

"You're getting just like George Halas," somebody said. The Chicago owner and coach has a reputation for getting excited.

"Halas?" Lombardi snorted. "Halas? Hah, hah. Halas. I can whip his ass. You whip the ballplayers and I'll whip him."

Everybody giggled at that.

After the workout, Vince spoke to us more seriously. "Nobody knows the tortures you go through, trying to stay on top as champions," he said. "It's not so damned tough to get there, but once you get on that pinnacle, everybody in the world is fighting you. It becomes increasingly difficult to win. Kansas City is getting a little taste of what it's like in the American Football League this year. They won their championship last year, and they're virtually out of the race now. They've been getting the hell beat out of them."

Vince smiled a bit. I think he's glad that their loud-mouthed coach—who said he'd whip us the next time he played us—may have to wait a long time to get in the Super Bowl again.

NOVEMBER 26

At our devotional service this morning we had a guest speaker, a retired doctor who spends his time traveling around the country talking to athletes about Christ. He gave us copies of his booklet *Athletes in Action*, and I began thinking about people who never make decisions about their own lives.

The other day, I saw a film called *Cool Hand Luke*, and Paul Newman played a wild character who courted disaster all his life. He had no goal, no fear, and toward the end of his life he escaped from prison two or three times. The last time he escaped, he came upon a church and went in and got on his knees and said something like, "Old Man, whadaya got planned for me? What's next, Old Man? Whadaya want me to do? What did you put me on earth for, Old Man?"

I ask the same questions. I often wonder where my life is heading, and what's my purpose here on earth besides playing the silly games I play every Sunday. I feel there's got to be more to life than that. There's got to be some reason to it.

Many people never take control of their own lives, never say this is the way it's going to be, and maybe I'm one of them. I didn't come up with any answers this morning. I just thought about it for a while.

When we got to the stadium everything was pretty tense, pretty tight. Our people seemed nervous; this was the most we'd been up for a game, physically and emotionally, in some time. It's another reflection of Coach Lombardi's brilliance, I guess. Several times during the season I felt we were low, we were dead, and perhaps it was all deliberate, all part of Lombardi's scheme to bring us along gradually. Beyond any question, we were up today.

There's a danger of getting too high, to the point where you're ineffective. Inexperienced ballplayers are especially vulnerable to this. They get so emotional they can't do anything right. We've got a lot of young boys, and today, before the game, Vince was kind of gauging them, trying to measure their emotions. "How you feel, Jerry?" he asked me. "You think everybody's ready?"

"I don't know about the rest of them, Coach," I said, "but I sure as hell am ready."

Lombardi called us together, and we were all jumping around, hopped up, chattering, tight as drums.

"OK, boys," Coach said, in a calm voice. "I want to tell you a little story." He paused, and we waited, very quietly, to hear what he had to say. "Did you ever hear," Vince said, "about why Belgians are so strong?"

In Green Bay, we tell Belgian jokes, the same jokes people in some areas tell about Italians and people in other areas tell about Poles.

"No," one of the guys said.

" 'Cause they raise dumbbells," said Lombardi.

That was his whole pregame speech. It was a silly, asinine little joke, but it worked. It took the edge off the tension. Most of the guys giggled, and we all loosened up. We went out and beat the Bears 17–13.

I had a good day. I handled Frank Cornish well on running plays and on passing plays. Usually when you play a good game as an offensive lineman nobody notices you. If you do your job right and keep your man away from the ballcarrier you've got to be inconspicuous. When you're screwing up and your man is making tackles, you get noticed. But I got lucky today. On the first touchdown of the game, when Bart scrambled out of the pocket and wandered around before he found Boyd Dowler in the end zone, I stopped my man at the line of scrimmage, then retreated into the backfield and, in the open, where everyone in the stands could see it, I cut down two Bears with one block. An open-field block is no harder, probably easier, than a good block at the line of scrimmage, but for an offensive lineman to cut down two men is just like scoring a touchdown. It's a beautiful feeling.

The Bears, rough and hungry, really made us work for the game. They tied us 7–7 in the first quarter, and then Travis Williams ran back a kickoff 69 yards to set up a touchdown that put us ahead 14–7. From then on, our defense got tough, and we hung on to win the game and clinch the Central Division championship.

We took the victory pretty calmly. Nobody went wild in the locker room. Nobody screamed. Nobody poured champagne. We walked around quietly congratulating one another for a job well done. There was an air of satisfaction rather than of exhilaration. Some of the visiting sportswriters in the locker room felt we were a little too blasé. They thought we should have been whooping it up a bit more. Henry Jordan had the perfect answer for them. "Sure it's a thrill," Henry said, "but we'll walk into the movies Tuesday morning, and we'll think we lost the game."

NOVEMBER 28

Henry hit it just about right. We came in Tuesday morning, and Lombardi cussed this guy and cussed that guy and hollered at all of us. "If you think we're going to let down," he screamed, "you're crazy. We're going to play just as damned hard as we've ever played in our lives." We watched the movies, and at one point he turned around and said, "Jerry, you had one of your better games. You had a helluva ball game. You knocked that Butkus right on his ass a few times." Vince hadn't talked to me like that for some time. He was absolutely right, of course.

Coach had a special treat for Jim Grabowski. "Grabo," Vince said, as soon as he spotted him, "that'll cost you $250." I wondered what Grabo had done, and then I found out that Jim, who had reinjured his knee against the Bears, hadn't reported to the training room for treatment Monday. He had stayed over in Chicago to see his friends and relatives. His little vacation had cost him $250.

NOVEMBER 29

Coach Lombardi wore his mouthful-of-sour-owls look today. He screamed and hollered as if we'd won one and lost ten, as if we were the worst team in professional football. Steve Wright blew a play, and as he trotted back to the huddle Ray Wietecha said, "C'mon, Steve, think! Have a little poise out there."

"Think!" Lombardi shouted. "You've got to be kidding, asking that guy to think. He can't think. He can't do nothing." He cussed Steve up and down, and he said, "We'll get rid of you next year. We'll send you down to one of those hinky-dinky teams, and you can be a big man on a hinky-dinky team. That's all you're good for, anyhow."

Steve, who's about 6'6'', just looked at Lombardi and then

looked down at his own shoes and then sort of shuffled back to the huddle. He didn't say a word.

What could Steve say? He knew Vince didn't mean the harsh words, but you can't argue with the man—unless you've got some good strong football reasoning behind you. If you just back-talk to him he gets all over you, and you get chewed five times as bad.

A minute or two after the lecture to Steve, Fuzzy missed a block, and Lombardi exploded. "Who was supposed to be on that man?" he demanded.

"I was," Fuzzy said. "I thought Zeke called a pass."

"WHAT IN THE HELL IS GOING ON HERE?" Lombardi shrieked. "What in the hell are you thinking about? What in the hell's wrong with you guys? I drive and I drive and I drive, and you guys don't give a damn. You've got too many restaurants, too much hunting, too many outside interests. I've had it. I'm disgusted with you guys. The hell with you. Let's go to defense. The hell with the offense." He was livid. He was fuming. "You guys," he said, "can stick it in your diddy-bag."

He was so angry, so hot, and when he came out with that word, "diddy-bag," he just sounded ridiculous. I was standing by Forrest Gregg—neither of us had the faintest notion what a diddy-bag was—and Trees whispered, out of the side of his mouth, "Don't you look at me." He was practically giggling. He was afraid he'd burst out laughing in Vince's face. We watched movies later, and Coach didn't crack a smile all day. He looked like the great stone face himself.

NOVEMBER 30

Lombardi came to work today full of remorse, genuinely sorry that he had been so rough on us. He bounced around the locker room laughing and smiling, trying to get back on good terms with everybody, and he walked over to a pile of autographed footballs lying on the table where we sign them, picked them up and started throwing them, one by one, like a pitchout, through a door into the equipment room. Vince kept giggling, enjoying himself, and, finally, he said. "That's pretty good. Ten in a row. I'm getting to be a helluva pitchout man."

And Max shouted, "Why don't you see if you can throw one in your diddy-bag, Coach?"

Everybody in the place broke up, including Lombardi.

The sun was in the sky again. Everybody was happy. We even found out that a diddy-bag is something sailors stow their gear in.

"I don't want to seem ungrateful," Vince said, at a meeting. "I'm awfully proud of you guys, really. You've done a helluva job." He couldn't resist adding, "But sometimes you just disgust me."

We play a rematch with the Minnesota Vikings Sunday, and we've got nothing going for us except our desire for revenge. They've been looking pretty good since the day they beat us. They've got a big, strong defensive front four. Coach Lombardi told us today that it's the best front four in the business, but, of course, he's exaggerating. They're tough, though, and my man, Alan Page, is especially tough. He's been named Associated Press Lineman of the Week twice already this year.

Gilly and Fuzzy and I have been doing a lot of talking this week in the movies and on the practice field. Since Gilly took my place against Page in the first game, and Fuzzy took Gilly's place against Paul Dickson, I've been asking Gilly about Page and Gilly's been asking Fuzzy about Dickson. "Page's stronger'n hell," Gilly told me. "He's the kind of guy you really have to meet. If you wait for him, he'll just start sweeping you back and you can't catch yourself. Make sure you hit him good and solid right on the line before he gets moving. Stop him and then get away from him."

Page is a lot like Frank Cornish, the Bears' tackle; they're both strong men, without too many tricky moves. They're not dancers. I'm not going to play cute with Page. I'm just going to hit him as fast and as hard as I can.

DECEMBER 1

At the start of our meeting this morning Coach Lombardi went over the itinerary for our trip to Minneapolis and the west coast. We're leaving straight from Minneapolis for Santa Barbara to work out there before we play the Los Angeles Rams. Lombardi got halfway into the itinerary and somebody said "Hey, there's a couple of guys still in the training room." Lombardi marched over to the training room and shouted, "What the hell's going on in here?" He was pretending to be angry. "I thought this damned meeting started at 10 o'clock," he said. "What are you guys doing in here?"

The time was then exactly 9:25 A.M. "I don't know what the hell you guys think," Vince said. "When 10 o'clock comes around, we're supposed to have a meeting."

We may be the Central champions, but we're still operating on Lombardi Standard Time.

I went to talk to Blaine Williams this afternoon because our portrait program is definitely in trouble. The Kraft people predicted that by mid-November things should really be steaming along, but now it's December and we haven't had more than 350 orders in a day. I'm afraid the whole thing sort of fell apart. We'll try to recoup, try to sell the portrait albums as Christmas gifts. I called Urban Henry in Louisiana and asked him to go on Paul Hornung's TV show and plug the portraits, and I called Bill Forester in Dallas and asked him to do the same thing in his area. I'm going to get in touch with Dick Schafrath or somebody from Cleveland and maybe Tom Matte from Baltimore, and see if we can get this whole thing straightened out. I signed a $50,000 note to get the business started, and I'd hate to lose the money.

DECEMBER 2

Ray Nitschke showed up at the plane this morning wearing a toupee and sunglasses, and he looked like a different individual. He kept jiving up and down the aisle, showing off his rug and his shades. "Which way's Hollywood, gang?" he said. We were all pretty damned anxious to get out to California and soak up a litle sunshine.

DECEMBER 3

We beat the Vikings today 30–27, when my roommate kicked his third field goal of the game in the closing seconds. For a balding old man, he kicks pretty well.

I couldn't get terribly excited about the game one way or the other, but I went out and played hard-nosed football. I played one of my best games of the season. I came off the ball fast and I pounded Alan Page, and he didn't do any damage. He's relying entirely on his strength now—and it definitely wasn't enough today—but I suspect that in a couple of years, when he picks up a few moves, I'm not going to have much fun with him. I think I'd better retire pretty soon.

Vince kept shifting players in and out of the lineup, giving everybody a chance to rest, giving the young boys a chance to show what they can do. Travis Williams got his first good shot at playing halfback, and he picked up quite a bit of yardage. I think Travis is going to be one of the great football players in the NFL. I hope he gets to play a lot in the last two games against Los Angeles and Pittsburgh, because if he just learns a little more about the way our offense functions, he could make a difference in the playoff games.

Bart had a good day, a very good day, which is certainly an encouraging sign. He's played two excellent games in a row. He was one of the few people who played the whole game today. "I rested enough earlier in the season," he told one sportswriter.

At the start of the fourth quarter Coach Wietecha asked me if I wanted to rest, and I said, "OK, but don't let me sit here on the bench for ten minutes and cool off and then send me back in. If I come out now, I'd like to stay out."

"OK," said Wietecha.

When I came out, we were leading 27–17, but with two minutes to play the score was tied 27–27, and Minnesota had the ball. Then they fumbled in their own territory and Tommy Brown recovered for us, and the offensive team ran out on the field, with Fuzzy in my spot. I was standing on the sidelines just enjoying the game. Suddenly, Coach Lombardi spotted me and shouted, "Jerry! What are you doing here? Get the hell in there!"

I jumped like a wounded rabbit and ran out on the field just as our huddle was breaking. Naturally, I had to tell Fuzzy to come out, and it made him look bad, running off the field by himself. He was bitter afterward. He was furious with me at first, but then he realized it wasn't my fault, and he started hating Vince. All the way to California after the game, Fuzzy boiled. He snapped at everybody.

DECEMBER 4

My roommate is a great human being. Last night, after we ate dinner in Santa Barbara, he went back to our motel to sleep and

I went out with a few of the guys to celebrate. We weren't celebrating our victory—just the sunshine and the freedom and the escape from the telephone that never stops ringing at home.

We let loose, more than any other night all year. We went to a bowling alley—I know that doesn't sound very exciting, but we're from Green Bay—and we went to a discotheque and we listened to music and we sang and Max bowled and we all had a few drinks. There was no curfew last night—starting tonight, it'll cost us $1,000 if we miss 11 P.M. bed-check, and $2,000 if we get caught sneaking out after the bed-check—so we got rid of enough tension to last us all season. I didn't really drink too much, but when you've been in training for months and your body's grown accustomed to no more than one drink or two drinks a week, you take more than a couple and you feel pretty happy. I came back to our room in the wee hours feeling loose and happy, and there was my roommate fast asleep—fast asleep in the single bed. He had left the big double bed for me. He has kicked seventeen field goals in twenty-three attempts this year, and he is a great human being.

"Sure I left the double bed for you," Don said this morning. "I knew darn well that if I didn't, you'd throw me out of it when you got home. I just wanted to sleep."

For the first time in several years the offense and defense had a joint meeting tonight to watch the Minnesota films, and the old man was in a screaming mood. He called me a big cow for getting to a linebacker late, and he heard Boyd Dowler whispering and he shouted, "I'll make the comments in here," and he hollered at Marvin Fleming, "Look at you, stupid, you big jerk. You don't have the mental capacity to retain anything for twenty-four hours."

It was really just a typical Lombardi performance, nothing special, but the defensive boys were deeply impressed.

"You don't have much fun in your meetings, do you, Jerry?" said Doug Hart. "We have lots of laughs in our meetings."

"You guys get more money than we do," said Kostelnik, "but you deserve it to sit through those meetings. I don't ever want to go to one again."

DECEMBER 5

We went out to practice this morning, and Elijah Pitts came limping around the field, wearing a blue turtleneck sweater that made him appear a little fat. "Dammit, Pitts," said Lombardi, "there's a chance we can activate you for the Super Bowl, but you look like a balloon. Where the hell are we gonna put you? At guard?"

Herb Adderley said, "Pittsie and Fuzzy now have the exact same waistline."

We're having some fun this week, but on Saturday, in the Los Angeles Coliseum, I'll be facing Merlin Olsen, and that's definitely work, not fun. Merlin is simply a great football player. He's about 6'5", and his weight varies, maybe 275 or 285 or 290. That may sound silly, but it's not like weighing 175 or 185 or 190. My weight last week fluctuated from 259 at the beginning to 250 1/2 at the end. I've seen Merlin at 260 and at 296 when we played together in Pro Bowl games. Merlin's not as quick as Alex Karras, but he's stronger. Both of them have great lateral movement. Merlin has tremendous hustle; he never quits. Alex sometimes will ease up if his club is far ahead or far behind, but Merlin never lets up. He'll run right over you no matter what the score is. When I play against a guy like that there's a lot of mutual respect, and there's never any holding or kicking or clipping, just straight, clean, hard football.

The other night Forrest Gregg was talking about Carl Eller, a good defensive end for Minnesota, and somebody said, "Man, if you get down around his knees, you can cut him off real easy. He's got bad knees. You can tear him up."

"Yeah," said Forrest, "but I hate to. He's a helluva guy. He's such a good clean competitor I wouldn't do anything like that."

That's the way I feel about Merlin.

DECEMBER 6

Somebody tried to rob our motel this morning. A guy came in around 2:15 in the morning carrying a small automatic and tried to hold up the night clerk. The clerk took out his own gun and shot the stickup man in the leg. He fled, and the police caught him.

The ironic part was that the night clerk didn't even have a dime. But I was sleeping on the ground floor, only a few doors off the lobby, with my door unlocked and several hundred dollars in my attaché case. From now on, I think I'll lock my door.

Lombardi's a little bit afraid of robbery, too. He's afraid that somebody from the Los Angeles Rams will try to steal a look at our practice sessions. We stayed in Santa Barbara last year and we worked out at the same field, the stadium of the University of California at Santa Barbara, and Vince gave the school $3,000 to buy a big canvas screen to put around the field. We're practicing behind the screen this week. Vince Lombardi believes in locking his doors.

DECEMBER 7

We want to beat the Rams Saturday for a very selfish reason. If we beat the Rams, they're eliminated from the Coastal Division race, and Baltimore wins the division title. But if the Rams beat us and then beat Baltimore the following week, they win the title. We play the Coastal Division winner in Milwaukee for the Western Conference championship, and we want to play Baltimore. We think the Rams are a much more dangerous team. We feel that we had the Colts beat in Baltimore, that we lost the game only through a fluke and that we'd certainly be able to beat them in the playoff.

There are only a few dissenting opinions on the team, and they all come from the defensive unit. They're not anxious to face Johnny Unitas again. I don't blame them. But, given the choice between going up against Unitas and going up against Los Angeles' defensive Fearsome Foursome, the consensus is: Bring on Unitas.

DECEMBER 8

We drove in chartered buses this afternoon from Santa Barbara down to Los Angeles, checked into our hotel and hurried out to do some shopping. A bunch of us went over to a knitting mill where they let pro football players buy clothes at half price. Sometimes I think we buy everything wholesale. I bought my wife a few dresses and bought myself half a dozen alpaca sweaters and eight or ten pairs of slacks. I do like to spoil myself.

DECEMBER 9

I understand now, better than I ever did before, what Vince means when he says, "The harder you work, the harder it is to surrender." We worked our butts off today, and when the game ended, when we finally surrendered, I felt like crying.

The game was on national TV, and it must have been beautiful to watch. The Rams were fighting for their lives, we were fighting for our pride, and both teams were up for the fight. Neither of us ever led by more than a touchdown. After we'd been in front 7–0 and 10–7, the Rams took the lead 17–10. Then they kicked off deep to Travis Williams—they had been kicking shallow all afternoon—and Travis caught the ball in the end zone, came up the middle, bounced off one of their men and spun to his left. I got a piece of a block on one Ram, then a piece of a block on another; the second man, after I'd hit him, stumbled toward Travis, reached out and barely missed him. I was surprised to see Travis running up the sidelines; I'd expected him thundering up the middle behind me. Travis sprinted all the way to a touchdown, a total of 104 yards, tying the score.

In the last minute of play, we were leading 24–20, and we had to punt from our own territory. Tony Guillory, a Los Angeles linebacker, lined up right on our center. On a punt, the center isn't responsible for blocking anyone; he's got his head down in a very awkward position and his main job is to get the ball back to the punter. Chuck Mercein, who was new to the punting team, was supposed to check Guillory. But Guillory jumped around Bowman at center, and Mercein didn't pick him up, and Tommy Joe Crutcher, who was back blocking for the punter, was looking from side to side, expecting someone to come charging in from the outside, and didn't even see Guillory coming up the middle. Guillory blocked the punt, the Rams recovered on our 5-yard line and, two plays later, Roman Gabriel threw a touchdown pass to beat us 27–24.

I was ready to fall down when the game ended. I contained Merlin pretty well, but I was beat from head to toe. I played about as hard as I've ever played in my life, and I took an incredible physical pounding in the middle of the line. So did everybody else; everybody gave 100 percent. Coach Lombardi told me I played a great game, but I was down, blue, disappointed, dejected, everything. I never came so close to tears on a football field.

We were pretty quiet in the locker room after the game, and Dave Robinson said to me, "The disappointment of losing a football game is in direct proportion to the amount of energy expended in trying to win it." Robby's an engineer, and I guess he likes to talk in formulas, but I didn't have to be a mathematician to figure out what he meant. It was a long ride home to Green Bay.

DECEMBER 11

I just stayed around the house yesterday and today, licking my wounds. The defeat still hurts; the clock ran out on us again. I watched a little television and I caught up on my reading. I read *In Cold Blood* and a book by Jeane Dixon, who says she can see into the future. Jeane Dixon predicts that the 1967 National Football League champions will be the Green Bay Packers. I hope the lady knows what she's talking about.

DECEMBER 12

Coach Lombardi said this morning that he was very proud of us for putting on the display we did against Los Angeles. He said he thinks we're a helluva bunch of young men to have worked so hard in a game that meant nothing to us in the standings. Then he began cussing. He cussed me and Gilly and Forrest and Ski and just about everyone on the team. He called us a bunch of fatheads and he said that we didn't have one brain among us. He's getting himself worked up more than anyone else, building up his own momentum to carry him through the playoffs. The rumors about his possible retirement are going around again, and I think he wants the third championship in a row more than anything in the world. I wouldn't mind it myself.

DECEMBER 13

The Associated Press announced its All-Pro teams today, and I was named first-string offensive guard. Forrest made first-string tackle to keep me company. We were the only Packers on the offense, but Willie Wood, Willie Davis, Dave Robinson, and Bob Jeter made it on defense. I felt badly about Ray Nitschke missing out. Ray had his best season, a great season, but the sportswriters passed him by.

My selection gave me a great deal of satisfaction. I've been All-Pro five times during the last eight seasons; the other three years I was sick and hurt and forgotten. Being chosen again is a strange feeling, sort of like having a fickle lover come back, I guess. I'm tempted to say that the selection doesn't mean anything, but it does. It really does. It means recognition—which may be part of the reason I keep playing this silly game.

DECEMBER 14

We're really in no shape mentally to play Pittsburgh Sunday. We know the game doesn't mean a thing. We know the coaches are spending all their time preparing for Baltimore and Los Angeles, getting ready no matter which one wins their big game in California. We're looking at the Pittsburgh game as if it were a good scrimmage, the last big scrimmage before a ball game, the final chance to polish our technique. Guys have been laughing and clowning on the practice field, and Coach Lombardi's screaming doesn't seem to have much impact. "You'll be laughing," Vince said today, "you'll be laughing down in Miami on January 7th. That's where you'll be laughing. You won't be laughing December 23rd." He kept referring to the 23rd, which is when we play the winner of the Rams-Colts game, and to the 7th, which is when the loser of the Western Conference playoff meets the loser of the Eastern Conference playoff. It's very unusual for Lombardi to refer to losing. Maybe he thinks we are going to lose.

DECEMBER 15

I've never heard a word from that Idaho classmate of mine who told me he'd become a doctor in New York City. I haven't received a check or a letter or even a postcard. And the university hasn't helped me at all. The tracer on him didn't turn up an address or a telephone number. It's kind of funny to go all the way to New York City to get suckered by an Idaho country boy. It won't be so funny for him, though, if I ever find him.

DECEMBER 16

Coach Lombardi told me this morning that I'd been picked to play on the Western Conference team in the Pro Bowl game—for the first time in four years—but I missed my chance for even greater honors: I didn't win one of the big awards presented today by Tom Brown, the commissioner of the Green Bay Packer Volleyball League.

We've played a volleyball game almost every Saturday morning all season, using a football for a volleyball and a goal post crossbar for a net. Lee Roy Caffey and Tommy Joe Crutcher have co-captained one team, the King Ranch Bullies, and Ray Nitschke's captained the other, the Cicero Sissies. I've been on the Sissies, but despite my heroic play the King Ranch Bullies won the championship. Lee Roy won the Most Valuable Player award, and Ron Kostelnik, from our team, won the Outstanding-at-Standing-Around-and-Doing-Absolutely-Nothing-but-Tearing-the-Grass award.

Lombardi handed out awards today, too, blocking awards for the last two games, and I got one for the Minnesota game. I got a 95 for passing and an 85 for running, the highest grades I've gotten all year, but I still don't put much faith in them. I've received blocking awards for only two or three games this season, and I didn't get one for the Los Angeles game, even though Vince told me right afterward that I'd played brilliantly. Ray Wietecha has the most to say about which linemen get blocking awards, and I'm beginning to suspect that he's still mad at me for beating the Giants in the 1961 and 1962 championship games. Ray was playing for the Giants in those games.

After our workout this morning, CBS-TV filmed an interview with Forrest Gregg and me for their pregame show tomorrow. The show's usually reserved for the big names, the backfield stars and a few defensive linemen. They must be getting down to the bottom of the barrel if they've got to interview a couple of offensive linemen. One of the Cleveland Browns once told me that if he ever had to go on the lam from the law, he'd become an offensive lineman.

It cheered me up when the producer of the CBS show told me he'd heard that I had a TV show and he'd like to see it; he asked me if I was interested in a future in television, and I told him I certainly was. It also cheered me up to hear from Blaine Williams that Kraft has tentatively agreed to make up whatever money we lose on the portrait program. Urban Henry has a saying, "The sun doesn't shine on one dog's rear all the time," and maybe the sun is starting to shine on mine.

DECEMBER 17

We emptied our bench today, poured every active player into the Pittsburgh game except Jim Grabowski, whose knee is still sore. Don Horn played most of the game at quarterback and Travis Williams played almost a full game at halfback. Travis had a beautiful day. He scored two touchdowns, ran for a lot of yards, and caught several passes. I think he's got the potential to be another Jimmy Brown. He's got an uncanny knack for picking the right holes. It usually takes a running back three or four years as a pro before he learns how to hit the holes, but Travis does it naturally.

We lost the game 24–17, which didn't mean much to us, but meant a great deal to the Steelers, particularly to the ex-Packers on their team. Kent Nix, the boy we traded during training season, played the whole game for them at quarterback and looked pretty good. My Idaho friend Dick Arndt played a little at defensive tackle; he faced Gilly, so I didn't have a chance to give him a proper greeting. I did bump into him in the tunnel before the game, and I asked him what his picture was doing in our program in a Green Bay uniform. "I've been gone fifteen weeks." Dick said. "You'd think that'd give 'em enough time to change the picture."

Pittsburgh treated us rough. They bruised Donny Anderson and banged up Ben Wilson, and Steve Wright cracked a rib. And Allen Brown almost died. He was playing on the kickoff-return team, and on one kickoff return one of the Steelers told Allen he was going to get him next time. Allen didn't pay any attention; neither did anyone else. Guys are always saying things like that without meaning anything by it.

On the next kickoff, Allen threw a cross-body block into the guy and turned his back a little bit, and the guy kneed him in the back. Allen got up under his own power and hobbled off the field, a very pained look on his face. I couldn't tell whether he was really hurt or shocked or just surprised, and I didn't think much about it. I figured he just got kneed or kicked, nothing serious. I found out after the game that the doctors had removed Allen from the stadium at half-time in an ambulance. He almost lost his blood pressure on the way to the hospital. They took him inside and examined him and discovered that he had two broken ribs and a punctured kidney. They put him on the critical list.

Poor Allen's really had a tough life as a Green Bay Packer. In 1965, his rookie year, he hurt his shoulder in the College All-Star game, underwent surgery and missed the whole season. In 1966, he injured his knee the third week of the season, had to go under the knife again, and missed the rest of the year. Now this. He must be trying to build up a medical history like mine.

It's curious the way the guys react to an injury like Allen's. Most of the guys try to wipe it right out of their minds. You'll see them turn their backs on an injured teammate on the field, sort of to pretend that it didn't happen. They're afraid to think about injuries, afraid to think that it might happen to them. The more you think about it, of course, the more likely you are to get hurt. I'm fatalistic myself. I don't really realize how brutal the game is until the off-season, when I go out to banquets and watch movies of our games. Then I see guys turned upside-down and backwards and hit from all angles, and I flinch. I'm amazed by how violent the game is, and I wonder about playing it myself.

I tried to stir up a little violence myself this afternoon. I kept looking for No. 50, Bill Saul, the linebacker who'd grabbed me by the shoulder pads and thrown me to the ground—after the play was over—during our preseason game. I was really looking to blast him. But I got only one shot at him and it wasn't a very good one. Pittsburgh was in a four-four defense, and Saul was directly behind Ken Kortas, my tackle. My assignment was to block Kortas if he tried to go outside me—or to block Saul if Kortas went inside me. Kortas charged to the inside, and I went for Saul, but I didn't hit him from the best angle. I still drove him back about five yards. He looked at me kind of oddly. I don't think he remembered what he'd done to me in the exhibition. He didn't have a tooth in his mouth; he was gummy and evil-looking.

I didn't play much of a game. I tried to make all my blocks crisp and low, perfect them for the playoffs, but the emotion wasn't there. Without the emotion, you can't play this game.

As soon as we got dressed after the game Don Chandler and I and a few other people hurried back to my house to watch Los Angeles play Baltimore on television. We were all pulling for the Colts—we didn't want to face the Rams again—but by the half we knew Los Angeles was going to win. They won the game 34–10, and they looked terrific. They're tough. They're hot. They're lucky. They're confident. They've got everything in the world going for them. They think nobody can beat them, and, by thinking that way, they just may be right.

This is the sixth time in eight years that we've gotten into the postseason playoffs; this is the second time we've had a chance to win a third straight National Football League championship. I'm positive that we're a good team, but I don't know how good. I'm a little bit worried. I've got a terrible feeling that maybe we're going to get our tails whipped. I don't think I've ever felt this way before.

WAR'S END

DECEMBER 18

It is dreary, cold, rainy, typical Green Bay weather. Even my head is foggy. I got banged in the head yesterday. The Steelers kicked me from my head to my toes, my neck, my ribs, my feet, every part of me. I can barely think, and when I do my thoughts are not at all reassuring.

If there is ever a year for us to get knocked on our butts, this it it. Compare the way we played against Pittsburgh yesterday with the way Los Angeles played against Baltimore, and you have to believe that the clock, finally, is about to run out on us. I hate to be gloomy. I hate to even think about defeat. I hate the idea that we could come so close to a third straight world championship and miss it. But I have a very bad feeling about this game.

I flew to Milwaukee this afternoon to buy my wife a piano for

Christmas—wholesale, naturally—and on the plane I bumped into Jim Flanigan, our rookie linebacker. Jim told me he was flying to Chicago on business.

"What are you going to do?" I asked. I'm a very prying individual.

"I'm going to buy an engagement ring for my girl," he said.

"Wonderful," I said. "I've got a friend in Milwaukee who runs a wholesale jewelry house. Want to see him?"

"I don't know," Jim said. "We went over to Tiffany's in Chicago and saw several rings we liked."

"How much you had in mind spending?"

"About $5,000," Jim said.

"Good Lord, Jim," I said. "That's a tremendous amount of money to spend for an engagement ring. You'd better get off this plane with me and come talk to my guy."

I brought Jim into Milwaukee and he picked out a two-carat diamond, a perfect diamond, a $5,200 ring, and paid only $2,700 for it. He saved himself a couple of thousand dollars. Rookies sure have more expensive tastes now than they did when I was a rookie. My whole rookie season, I only earned $7,750.

Now Jim Flanigan's got a chance to earn $25,000 in the next four weeks. If we can beat Los Angeles, if we can beat the Eastern Conference champions, if we can win the Super Bowl game, we'll earn about $25,000 a man.

I keep seeing the figure running through my head. Each week during the season, when I tried to work up a hatred for my opponent, I was really just using a gimmick to get myself emotionally ready. I called it hatred because there was nothing else involved. But now I call it $25,000. I keep telling myself that I've got $25,000 in my pocket and somebody's trying to steal it from me. There's no problem getting emotionally ready this week. I just wish that bad feeling would go away.

DECEMBER 19

I've started daydreaming about Merlin Olsen. I see myself breaking his leg or knocking him unconscious, and then I see myself knocking out a couple of other guys, and then I see us scoring a touchdown, and always, in my own dreams, I see myself the hero.

I lay in bed last night and my mind began drifting. "Third-down situation," I told myself. "Passing situation. Merlin likes an outside rush on a third-down situation. His favorite move is to come into me with his head, pull me with his left hand, throw his right hand across my head and go to the outside to get to the passer. Now, in this situation, I'm going to hit him, then I'm going to come off him a little bit and then I'm going to drive him. I'm going to drive him to the outside just as hard as I can, and I'm going to knock him down."

And then my thoughts wandered to other situations: "Lundy plays wide, so on a sweep-left, we're gonna have to run inside him. I'll pull and turn upfield real quick and I'll look for the middle linebacker, Woodlief, and knock him down, knock him unconscious, of course, and then I'll go get the safety, Meador. But when we sweep the other way, outside Davy Jones, it's hard for a back to cut him, so I'll knock him down and then I'll get the linebacker, Pardee, and then I'll look for the halfback." Before I knew it, I had played a terrific half a football game. Finally, I fell asleep.

When we reported to practice this morning, Coach Lombardi greeted us with a little inspirational talk. "We may be wounded," he said. "We may be in trouble. Some people may be picking Los Angeles over us. But I'll tell you one thing: That damned Los Angeles better be ready to play a football game when they come in here 'cause they're going to have a battle. I'll guarantee that. This team has a history of rising to the occasion. This is it. There's no tomorrow. This is really the start of the big push."

Vince hollered and screamed a little while we watched the movies of the Pittsburgh game, but he didn't have his heart in it. He wanted to get on to the Ram game. He gave us a few new plays to learn, and we went out and had a real good workout. We didn't play our usual game of touch. We combined the regular Tuesday and Wednesday practices because this is a short week. We play the Rams in Milwaukee Saturday.

I found a few early Christmas presents in my locker. I got a box of candy from a candy manufacturer up in Michigan, a bottle of cologne from some cologne manufacturer, and a spice rack from Channel 11 in Green Bay, all gifts to wish us well against the Rams. The whole team got a letter in Braille today from a class of blind schoolboys.

Don Horn, the rookie quarterback, came on my TV show tonight, and his answers to a few of my questions showed how far he's come since training camp. He's changed his attitude—he isn't cocky anymore—and, like all the other first-year men he's become a part of the Green Bay Packers.

"Don, you've got what's known as a quick release," I said. "How'd you develop that?"

"I guess I do get rid of the ball quickly," said Horn. "When you see all those big linemen coming at you, you're scared to death, and you've got to get rid of the ball quickly."

"How long does it take to make a good pro quarterback?"

"When I first arrived here," Don said, "I didn't think it would take any time at all. Now, after learning a little from Bart and Zeke, I figure it's got to take three to five years, if I'm lucky."

The pressure is here. The tension is here. Generally, the tension builds up gradually, but this week it's a constant thing—morning, noon, night. God knows what it'll be like by Saturday. At this stage of the season, you can't do anything about your physical condition, but if you can get the mental thing going for you, that's something. That's what Vince is working on. That's what the whole club is working on. All I keep thinking is: Olsen, Olsen, Olsen.

DECEMBER 20

I'm having terrible trouble sleeping. I can't stop seeing those plays running through my mind. I got to bed last night at 9 P.M. and read for half an hour and wasn't tired. Then I watched TV for half an hour and wasn't tired. I read for another hour and, at 11, I took a tranquilizer, and I still wasn't tired. At 11:30, I took a sleeping pill and, about 1 o'clock, I finally dozed off.

I got up bright and early this morning, picked up Chandler, and drove over to the stadium. Lombardi had that gleam in his eye, that hungry, lively look. He was excited, very excited, and he got everybody else excited. The bad feeling is starting to go away. The memory of how good Los Angeles looked against Baltimore is starting to fade. We're all getting rid of our misgivings, getting a little confidence, beginning to believe in ourselves once more.

We had a lovely practice, the first and last practice this week with pads on. The backs were hitting the holes well, sharply, precisely. Lombardi kept screaming, "Tremendous. Beautiful. Way to go." He kept building everybody up, nursing their confidence. He looked young and fresh again.

We're just in fair physical condition. Allen Brown is still in the hospital, coming along, but critical, leaving Marv Fleming as the only tight end. Ben Wilson and Jim Grabowski make up about one fullback between them. Grabo says he can block, but can't run, and Ben's limping a little. Chuck Mercein's our only able-bodied fullback, and, of course, he's still learning to fit into our system.

Coach Wietecha gave the offensive line a speech this morning on how he felt about the Ram game. He said that we have to approach the game positively; we can't afford to think of the past or of bubbles that have to burst. "If you guys handle yourselves properly and prepare yourselves properly," Wietecha said, "you can keep winning for the next thirty years."

We concentrated on a few new plays, plays I suspect Lombardi has been saving for several weeks, saving especially for this game. We've put in some quick-hitting plays up the middle, a 21-quick, a 41-quick, a 61-quick, all through the "one" hole, the hole between me and the center. The difference between these plays and our regular plays is that we're utilizing "quick," or direct, blocking. Instead of, for instance, the center blocking on the tackle and me stepping behind the center and blocking the middle linebacker, we just block straight ahead, strict zone blocking. The back has got to hit the hole as fast as he can, no jab step, no hesitation, no looking for an opening. It's a little different from Coach Lombardi's standard theory of running to daylight, because with these plays we anticipate the holes. The beauty of the plays is that they're a change of pace; they're just the sort of plays other teams don't expect from us.

After our workout we watched movies of our last game against the Rams, and I tried to watch me exactly as Merlin Olsen would watch me. I tried to use the mind of a defensive tackle to study myself. I think I know what Merlin'll try to do, and I think I know how I'll stop him.

When I got home this afternoon I stepped into a headache. I had a whole bunch of tickets for the players' wives, and I've got to straighten out who's going to sit with whom. It's not enough I've got to worry about hurting Merlin Olsen; I've got to worry about hurting people's feelings, too.

DECEMBER 21

Coach Lombardi was jolly and jovial in the locker room this morning. He was alive, intensified, bouncing around. It's as though he had been lying dormant for fourteen weeks, just going through the motions to get all that unimportant stuff, all those regular-season games, out of the way.

Someone in Vietnam, a Packer fan in a foxhole, had sent Vince a smiling Buddha, not a sitting Buddha, but one standing up with his arms stretched over his head and, of course, a large, protruding stomach. The soldier had told Vince that it was good luck to pat the stomach of a smiling Buddha, so Vince passed the statue around the room. It was beautiful to see the looks on some of our big football players' faces while they gently rubbed Buddha's belly. "That's what Fuzzy's going to look like in five years," Lombardi said. "Or Pitts." He stopped and smiled, showing all his teeth. "Come to think of it," Vince said, "that's what Pitts looks like now."

The only thing upsetting Vince a little was that some of the guys seemed to be thinking negatively about the game—saying things like IF we did something or other, we'd kill L.A., or IF we had some luck, we'd win. Vince didn't like that tone at all. He was unhappy with my remark to one of the Milwaukee sportswriters. "Merlin Olsen is very big, very strong, has great speed and great agility," I said, "is a very smart ballplayer, gives at least 110 percent on every play, and these are his weak points." Lombardi cussed everybody for worrying about the Rams. "Just knock the hell out of somebody," he suggested.

We've watched a few extra reels of the Rams in action, sent to us courtesy of George Halas, the coach and owner of the Chicago Bears. Halas wants us to whip the Rams. He hates the Rams because their coach, George Allen, used to be one of his assistants and broke his contract to take the job in Los Angeles.

I'm beginning to get a good feeling about the game. I'm very happy with our plays. I'm very happy with my own chances against Olsen. I'm very happy with my weight; I've lost ten pounds, down to 251, in about ten days. I'm getting a positive approach to the whole thing. There's one strange thing, though. We've never, as long as I can remember, gone into a game with so much respect for an opponent. We always say we respect an opponent, we always try to sweet-talk him to death, but we don't always believe it ourselves. We believe it this week. We respect their front four. We respect Roman Gabriel. We respect just about everybody on their team, except maybe Jack Snow, their split end. He told some sportswriter that he's not going to have his hair cut until after the Super Bowl game. He shouldn't have said that. He's got us a little angry. We want to give his barber some business a little early.

DECEMBER 22

We worked out in Green Bay this morning—the weather turned colder, which is good for us and bad for the Hollywood crowd—then drove down to Milwaukee in our chartered buses. I spent most of the afternoon playing poker, but I didn't enjoy myself as much as usual. I couldn't concentrate on the cards. I kept throwing my money into the pot and thinking about the Rams. Everybody seemed a bit nervous and tense, everybody except Max. He never gets nervous. He was the big winner in the poker game.

I went to Frenchy's for dinner tonight, not wanting to eat too much, and my appetite wasn't helped by the fact that (1) Coach Lombardi and Mrs. Lombardi were eating at one table nearby and (2) a bunch of the Rams had picked Frenchy's for dinner. Merlin Olsen was sitting about three tables away from me, and I walked over and said hello to him, and we sweet-talked each other something terrible. "Gee, Jerry," Merlin said, "you're having a helluva year. You really looked great against us." He told me how glad he was that I'd made it through the whole season without serious injury for a change, and he told me how he was looking forward to getting together with me in Los Angeles during the week of the Pro Bowl game.

The horrible part was that Merlin meant everything he said. He and I have always gotten along very well. I honestly like him, both as a football player and as a person, and I know he likes me. I told him how great he looked against Baltimore and how great his whole team looked, and we both agreed the game tomorrow should be a real struggle. We smiled and we shook hands, and then we both sat down to our dinners and sort of picked at our food. I was so tense I passed up the *escargots*.

A few other Rams were sitting at the table next to mine, and we kept offering to buy each other Martinis and, of course, we kept sipping soft drinks. They've got an exotic menu at Frenchy's, with things like African lion chops and kangaroo steaks, and Joe Scibelli of the Rams said to me, "C'mon, Jerry, eat some raw possum." We'll feed him raw possum tomorrow.

DECEMBER 23

I couldn't get to sleep last night. I started reading *Only a Game*, a novel about pro football, and I put it down around 10:30 and tried to sleep. I lay in bed and I thought to myself, "Sleep, sleep, sleep, a thousand and one, a thousand and two, a thousand and three, sleep, sleep, sleep, got to go to sleep, going to sleep any minute, going to sleep now . . ." I couldn't sleep. I got an itch on my leg and then an itch on my shoulder, and I turned over and changed my position, and I thought, "Sleep, sleep, sleep." At

11 o'clock, I got up, went in the bathroom so I wouldn't disturb Chandler, and read a little more of the book. I got back in my bed at midnight, tossed and turned for another hour, then took a sleeping pill. Olsen, the game, the $25,000, the third straight championship—everything kept marching through my head. Lord knows when I finally fell asleep.

We had our usual prayer meeting this morning, conducted by Carroll Dale, and we had a guest speaker, a Milwaukee lawyer named Paul Connors. He talked about how three men had impressed him and influenced him during World War II: A chaplain he met in a foxhole just before the chaplain was killed; his commanding officer, William Darby, of Darby's Rangers; and the war correspondent, Ernie Pyle.

When Connors landed in the invasion of Africa, he told us, he was very scared, and he saw Ernie Pyle next to him. "Son," Pyle said to him, "you're in the big leagues now." The application to us, and to our situation, was rather obvious. At the end of the meeting, we prayed that we'd all come through the game healthy.

In the locker room, before the game, Coach Lombardi took his text from one of St. Paul's Epistles. I don't know which one. Maybe Vince was just using St. Paul's name to back up his own theories, but anyway he said the key phrase was, "Run to win." Coach said that many people enter a race and just think about finishing, or about coming in second or third, but that when we enter a race, we're only looking for one thing: We run to win. Vince has a knack for making all the saints sound like they would have been great football coaches.

They kicked off to us, a short kick to keep the ball away from Travis Williams—the Rams had learned their lesson in Los Angeles—and while Jim Flanigan was returning the ball almost to midfield, I got in a good lick and shook my butterflies. We lined up and Bart called for one of our new quick openers through the middle, and Donny Anderson hit the hole just right and picked up seven or eight yards. The Rams seemed a little surprised, and the next play Bart came right back with Donny through the middle, and he picked up a first down inside their territory, and I was lying on the ground near Roger Brown, their big tackle, and I could read the look on his face. "What the hell are they doing?" he seemed to be thinking. "They can't be doing this to us."

A fumble stalled us before we could score, and then we got a little sloppy on our blocking assignments, and after two or three exchanges of punts, they got a break. We fumbled again, and a couple of plays later Gabriel passed for a touchdown. The Rams led, 7–0.

For a few seconds, I had that bad feeling again, that sinking feeling, a hint of disaster that quickly disappeared. But we definitely were disorganized after their score. We lost a few yards on the ground, and then Bart threw a pass that was intercepted and they took over on our 10-yard line. They could have broken the game open right there. They could have put us in a terrible hole. But our defense, as usual, rose to the challenge, pushed the Rams backwards a few yards, and then, on fourth down, when they attempted a field goal, Dave Robinson burst through and deflected the kick and saved us.

Then we started to move. Unconsciously, they began closing off the middle, tightening things up, and a few minutes later, after Tommy Brown returned a punt about 40 yards to their 46-yard line, we went into our huddle and Bart decided to capitalize on their concern with the middle. He called a 67, a play in which Travis Williams cuts off right tackle, outside Forrest Gregg. "Run to win," I said, in the huddle, quoting either Vince Lombardi or St. Paul.

Gilly pulled out from left guard, came over, and, with Gregg, double-teamed Davy Jones, forcing him to the outside. I blocked

Merlin Olsen to the inside, and he got caught in a pile of his own men, Roger Brown and Jack Pardee and a couple of others. As Travis brushed past me at the line of scrimmage, with the other Los Angeles linebackers already out of the play and Bob Hyland leading a path downfield, I knew Travis was going to go all the way. I raised my arms over my head, signaling a touchdown, when Travis was still 40 yards from the goal line. And I was right. I knew I'd done my job perfectly, and I felt somehow that this was the turning point, that this was the game for us.

After the kickoff, while Los Angeles controlled the ball for a few minutes, I chatted with Bart on the sidelines. I don't like to bother him in the huddle, so whenever I have any thoughts, I pass them to him on the sidelines, usually after checking with the rest of the offensive line. I didn't bother to check with anybody else this time; I trusted my own instinct. Travis's touchdown run had come from a brown right formation—the tight end, Fleming, lined up on the right side; the halfback, Williams, lined up directly behind the left tackle, Skoronski—and I said, "Bart, if you can come up the middle with something from a brown right, I think it'll go. They're scared to death of the 'seven' hole right now."

We didn't even have a brown right 41-quick in our game plan, but when we got the ball again, after they missed another attempted field goal, Bart probed the seven hole a few times and then—I spoke to him again during a time-out—called a brown right 41-quick. He didn't have to explain the play in the huddle because we had been using a 41-quick from a different formation. The Rams must have been looking for Travis to hit the seven hole again, and when we zone blocked and opened a quick hole in the middle, he broke through for fifteen yards. Three plays later, a pass from Starr to Dale put us in front 14–7.

At half-time, Vince said, "Magnificent. Just magnificent so far." He didn't say much more. Some people think we get big pep talks between the halves, but that stuff went out with Rockne. There isn't any time for it. We lick our wounds and drink our Gatorade and review our plays and go to the john and that's it. Today, everybody kept patting everybody else on the back and saying, "Great job. Great job. Keep it up. Let's get 'em."

We kept getting them in the second half. Our defense played a fantastic game. Ray Nitschke and Henry Jordan, in particular, were incredible. Both of them had been left off the All-Pro teams and the Pro Bowl squads, and both of them have tremendous pride. Each feels he is the best man in football at his position, and each set out to prove it today. Henry seemed to spend all his time roaming around the Los Angeles backfield; he had his arms around Roman Gabriel so often they should have been engaged. Nitschke stopped everybody who cracked the line of scrimmage; he stopped them in the middle, on the left, on the right, everywhere. Willie Davis, who'd looked bad in Los Angeles, ate up the man in front of him, and Kostelnik and Aldridge enjoyed themselves, too. In the whole third quarter, I found out afterward, the Rams gained a net total of seven yards.

Bart kept mixing up his plays beautifully, exploiting first one hole, then another, taking to the air whenever he felt like loosening up the Rams. He had his finest passing day of the year, and his play calling was even better. It was a great feeling in the line, sensing the frustration of the Rams, sensing their confusion, knowing how helpless they must have felt. Late in the third quarter, Chuck Mercein, cast off by the Giants and by the Redskins, leaped through a quick opening in the middle, kicked off a few tacklers and went six yards for our third touchdown. I never saw a Yale man get so excited. Of course, playing pro football, I hadn't seen too many Yale men before.

We could do no wrong, on offense or defense. Travis dove for another touchdown in the final quarter, even though I only gave

Merlin half a block, and we won the Western Conference championship, 28–7. The fans carried Travis off the field—he had a fantastic day—and we rushed to the locker room, laughing and shouting and absolutely floating.

"Magnificent," Coach Lombardi said, when we all reached the locker room. "Just magnificent. I've been very proud of you guys all year long. You've overcome a great deal of adversity. You've hung in there, and when the big games came around . . ." He couldn't finish the sentence. He broke up, and the tears started trickling down his cheek. He just knelt down, crying, and led us in the Lord's Prayer. We thanked God that no one had been injured.

Guys walked around the room, hugging each other. Nitschke actually was kissing and hugging everybody. He came up to me and said, "Thank you, Jerry," and then he turned to Gregg and said, "Thank you, Forrest," and he thanked all his teammates. "I just wish the game hadn't ended," Henry Jordan said. "I could have played another half. I had so much fun. Sure, it was a money game. I'm broke, and I have an expensive wife."

"Hey, Jerry, I don't have to send the coat back," Fuzzy said. He had bought his wife a mink coat for Christmas on an "if" basis. If we won the game, she got the coat.

I was misty-eyed myself I felt so good. I felt so proud, proud of myself and proud of my teammates and proud of my coaches. I felt like I was a part of something special. I guess it's the way a group of scientists feel when they make a big breakthrough, though, of course, we aren't that important. It's a feeling of being together, completely together, a singleness of purpose, accomplishing something that is very difficult to accomplish, accomplishing something that a lot of people thought you couldn't accomplish. It sent a beautiful shiver up my back.

DECEMBER 24

All our coaches were told to report to work at 8 o'clock this morning, but Coach Lombardi got soft and changed his plans and didn't make them come in until 11 A.M. You wouldn't think they'd be working so hard the day before Christmas, but it's typical of Coach Lombardi. He may drive his players hard—and treat us all like dogs, as Jordan says—but he drives himself and his staff even harder. During the season, they work every night of the week except Thursdays. They put in fifteen, sixteen hours a day. Someone once figured out that, on an hourly basis during the season, a Green Bay coach earns less than a Green Bay garbageman.

(The coaches don't let up too much during the off-season, either. They don't get a vacation until about May or June. I once walked into the office during the off-season, and all the assistant coaches were working on a game plan for a theoretical game between our offense and our defense. The offensive coaches were concentrating on finding the weaknesses in our defense, and the defensive coaches were concentrating on finding the weaknesses in our offense. It was a smart way to evaluate our personnel, to find out which special talents we needed to develop.)

The coaches guessed that Dallas would beat Cleveland for the Eastern Conference title today, so they spent the morning looking at Dallas movies. When the Dallas-Cleveland game began, they left the movies and watched about the first ten minutes on TV. "OK, that's enough," Lombardi said. "It's Dallas."

He was right, of course. Dallas destroyed the Browns, 52–14, and I didn't enjoy the show as much as I had expected to. I settled back to watch the game with a big cigar in my mouth and a glass of beer in my hand, enjoying the fruits of victory, I suppose, and I started getting antsy about the middle of the second quarter, seeing how good Dallas looked. My man, big Jethro Pugh, looked very tough. I thought I was going to have a few days to savor that victory over the Rams, but I'm getting tense already. The pressure is here—not so intense as it was before the Los Angeles game, but it is definitely here.

I don't think Dallas has as powerful a team as Los Angeles, but the Cowboys have something special going for them that can mean even more than talent. They've had a full year to brood about their loss to us in the 1966 NFL championship game. A defeat like that—with the score 34–27, we stopped them just short of the goal line in the closing seconds—really eats at you. They're going to want to beat us so badly it's unbelievable.

Coach Lombardi told some sportswriters in the dressing room yesterday that the Los Angeles game was our first real challenge all year, and I agree with him. But Dallas is in a position similar to ours. They won their own division without being seriously pressed, and they didn't even have to get up too high for their conference championship game. They had beaten Cleveland during the regular season. But they are going to be up this week. They may consider us their first real challenge of the season.

This evening Barbara and I went over to the Nitschkes' for Christmas Eve eggnog. Jackie Nitschke had invited a bunch of the players and their wives to stop by for a glass or two, and Ray couldn't understand why so many of us hung around, filling up his living room, sitting on his floor. He ran out of both chairs and glasses. About 9 o'clock, Ray found out why we were all waiting. Jackie told him to look out the window; she said she heard a strange noise or something. Ray went to the window and looked out and saw, perched on his front lawn, a 1968 Lincoln Continental. It was his Christmas present from Jackie. Ray got tears in his eyes he was so thrilled. He was like a little boy. He had to take the car out for a spin right away.

Ray didn't have an easy childhood. He grew up without any

luxuries, without anybody ever coming close to spoiling him. "You know," he told me tonight, "once, when I was a little kid, someone gave me a ride in a Lincoln. Ever since then I've dreamed of owning one. I never thought I would." I swear Ray was ready to bawl. I don't suppose any NFL ballcarrier would believe that.

DECEMBER 25

I celebrated Christmas this morning in the sauna bath at the stadium. Forrest Gregg joined me, sweating out the eggnog, and he said, "Jerry, I took a page from your book Saturday. I worked it just the way you did against Alex Karras. I let Davy Jones have a real good game against me the first time, out in Los Angeles, just so everybody would watch the two of us the next game. It sure did work beautifully."

Everyone around the Green Bay Packers, of course, had a very merry Christmas. It was a diamond year. Don Chandler bought his wife a diamond ring, and his wife and mine both bought us diamond stickpins. Lee Roy Caffey bought his wife a gold-and-diamond watch, and I wouldn't be at all surprised if Max bought a whole gross of diamond rings, to hand out to all his fiancées.

DECEMBER 26

The guys came in this morning in high spirits, feeling pert and sassy. We were all kidding about quitting the game. "They're gonna have to move you to right tackle next year, Jerry," Forrest Gregg said, "to fill my spot. Be good for you. Won't have to run so much at tackle."

"They're gonna have to come down to Louisiana to get me," I said.

"You ain't gonna quit," Forrest said. "You can't quit."

"I sure as hell won't quit till you do," I said.

"I'm not quitting till Bart quits," said Ray Nitschke, "and he ain't ever gonna quit."

"This is my last year," said Henry Jordan. "This is it."

Lombardi was in a cheerful mood, relaxed, not whipping himself or us yet. He had good words for almost everybody, starting with Jordan. "Henry had a great game," Vince said, "probably the greatest game I've ever seen him play." Maybe Coach heard Henry talking about retiring and wanted to change his mind. Vince also had a million good words for Nitschke and said that Ray was having his finest season.

When we watched the films of the game, Vince tried to holler a bit, but he couldn't really get angry. He said that Donny Anderson had come of age as a Packer, that he'd played his best game. Andy made a great catch on a high center when he was punting early in the game. If the ball had been just a little higher, it would have been eighty-eight and out the gate. We would have been in bad shape.

Wally Cruice, our super scout, gave us a rundown on Dallas. He said that they'd put everything together Sunday, everything they had been working on all year. He had nothing but praise for them, which seemed only fair, the way they played Sunday. "Cruice scouts the players and I scout the coaches," said Lombardi. "Tom Landry took a course in psychology during the off-season." Landry must have taken a course on how not to antagonize your opponents, judging from the way his players talked on television after the Cleveland game. They were so sweet. They said they were thrilled to have an opportunity to be on the same field with the Green Bay Packers. They said it was a privilege for them to play against the greatest team in the history of football. They were poor-mouthing something terrible. They sounded just like us.

You learn through experience never to bad-mouth an opponent, and the best example I can remember came when I was hurt a few years ago. We had a kid named Dan Grimm filling in for me, a pretty good kid, and the first time we played Detroit, he handled Alex Karras very well. "Karras isn't so tough," Grimm told some sportswriter after the game. "Not as tough as I thought he was. He didn't show me many moves." The sportswriter quoted Grimm in the paper. The kid didn't know that Alex was playing with a pulled groin muscle. The next time we faced the Lions, Alex ate him up. He tore the kid's helmet off, knocked him down, chewed him up and spat him out. After one vicious attack, Alex looked at the kid and said, "How do you like those moves, ass-face?"

I've got only nice things to say about Jethro Pugh, the man I'll be facing Sunday. He's just in his third year as a pro and he went to some school called Elizabeth City State, but he had a great year. He beat me a couple of times real quick in our exhibition in Dallas. He's got good strength in his hands. He doesn't run over you, but he likes to put his hands on your shoulders and pull. He likes to go to the outside, to my right, to get to the quarterback.

Jethro is definitely mobile, agile, and hostile. I watched him in the movies playing against San Francisco, against Howard Mudd, who's a real fine guard, and Pugh gave Mudd a hard time. My first thought after seeing him against Mudd was that I'd better spend a little time this week working out against Henry Jordan, just to get myself used to moving against somebody fast. I'd also like to lose a few pounds. I'm back up to about 255.

I can't afford to make any mistakes Sunday. If the fans hear this guy's name once on the PA, they'll never forget it. And if they hear it twice, they'll think they've been hearing it all day long.

They'll think he made every tackle in the game. I wish he had a name like Smith.

DECEMBER 27

It was bitter cold this morning. Somebody said it hit 10 below zero, which is cold even for Green Bay. Herb Adderley said his car froze to the ground. "We've got Jack Frost on our side," said Coach Lombardi. Our field's heated electrically so that it'll be playable Sunday, but Vince said if he has to he'll pull the plug on Dallas.

We don't seem to have much fire yet, much emotion, not even a tenth of the emotion we had for the Rams. We're cocky and flat, and Coach Lombardi's trying to get us excited. Vince talked today about the third straight championship, talked about how no team has ever won three NFL playoffs in a row, and he said that if we could do it we'd earn lasting recognition, recognition through the years. "The hell with recognition through the years," Nitschke called out. "Let's get the money. Let's get my car paid for."

When we went out on the field, Lombardi reminded me that Jethro Pugh had given me trouble in the exhibition game and, just to make sure I wouldn't forget, he chewed my butt all through practice. I was working hard, anyway, but he wanted to get me up on the bit, so he cussed me out four or five different times, which is some kind of record. One time I pulled to the left and I bumped into the center, and Vince screamed, "C'mon, c'mon, Jerry, you're slow. You're too damned slow." Another time we tried a drive play right up the middle, and I knocked Jim Weatherwax back about five yards before he got away from me, and Lombardi hollered, "How in the hell could you let that man slip away from you like that?"

"The primary reason," I said, "is because he's five yards downfield. That's why he got off me to the inside." I was getting hot with Lombardi.

"OK, OK, OK," he said. He wanted to push me, but not too far.

I thought I had an excellent workout today; Vince obviously disagreed. I worked real hard on pass protection, put in more than my usual share of time on the blitz drill, and later got off on the side and worked with Henry Jordan, a good, helpful session. I was very happy with myself.

"Jerks, jerks, jerks," Lombardi chanted, as we ran off the field, a fairly typical comment for him. If I listened to him, I'd think I never saw a good Wednesday practice before a Sunday game, no matter how good it was, and I'd think I never saw a bad Thursday practice, no matter how bad it was.

We had a meeting to vote for championship shares, and it was just like a hen party. Dave Robinson kept chattering like a magpie, bringing up parliamentary procedure and points of order, everything he could think of. He is the most argumentative man in the world. Robby'll argue any side of any question, just for practice. I once heard him argue for half an hour that black-eyed peas are really black-eyed beans. Maybe they are, but who cares? Most of the guys don't say much of anything in the meeting; some of them are willing to give shares to just about anybody who has anything to do with the ball club. Of the ones who do speak up, the majority are out to protect their own shares. They say things like, "Damn, I didn't see that guy hustle any, I don't want to give him any of my money," or, "Hell, that guy sits up in an office, never getting hit on Sunday, I don't want to give him any of my money." The discussions get pretty heated.

Only the active players are eligible to vote, and we were all kidding Elijah Pitts, telling him that he was only going to get half a share because he missed half the season, but, of course, there was no question about voting him a full share. The major arguments were over front-office people and maintenance people and the guys on the taxi squad. We decided we didn't want to give one cab player a cent because (1) his attitude wasn't good and (2) he had received a big bonus. "No sense in giving him any money," somebody said. "Just put him in a higher tax bracket."

The meeting dragged on and on and on—we did decide to give the other taxi players cash awards—and finally Coach broke it up before we finished. "Finish it tomorrow," he said. "You've got to watch some films." I was the first one out of the meeting, and the first thing I saw was a golden head on a pair of sloped shoulders—Paul Hornung. I thumped him hard on the head. I was really happy to see him, happy that he had decided to come up from New Orleans for the championship game. Even though I played on the same team with him for nine years, Paul's always been an idol of mine. I know that sounds a little ridiculous, especially since, as I always tell Paul, I did so much to make him as great as he was.

Paul said hello to everyone and sat with us while we viewed the films, biting his fingernails the way he always did. Paul and Max sat together, and they got Gregg and Skoronski giggling during the movies. The old man didn't get upset. He was practically giggling himself he was so glad to see Paul. He's always had a weakness for Paul. I guess that's natural, the stern father being fond of the wild son.

DECEMBER 28

We had a heat wave today. The temperature was up to around 10 degrees above zero, and it seemed like the tropics. We had a short pre-workout speech, mostly about the voting for championship shares. Lombardi was sore at us for taking so much time yesterday and not finishing. "After the workout today," he said, "you'll go in there and finish voting for those shares, and you'll finish in five minutes. Enough of that nonsense."

As we started out toward the field Lombardi shouted, "Let's have a good workout today. Let's get a little fire, a little spirit. You look a little sloppy. You're walking through the motions."

I happened to be standing near him, and I said, "Hey, I worked as hard out there yesterday as I've worked in three months."

"I know you did," he said. "I know you did."

I worked hard again today. I spent some time with Bob Brown and Jim Weatherwax because they're both tall like Jethro Pugh. I played a little brother-in-law with Wax, telling him what to do to me during practice. Usually, when we brother-in-law, it's during a blitz drill. I say something like, "Take an inside, Kos," or, "Wax, take an outside this time." You just do it because you can't explode off the ball every play in practice and you don't want to fall down and look bad and get yourself chewed. You do it for self-preservation. But today I was looking for help. I told Wax, "It's a pass situation, Wax. Grab me. Pull me. Use your hands. All hands. Butt me once in a while, but keep using your hands." I wanted him to come at me the way I think Jethro Pugh will.

I'm trying to get a set plan in my mind, and it's shaping up pretty well. I'm really not too concerned about the running plays; I seldom have much trouble on running plays. I've got to concentrate on my pass blocking. I've made up my mind to try to keep my head up, my back straight, and my hands out. If I can keep his hands off me, if I can keep moving, if I can keep my head up and watch him all the time, I think I can defeat him.

At one point during the practice, Lombardi came up to the offensive line and said, "The defense says they can tell when you linemen are gonna run and when you're gonna pass."

"Which linemen?" I said. "Who and when?"

"Fuzzy and Ski," Lombardi said.

I felt better, because I'm always watching out to make sure that I'm not tipping the play. I tell Kostelnik every day, "Watch me. See if you can tell anything." If he calls the play right half the time, he's only guessing. If he's right more than half the time, I've got to check myself. In the middle of this season I started tipping my cutoff block, a real quick throw-out at the tackle's legs. Every time I got set to try it, Kos yelled, "Cutoff, cutoff, cutoff." I said, "How'd you know?" And he said, "You're cocking yourself." I started studying a piece of grass on the ground, watching it to make certain that I didn't move at all.

We're in a little better shape for this game. Grabo looked good today. He made several sharp cuts, several good moves. "Way to go, Grabo, way to go," Lombardi shouted. "How you feel?"

"Ready, Coach, ready," Grabowski said.

Of course, if Grabo cuts the wrong way one time, he can hurt the knee again.

Coach Lombardi's having a struggle with himself, trying to decide whether to start Donny Anderson or Travis Williams. He feels he owes it to Anderson, but he knows Williams is more explosive, more of a threat for the long run. Coach is also thinking about starting Kenny Bowman at center. The Cowboys' middle linebacker, Lee Roy Jordan, is only about 230, smallish for a linebacker, but he's very, very quick. Bowman, at 235, is quicker than Hyland, at 265, and he may have a better chance to get to Jordan. Either way, we shouldn't be hurting at center. Hyland's been coming along very well.

We haven't put in any special plays for Dallas yet. The Cowboys use a staggered defense, one tackle up tight and one off half a yard, the same with the ends, varying according to our formations. They're pretty good at stopping runs from tackle to tackle, and I think we're going to aim a lot at the seven hole, outside For-rest Gregg, the spot Travis hit on his long touchdown run against the Rams.

As we were coming off the field, Lombardi seemed pleased with the workout. "Pretty good practice," he said. "Pretty good practice, I'd say. What do you say, Dick Capp?"

Dick said, "Yes, sir." He's been on the cab squad most of the year, but he's learned the right lines.

We went right into the meeting room to resume voting on the shares, and we got into a miserable hassle. We fought over the public relations man and the groundskeeper and the chief scout and the personnel manager, and somebody argued, "They're not getting knocked on their asses. They've got long careers. We're fin-ished fast." Finally, after a lot of screaming, we broke everything down, decided on shares and parts of shares for everybody, and called Coach Lombardi in. Willie Davis had written the shares on the blackboard.

Lombardi stared at the list. "You really outdid yourselves, didn't you?" he said. "You really gave a lot of your money away. You're really just a great bunch of guys." He couldn't have been more sarcastic, more cutting. "I'm ashamed of you," he said. "Just take my share off that list. Just take it off and split it up. Split it up, if that's the way it's gonna be. Just split it up."

Willie Davis didn't hesitate. He immediately erased the place where it said seven shares for the coaches and changed it to six.

"The hell with all of you," Lombardi said.

Coach spun around and walked out of the room, on the verge of crying. He seemed terribly upset, terribly disappointed in the guys. He believes in charity. Of course, he's wealthy enough to be-lieve in charity—and he doesn't believe in charity at contract time.

We went and watched movies for a little while, and then Vince said, "That's enough. Go back in there and vote again on that damned thing. Get back in there and straighten it out." He took Willie and Ski aside and told them what he wanted. He thought Wally Cruice, the scout, and Pat Peppler, the personnel man, and Chuck Lane, the public relations director, deserved larger shares. We went back in the room and wrangled for another half hour and came up with a solution. We called Lombardi in and he said, "OK. That's better. It's not great, but I'm happy. I give up." Naturally, he got his share back in the process.

But even the squabble over the shares couldn't shake the air of confidence in the dressing room. The difference between last week and this week is incredible. We were afraid to look beyond the Rams, and now we're not even looking at the Cowboys. I don't quite know what to make of it. I'm worried.

I chatted a little with Chuck Mercein, who'd been on my show this week. He said he'd watched the show last night and thought that he'd sounded a little too serious, but that Tommy Joe had made up for him. It wasn't really fair to throw Tommy Joe in against the Yalie.

"Do you own part of Channel 11 now?" Boyd Dowler asked me. "I turn the set on and I see you advertising bread, I see you advertising clothes, I see you advertising Pepsi, I see you advertising Citgo, I see your show. It's getting sickening. You might be overexposed."

"Who the hell ever heard of a guard getting overexposed?" I said.

I had an autographed football with me, and I asked Bob Jeter to sign it. I'd brought the ball home the other day for my son Tony, and he'd looked the ball over carefully and he'd told me that Jeter's name was missing. "He's my favorite Packer, Daddy," Tony said. "I like you as a person, but I like Jeter as a player."

DECEMBER 29

Coach Lombardi talked to us this morning about the third world championship, about how much it would mean to all of us all our lives. He mentioned that Green Bay had won three straight championships in 1929, 1930, and 1931, in the days before playoff games, but he said that those years didn't count. "The Little Sisters of the Poor could have won then," he said.

"I want that third championship," Vince said. "AND I DESERVE IT. WE ALL DESERVE IT."

Then he lowered his voice and talked about the type of men who play for Green Bay. "Lots of better ballplayers than you guys have gone through here," he said. "But you're the type of ballplayers I want. You've got character. You've got heart. You've got guts." He got worked up, very emotional, and then, abruptly, he stopped. "OK, that's it," he said. "That's my pregame speech. Let's go."

We went out on the field and he gave us two new plays to use against Dallas. One looks particularly good. The fullback, either Wilson or Mercein, will lead the halfback right up the middle. The fullback will go for the middle linebacker, and either Gilly or I will pull and block the tackle on the opposite side. Because their middle linebacker, Jordan, is so fast, we're hoping that he'll be moving, following the guard, and our fullback will be able to handle him.

"You'd better not miss that block, Gillingham," Vince yelled, before we even tried the play. "You'd better not miss it."

"Damn," said Gilly. "That's the first time I ever got chewed out for a block before I got a chance to make it."

Most of the time, Vince was in a good, cheerleading mood. He kept smacking his hand and saying, "We're ready, we're ready." And he kept looking to Paul Hornung, who watched the whole practice, for his approval. Paul was having fun. He asked Max, "What kind of year have you had?" And Max said, "Coach Schnelker and I have had about the same kind of year. We've both kept real warm and haven't had too much contact."

After the workout we watched movies of our 1966 championship game with Dallas and half of their game with Cleveland. Everybody still seems to have that confident feeling, no tightness, no real strain. Chandler's a little concerned, and so am I. The guys can't possibly be thinking of anything but the game. I know I can't think of anything else.

I'm not daydreaming about Jethro Pugh, the way I did about Merlin Olsen. My thoughts are of a more precise nature: What am I going to do on pass protection? Head up, keep moving, keep his hands off me.

I noticed something about Jethro in the movies today and I mentioned it to Lombardi when we were talking about our goal-line plays. "Pugh's high, Coach," I said. "He doesn't get down. He doesn't bury himself the way Bob Lilly"—their other tackle— "does. If we're gonna wedge, we should wedge Pugh."

I'm thinking about Jethro all the time. This morning, in fact, I started calling my wife Jethro. "C'mon, Jethro," I yelled at Barbara. "Get me breakfast, Jethro. Get me my coat, Jethro. Get me my car keys, Jethro." I don't know if it's going to help me much Sunday, but it's kind of fun today.

DECEMBER 30

The tension really hit me last night. I went to bed at 6:15, slept a few minutes, woke up, slept, woke up, slept, woke up, finally had to take two sleeping pills, a little one, then a big one, to knock me out. I had a wild dream about the game. I dreamt I suffered a concussion and woke up three days after the game and asked who won, and my daughter, Diane, said we won, 60–4, and Barbara said we lost, 17–7. And then I started remembering the game, and Dick Modzelewski, the old Cleveland tackle who hasn't played in years, was opposite me, and he and Forrest Gregg started fighting over a fumble. They both bobbled it, and I recovered the ball, and something hit me, and I staggered off the field and asked someone, "Who's the coach?" Then I told the coach that I didn't feel I should continue to play.

I've never had a dream quite that wild. I don't know how Dick Modzelewski got in there, and I never heard of a game anywhere ending with a score like 60–4.

We played a world championship volleyball game this morning, and we used a real volleyball for the first time all year. My team, the Cicero Sissies, was beating the King Ranch Bullies 5–4 when the commissioner, Tom Brown, made an extremely bad call. The call totally demoralized our team and we lost, 9–6. We filed a protest against the commissioner with the commissioner, but we don't expect it to be acted upon favorably.

I suggested to Coach Lombardi that we have Paul Hornung sit on our bench tomorrow. I said it would help the team and make us play better. Vince said he'd check to see if it was OK with the commissioner. He meant Pete Rozelle, the commissioner of the National Football League, not Tom Brown.

Just before we left the field today, Coach Lombardi gave us a brief talk. He simply said that this is for the NFL championship and that we all know what it means. I know. The championship game was the biggest game of my life the first time I played in it, and the second time, and the third time. This is the sixth one for me—the ninth one for Don Chandler—and the more you play in it, the more you realize how much it means, especially if you lose. We lost the title game to Philadelphia in 1960 and the defeat obsessed me for the next six months. I thought about it almost every night. Over and over and over, I kept seeing a play I had blown. I had one of the most miserable winters of my life.

The Cowboys have just gone through a terrible winter remembering the game they lost to us. I was in Dallas last spring to set up their participation in the portrait program, and I visited Bob Lilly and his wife. She didn't know quite what to think of me. She was still hating the Green Bay Packers. To break the strain—or maybe to increase it—I said, "Katsy, if you like, I could leave this package of Green Bay Packer portraits with you. Maybe you'd like to put them up around the house." She wasn't too amused. "I've heard enough about the Green Bay Packers," she said. "That's all I've heard all winter." When I left the Lillys' house, Katsy Lilly said, "We'll see you in Green Bay in December."

I guess she's here for the game.

I thought I wasn't too nervous today, but when I got home this afternoon, I discovered that, in the dressing room, I'd put my shorts on backwards.

DECEMBER 31

When I woke up this morning, after a good night's sleep, I knew it was cold. "It must be 10 below zero," I told Barbara. I thought I was kidding.

During breakfast, I found out the temperature was 16 degrees below zero, the coldest December 31st in Green Bay history, and I started to shiver. Still, I figured it would warm up a little by noon. It warmed all the way up to 13 below by game time.

Chandler and I bundled up driving over to the stadium and we didn't realize quite how bitter the cold was. As we ran into the dressing room we saw a helicopter hovering over the stadium, blowing snow off the seats.

When I got inside and began dressing, Gilly came over to me and said, "You gonna wear gloves?"

I hadn't thought of it. I'd never worn gloves before in a football game. I was about to say no, and then I thought, "Who the hell am I kidding? I don't use my hands out there."

"Hell, yeah," I told Gilly.

Maybe, if it were 5 above zero or 10 above, I would have passed up the gloves and tried to psych the Cowboys into thinking that the cold wasn't bothering me. But at 13 below I wasn't going to be psyching anyone. Everybody in the whole United States was going to know I was cold.

Gilly, Forrest, Ski, and I—the interior linemen—got gloves from Dad Braisher, the equipment manager. We're the only ones who don't have to use our hands in a game. We decided we'd wear the gloves outside to loosen up and see if we needed them for the game.

"With this cold," Ron Kostelnik mentioned to me, "it's gonna hamper us on defense. We won't be able to grab, to use our hands too well. You won't have to be afraid of popping people, Jerry. They won't be able to throw you with their hands." The thought warmed me up slightly.

We got dressed in our long stockings and our silk pants, and when we stepped out on the field—I was wearing my thermal underwear, but only knee-length and elbow-length, so that it wouldn't restrict my mobility—icy blasts just shot right up our skirts. It took Gilly and Forrest and Ski and me about three seconds to decide we'd keep on the gloves. "Hell, let's get another pair," I told Gilly.

I looked over at the Dallas Cowboys and I almost felt sorry for them. As bad as the cold was for us, it had to be worse for them. We were freezing, and they were dying. They were all hunched over, rubbing their hands, moving their legs up and down, trying to persuade themselves that they weren't insane to be playing football in this ridiculous weather.

We kicked off, and our defense held, and when I came out on the field for the first time we had the ball around our own 20-yard line. Bart started right off with the 41-special, the new play we'd put in for the Cowboys. Gilly pulled out to his right, faking Lee Roy Jordan, the middle linebacker, into thinking the play was going that way, and Bob Hyland blocked on Gilly's man and I blocked on Jethro Pugh, and Chuck Mercein, at fullback, leading Donny Anderson into the line, blocked Lee Roy Jordan trying to recover. The play worked just the way we hoped it would. Donny picked up five yards before he got hit. He fumbled, which wasn't part of our plan, but Mercein recovered for us. With Bart calling that 41-special a couple of times, and with the aid of a few penalties, we marched all the way down the field for a touchdown. Bart passed to Dowler in the end zone, and, midway through the first period, we were leading 7–0.

The cold was incredible, cutting right through us, turning each slight collision into a major disaster, but, for me, the footing on the field wasn't too bad. The ground was hard, but by putting most of my weight on my toes, I could dig in and get a foothold. I handled Jethro pretty well, popping him more than I would under normal conditions, keeping his cold hands away from me, moving him on running plays and checking him on passing plays. We didn't say a word to each other; even if we'd had anything to say, it was too cold to talk.

The only conversation I had all day was with Lee Roy Jordan. When we tried a screen pass, Bob Lilly or one of their linemen read the play and grabbed the back, the intended receiver, by the jersey. Bart had no one to throw to. "Look, he's holding, he's holding," I screamed at the referee. But the referee didn't see the infraction, and Jordan smiled and said to me, "He wasn't holding, Jerry. Your guy just slipped and fell down, and we were just helping him up."

We had more conversation on our own bench, mostly over who'd get the good seats by the warmer. Hornung usually had one of them; the commissioner had said he could sit on our bench. At one point, the warmer ran out of fuel and started to smoke, and we all jumped off the bench. Another time, Donny Anderson was sitting on the bench freezing, and he saw the CBS sidelines microphone, sponge-covered to kill the wind sound, dangling in front of him. He reached up and put his hands around the microphone, thinking it was some new kind of heater.

Early in the second quarter, when we had the ball on a third-and-one situation just past midfield, Bart crossed up the Dallas defense, faded back and threw a long touchdown pass, again to Dowler. We were ahead 14–0, and I felt warmer. I was only worried about our tendency to let up when we get a few touchdowns ahead.

Less than a minute later, Herb Adderley intercepted one of Don Meredith's passes and returned the ball almost to the Cowboys' 30-yard line. If we can get this one now, I thought, we can forget it, the game's over, the whole thing's over. I had a beautiful feeling about the ball game—until we didn't score. Bart lost some yardage eating the ball when he couldn't find an open receiver, and we had to punt. I felt frustrated, terribly let down. I'd been so certain that we were going to get at least something, at least a field goal.

Then, late in the second period, deep in our own territory, again Bart faded to pass and again he couldn't get rid of the ball, and Willie Townes, their big defensive end, hit Bart and knocked the ball loose, and George Andrie, their other defensive end, swooped in and picked up the ball and charged to the end zone for a touchdown.

Forrest Gregg tackled Andrie just as he crossed the goal line, and I was only a step or two behind Forrest, and I suddenly felt the greatest desire to put both my cleats right on Andrie's spinal cord and break it. We had been victimized by these stupid plays — scooped-up fumbles, deflected passes, blocked kicks, high-school tricks — so many times during the season that I felt murderous. I'd never in my career deliberately stepped on a guy, but I was so tempted to destroy Andrie, to take everything out on him, that I almost did it. A bunch of thoughts raced through my mind — I'd met Andrie off the field a few times and I kind of liked him — and, at the last moment, I let up and stepped over him.

We couldn't do a thing when we got the ball — Jethro caught Bart for a loss one time, but I thought I'd checked him long enough; I thought Bart held the ball too long — and they took over again and added a field goal, and so, at the half, instead of leading 17–0 or 21–0 or something like that, we were barely in front, 14–10.

Ray Wietecha chewed us out pretty good between the halves. "One guy's giving the quarterback all the trouble," he told us. "One guy. C'mon. Don't let up out there. There's a lot of money riding. Get tough, dammit, get tough." Ray didn't mention any names, but we all knew that Ski was having a lot of trouble with Andrie, that Andrie was doing most of the damage.

We just couldn't get unwound in the third quarter. I still felt I had Jethro under control, but he caught Bart two more times, not back deep, but out of the pocket, after Bart had had enough time to throw if he could have found anyone open. The ends were having trouble cutting. On the first play of the last quarter, they used the halfback-option — an old favorite play of ours — and Dan

Reeves passed 50 yards for a touchdown. We were losing, 17–14, and the wind was whipping us, too.

Five minutes later, my roommate was wide with an attempted field goal, and when the ball sailed by to the left I had a little sinking feeling, a little fear that the clock might run out on us. I thought maybe the time had come for us to lose. Dallas controlled the ball for about ten plays, staying on the ground as much as they could, eating up the clock, and all the time my frustration built up, my eagerness to get back on the field, to have another chance to score.

With five minutes to go, we got the ball on our own 32-yard line, and, right away, Bart threw a little pass out to Anderson and Andy picked up five, six yards. The linebackers were laying back; they were having trouble with their footing, trouble cutting. Chuck Mercein ran for the first down, and then Bart hit Dowler for another first down, and we were inside Dallas territory. I began to feel we were going to make it, we were going to go for a touchdown. At the worst, I figured we'd go down swinging.

On first down, Willie Townes got through and caught Andy for a big loss, and we had second and about twenty. But Bart capitalized on the Dallas linebackers' difficulties getting traction. Twice, with the ends still having problems with their footing, he threw safety-valve passes to Anderson and twice Andy went for about ten yards, and we had a first down on the Dallas 30, and I could feel the excitement building in the huddle. But we had only a minute and a half to play. Bart passed out to Mercein on the left and Chuck carried the ball down to the Dallas eleven. I walked back to the huddle, wondering what Bart was going to call, and he called a give-65, and I thought, "What a perfect call. We haven't used it all day. What a smart call."

It's a potentially dangerous play, a give-65. We block as though we're going through the "five" hole, outside me. Gilly pulls and comes over my way, and everything depends on the tackle in front of him, Bob Lilly, taking the fake and moving to his left. The play can't work against a slow, dumb tackle; it can only work against a quick, intelligent tackle like Lilly. We figured Lilly would key on Gilly and follow his move, but we didn't know for sure. Everybody blocks my way on this play, Anderson coming for the hole as though he's carrying the ball, and nobody blocks the actual target area, Lilly's area. If Lilly doesn't take the fake, if he ignores Gilly pulling, he kills the actual ballcarrier, Mercein.

But Lilly followed Gillingham, and the hole opened up, and Chuck drove down to the 3-yard line. With less than a minute to play, Anderson plunged for a first down on the one, and, with only two time-outs left, we huddled quickly. "Run over there," Gilly said, in the huddle. "Run that 55-special. They can't stop that."

Bart called the 55, and I thought to myself, "Well, this is it, toad. They're putting it directly on your back, yours and Forrest's." I didn't make a very good block, and the five hole didn't open up, and Andy got stopped at the line of scrimmage. We called a time-out with twenty seconds to play. Then Bart called the same play again, and this time Andy slipped coming through the hole—I don't know whether he could have gotten through—and slid to about the one-foot line, and we called time-out with sixteen seconds to play, our last time-out, and everybody in the place was screaming.

We could have gone for the field goal right then, for a tie, hoping that we'd win in overtime. We decided to go for the victory. In the huddle, Bart said, "Thirty-one wedge and I'll carry the ball." He was going to try a quarterback sneak. He wasn't going to take a chance on a handoff, or on anybody slipping. He was going to go for the hole just inside me, just off my left shoulder. Kenny Bowman, who had finally worked his way back to the lineup, and I were supposed to move big Jethro out of the way. It might be the last play of the game, our last chance.

The ground was giving me trouble, the footing was bad down near the goal line, but I dug my cleats in, got a firm hold with my right foot, and we got down in position, and Bart called the "hut" signal. Jethro was on my inside shoulder, my left shoulder. I came off the ball as fast as I ever have in my life. I came off the ball as fast as anyone could. In fact, I wouldn't swear that I didn't beat the center's snap by a fraction of a second. I wouldn't swear that I wasn't actually offside on the play.

I slammed into Jethro hard. All he had time to do was raise his left arm. He didn't even get it up all the way and I charged into him. His body was a little high, the way we'd noticed in the movies, and, with Bowman's help, I moved him outside. Willie Townes, next to Jethro, was down low, very low. He was supposed to come in low and close to the middle. He was low, but he didn't close. He might have filled the hole, but he didn't, and Bart churned into the opening and stretched and fell and landed over the goal line. It was the most beautiful sight in the world, seeing Bart lying next to me and seeing the referee in front of me, his arms over his head, signaling the touchdown. There were thirteen seconds to play.

The fans poured on the field, engulfing us, engulfing the Cowboys, pummeling all of us. Chuck Howley, the Dallas linebacker, got knocked down three or four times accidentally, and he was furious. I had to fight my way through the crowds to the sidelines; Bart came off the field looking like he was crying, and he probably was. The Cowboys still had time to get off two plays, two incomplete passes, and the game was over. I tried to get to the dressing room quickly, but I got caught around the 30-yard line, trapped in a mass of people beating me on the back, grabbing at my chin strap, grabbing at my gloves, trying to get anything for a souvenir. I had a sudden moment of panic, wondering whether I was ever going to get out of that mess alive.

Finally I reached the dressing room and I was immediately aware that the whole place was wired for sound. Cameramen and cameras were all around, and Coach Lombardi cussed the cameramen and ordered them, flatly, to get the hell out. When we were alone, just the team and the coaches, Vince told us how proud he was of us. "I can't talk anymore," he said. "I can't say anymore." He held the tears back and we all kneeled and said the Lord's Prayer, and then we exploded, with shouts of joy and excitement, the marks of battle, the cuts, the bruises, and the blood, all forgotten.

The TV people returned, and I was one of the first men led in front of the cameras. "There's a great deal of love for one another on this club," I said. "Perhaps we're living in Camelot." I was referring to the idea of one for all and all for one, the ideal of King Arthur's Round Table, and I meant it. And then I talked about Lombardi.

I'd been waiting for a chance to talk about Vince. A story had appeared in *Esquire* magazine a few weeks earlier making him look like a complete villain, like nothing but a cruel, vicious man. The story had hurt Vince; I had heard that his mother had cried when she read the story. I thought the story gave a distorted picture of the man; it showed only one of his many sides. "Many things have been said about Coach," I said on TV, "and he is not always understood by those who quote him. The players understand. This is one beautiful man."

I loved Vince. Sure, I had hated him at times during training camp and I had hated him at times during the season, but I knew how much he had done for us, and I knew how much he cared about us. He is a beautiful man, and the proof is that no one who ever played for him speaks of him afterward with anything but respect and admiration and affection. His whippings, his cussings, and his driving all fade; his good qualities endure.

Over and over and over, perhaps twenty times, the television cameras reran Bart's touchdown and my block on Jethro Pugh. Again and again, millions of people across the country saw the hole open up and saw Bart squeeze through. Millions of people who couldn't name a single offensive lineman if their lives depended on it heard my name repeated and repeated and repeated. All I could think was, "Thank God for instant replay."

Kenny Bowman came up to me smiling and said, "Don't take all the credit, Kramer. Don't take all the credit. I helped you with that block."

"Shut up, Bow," I said. "You've got ten more years to play. You've got plenty of time for glory. I ain't telling anybody anything. If they think I made that block alone, I'm gonna let them think it."

I was only kidding Bowman, of course. But I've got to admit that I didn't tell many people about Bowman's part in the block. I stayed around the locker room as long as I ever have, talking to all the reporters, answering all their questions, accepting all their kind words. I felt like a halfback. I stayed till the last dog was dead.

I drove home from the stadium in an icebox. The heating unit in my Lincoln was frozen, and so was I. For an hour or two I relaxed with a few friends and with my family, letting the circulation come back all over my body. I watched part of the American Football League title game, watched the Oakland Raiders kill the Houston Oilers, and then I went in my room and changed into my fancy, black-striped walking suit, putting it on over a white turtleneck sweater. I put on my black cowboy hat and stuck a fat cigar in my mouth, and I felt like a riverboat gambler. And then we all took off for Appleton, about thirty miles away, for the Left Guard

Steak House, owned by Fuzzy and Max, for a big, beautiful celebration.

It was 20 degrees below zero outside, and the heating broke down in the restaurant, but the cold didn't bother me at all. I drank toasts with Hornung and toasts with Jordan and toasts with Max, and, somehow, I managed to notice that Donny Anderson had, for company, a girl who had once been a Playmate-of-the-Month. Donny had certainly earned a big night out; he'd played almost the entire game, while Travis shivered on the bench.

I had a great time. At least everyone told me I had a great time. Fuzzy and I got carried away by the whiskey man, and we ended up the evening greeting the New Year with toasts—toasts, naturally, to the two greatest guards in the history of the whole world.

JANUARY 1

When I woke up this morning, my first thought was that the game against Dallas and the block on Jethro Pugh were only dreams. I thought that we hadn't really played the Cowboys yet. Then I felt the soreness in my legs, in my body and in my head, and I realized that I hadn't been dreaming, that we had played the game, that we had defeated Dallas, 21–17.

For the third straight year, we had won the championship of the National Football League. Even the soreness felt great.

JANUARY 2

I woke up today wondering who'd won the game. I was almost as foggy as I was yesterday. After Barbara assured me that we had actually won the game, I got dressed and drove over to the stadium for a sauna. We had an extra day off from practice because we're not playing Oakland in the Super Bowl in Miami until January 14.

Outside the training room I saw Coach Wietecha and asked him how Oakland looked. I knew he'd been working on the movies already.

"Hard to say," he said. "They have a lot of defenses. They jump around a lot."

"Who's my man?" I asked.

"Three people," said Wietecha. "They change defenses so much you'll be seeing three different people. They look pretty good."

I didn't ask any more questions. I didn't want to start thinking about Oakland just yet. I wanted a few more days to enjoy the victory over Dallas.

I found out today we won't be leaving for Florida till Sunday. We're going to be working out here all week, on the frozen ground, in subzero temperatures. I'm a little disappointed, and so are all the guys. Maybe Vince is afraid we'd get soft in the sunshine.

Phone calls and telegrams and letters have been coming in from all over. A fan called from New Jersey just to say congratulations. A kid at the Alpha Tau Omega fraternity house at North Dakota State phoned and said that he simply wanted to talk to a Packer and that he'd gotten my number from information; we chatted for ten minutes. A guy in the Philippine Islands wrote and offered to get me a job as a Japanese sumo wrestler. I'm not that big; he must've been thinking about Fuzzy.

A sportswriter from Philadelphia phoned and wanted to know what I meant by my remark on television that perhaps we're living in Camelot. I told him I felt that Camelot was the ideal situation, the perfect place, the epitome of everything good. For example, I tried to explain to him the attitude of the guys on the club. I mentioned Doug Hart. "He was a starter in '65," I said. "He played the whole year, did a great job, then lost his position to Bob Jeter in 1966. He should be upset. He should be sulking or demanding to be traded. Right? Wrong. Not here. He's one of the best men we have on our special units. He hustles harder than anybody on the club."

Then I told him about Fuzzy. "When Gilly took over this year," I said, "I'm sure it hurt Fuzzy. I'm sure he felt bad about losing his job. But he sat behind Gilly in every movie, he talked with him, he coached him, he was just like a big brother. He did everything he could to make Gilly a better ballplayer. This is why we win, I guess." The sportswriter didn't argue with me.

JANUARY 3

We certainly are tickled pink to be working out in Green Bay. When we reported to the stadium this morning, the temperature was a whopping 5 degrees above zero. I stepped on the scales and found out I was up to 260 pounds, and I know I'm not going to sweat off any pounds up here. I think I've also got a case of walking pneumonia.

While I was weighing myself, Ray Nitschke climbed up on the trainer's table to have his toes treated for frostbite. Both his big toes were bandaged. Ray said the doctor had told him the only way he could avoid getting frostbite again was to stay out of the cold.

"How the hell do you do that," Ray said, "and go out and practice in 5 degrees?"

Just then, Coach Lombardi wandered in. "You just go out and get up a good sweat," he said.

Ray started to ask how you get up a good sweat at 5 above zero, then gave up and said, "Aw, forget it, man."

Lombardi eased over to me, came up close to me and said, "I want to thank you for the things you said on television."

"Coach," I said, "it was something that needed saying and I felt very happy to have the opportunity to say it."

"I've had a lot of calls about it," Vince said. "A lot of people have commented on it. It was a wonderful thing to say in front of 50 million people."

Coach really seemed grateful, and it made me feel even better about what I'd said. It proved my point.

We watched the films of the Dallas game, and Coach did a lot of hollering and screaming, mostly at Gilly and Ski and Marvin. He was particularly rough on Gilly; he chewed him for everything. Vince talked a lot about Boyd's great catch for our second touchdown, but he didn't say hardly anything about my part in the game. I had quite a few good blocks, but I guess he felt that I'd come in for enough praise already. When we watched Bart score the winning touchdown, Lombardi said, "Well, gentlemen, we finally scored, with the help of God."

"Yeah," somebody shouted. "And with the help of a helluva block."

On the way out of the movies, Gilly, naturally, was dragging a little. "Hey," he said, "how bad did Dallas beat us?"

On the field, Coach talked a little about Oakland, about how good they looked and about how bad we'd look if we lost to them. The ground had softened, and steam covered the whole field. It looked like the Scottish moors, very eerie, very mysterious. We warmed up, ran through our calisthenics, then played our touch game. We killed the defense, of course. Tommy Brown began organizing another volleyball game for Florida. Our team, the Cicero Sissies, demanded a new commissioner or at least a new head linesman.

Then we ran through a few plays and heard about a few of the

Oakland defenses. Sometimes I'll be blocking the defensive end, Ike Lassiter, and sometimes I'll be blocking the defensive tackle, Dan Birdwell, and sometimes I'll be blocking the left linebacker, Bill Laskey. The scouting report on their tackles wasn't too encouraging. They've got one guy who's 7 feet tall and weighs 300 pounds. Fortunately, he's a second-stringer. I bet he's a real darling.

We found out after practice that Jim Grabowski was going to the hospital tonight for a knee operation. My older brother, Russ, who came down from his home in Alaska to see the Dallas game, went in tonight, too, for the same operation. Russ figured that as long as he was here, he might as well get his knee fixed up. They'll both be operated on in the morning.

My cold's killing me. The doctor gave me a shot in the training room this morning and came by the house this evening to give me another shot. The cold's all down my bronchial tubes and into the stomach. I can't wait to see Florida.

JANUARY 4

It was 6 degrees below zero this morning, with 15-mile-an-hour winds. The doctor gave me another shot and checked me out for pneumonia. He took his stethoscope and listened to my lungs and said, "I can't hear any rattle. Go ahead and practice."

I didn't want to practice in the worst way. "I won't go out if you don't go out," Lionel Aldridge offered. Nitschke was getting treatment for his frostbit toes again, and he said he wouldn't go out, either. Coach Lombardi came into the dressing room, and Willie Davis called, "Hey, Coach, what's the temperature down there, anyway?"

"Down where?" Lombardi said.

"Down in Florida," said Willie.

"About 78 degrees. Why?"

"Oh, nothing, Coach. I was just wondering."

We were all wondering what in the world we're doing in Green Bay. When we went outside, we all got ice on our eyelashes, and our eyes wouldn't stop tearing. Chandler wore a surgical mask over his mouth, and everybody wore stocking caps. Half a dozen guys felt they were coming down with the flu. We were supposed to stay outside for an hour, but after forty-five minutes Vince said, "The hell with it. Let's go in." I was the first one inside, and, instead of going into the dressing room, I went right into the sauna room and thawed out for about five minutes.

We watched some Oakland movies, the Raiders against the New York Jets. We didn't see anything funny about the Raiders—the previous year, before the Super Bowl, we actually laughed out loud at some of the antics of the Kansas City Chiefs—but the Jets did have a few linemen who were kind of humorous to watch. Lombardi delivered two conflicting speeches, which is not unusual for him. First, he said, "Our prestige and the prestige of the National Football League is at stake. You damn well better not let that Mickey Mouse league beat you. It'd be a disgrace, a complete utter disgrace."

Then, he added, "They've got a helluva good football team. They've got some good football players. You'd better be ready to play or they'll knock your blocks off. We're not going down there for a vacation."

When Vince finished, I looked at Gregg and Gilly and said, "Can you imagine anyone fool enough to think that going anywhere with this man would be a vacation?"

"Sure ain't my idea of a vacation," said Forrest.

Gilly, Fuzzy, and I sat together to watch the Oakland movies, and we concentrated on the pass rushes by the defensive tackles and ends. Gilly occasionally will have to handle Ben Davidson, their right defensive end, who's about 6'7" and 280 pounds and wears a flowing moustache. Ben played here in Green Bay one year—he wasn't too much of a ballplayer then—and I was teasing Gilly, "You're gonna try to block that big fellow and he's gonna knock you right on your can."

"No, he won't," Gilly said. "I'm gonna grab him by that big moustache, and I'm just gonna hold on."

We're supposed to practice indoors tomorrow. The temperature's supposed to hit 25 below zero during the night, and Vince couldn't get me outside with a whip.

JANUARY 5

My lungs are giving me trouble—I'm pretty sure I got them frostbit or something—but I worked out today, in sneakers, in a local high-school gym. We had a pretty good session. Then we saw a few movies, and my tackle, Dan Birdwell, looked like he's going to be a chore. He's quick. I think he's the best pass rusher on the Oakland Team.

I'm driving myself now. Just one more week of concentration, I keep reminding myself. Just one more week to drive that mind and drive that body. One more week and it'll all be over.

As we were emptying out of the locker room today, Fuzzy yelled to everybody, "Gentlemen, next week we begin the big push."

JANUARY 6

We had today off, and I spent the whole day running around with my brother, helping him shop for a car. He left the hospital less than forty-eight hours after his knee was operated on, and he feels pretty good. Grabo's in good shape after his operation, too. He can start getting ready for next year.

From Miami, I'll be going straight to Los Angeles for the Pro Bowl game January 21. I'll be away from home for at least two and a half weeks, so when I packed tonight, I packed eight suitcases, enough to last for about a year or a year and a half. I spent an hour and a half searching for my blue golf shoes, and I finally had to give up. I could only find my black-and-white golf shoes. I was very disappointed. How can I go to Florida without the proper clothes?

JANUARY 7

We left Green Bay today with great reluctance, of course. The temperature was 7 degrees below zero, and when we landed in Florida the temperature was 75. During the flight, Marie Lombardi, Vince's wife, walked over to me and said, "I've got to kiss you." And she did. "That was a wonderful thing you said on TV in front of 50 million people," she said, "and you meant it, didn't you?"

"Of course, I meant it," I said. "I meant every word of it."

We're staying at the Galt Ocean Mile Hotel in Fort Lauderdale, a typical Lombardi maneuver. We're about an hour or more from Miami and Miami Beach, far enough to discourage us from going off to sample the night life. And just in case we get bored, I suppose, Coach has scheduled a meeting almost every afternoon and every evening. We had the first one tonight. Vince reminded us that we're not down here to vacation. Nobody seemed very surprised.

Dave Hanner told me that he'd picked out the Galt Ocean Mile Hotel when he was down in Florida on a recruiting mission for Coach Lombardi last February or March. Coach told him to see if he could find a good place for us to stay when we played in the Super Bowl. Vince does believe in planning ahead.

JANUARY 9

Dozens of reporters and photographers covered our workout this morning, and I'm getting more attention than I ever got before. I've always been a good source for certain sportswriters—they've phoned me whenever they needed a comment on just about anything—but now, suddenly, everyone's coming up to me. Everyone wants to talk about the block I made on Jethro Pugh, about the remarks I made on television. It seems that a lot more people know my name this week than knew it two weeks ago.

I've learned to live with the obscurity of being an offensive lineman, which is probably why—when I'm honest with myself—I've never had a great deal of regard for myself as a football player. I've always felt that I play a secondary position, and I've never been terribly impressed with the fact that I play professional football. I remember reading John O'Hara's *The Last Laugh,* about a movie star who had been an SOB all his life and at the end of the book, after he had gone completely downhill, he said something like, "At least I've been a big-time movie star and nobody can take that away from me. Ha, ha, ha, ha." Big deal. Who cares? It's not as though you were a doctor or a lawyer, not as though you were doing something constructive.

I guess I wouldn't get these occasional feelings of depression if I were to carry the ball or pass the ball or do something important.

JANUARY 10

Vince has started calling Bob Hyland "the Boston stronghead." Hyland got quoted in the papers the other day saying that he thought it was a smart thing for professional football players to have agents, business representatives. I think he's probably right, but you shouldn't say such things where Lombardi can hear them, or hear about them. Vince has very strong feelings against agents for football players; Hyland's getting the brunt of those feelings now.

There are several different stories about why Lombardi traded Jim Ringo, who was then our captain and an All-Pro center, a few years ago. The most logical story, the one I believe, is this: The day Vince asked Ringo to come in and discuss his contract, Ringo showed up in Lombardi's office with another man. "Coach," Ringo said, "I'm not very good at negotiating for myself. This is my agent. He'll discuss my contract with you."

Lombardi asked to be excused for a moment. He left his office, walked down the hall and came back in a few minutes. "I'm afraid you're negotiating with the wrong man," he told Ringo's agent. "Jim Ringo has just been traded to the Philadelphia Eagles."

JANUARY 11

We've been working hard preparing for Oakland. They're a much better team than Kansas City was last year. Once, watching the films, when we saw the Raiders' safety men collide, we laughed, but it isn't like last year, when we were laughing all the time. The Raiders look tough, and their five-two defense is a real problem for us. We haven't seen anything quite like it in the NFL. Over and over, Vince has been showing us the movies of the Oakland–San Francisco preseason exhibition. The 49ers won 13–10, but Oakland put up a tremendous struggle. San Francisco didn't score a touchdown until the final period. That movie keeps us from getting too cocky.

The difference between our attitude for this game and our

attitude for the Los Angeles and Dallas games is obvious, I guess. For those two games, Vince didn't have to keep telling us how good our opponents were, and we didn't have to persuade ourselves. We knew the Rams and the Cowboys were tough. We have to keep saying it about the Raiders; we have to force ourselves to be respectful of Oakland. We know the importance of winning Sunday—each winning player gets $15,000 in the Super Bowl, and each losing player gets $7,500—but, still, there's not really any doubt on the club. We don't say IF we win; we say WHEN we win.

Before our calisthenics this morning, Lombardi gathered the whole team for a brief talk. "This is the most important game of your lives," he said. "It's certainly the most important of my life." His remarks reminded me of his comment last year before the Super Bowl game. "This isn't the most important game you've ever played," he said then. "Next year it may be, but this year it isn't."

His words—the emphasis he placed on this game—raised the question of his retirement once again. It's on everybody's mind. Bart and I talked about it tonight at supper, and we agreed we wouldn't be a bit surprised to hear Vince announce his retirement in the locker room, as soon as the Super Bowl ends.

JANUARY 12

We had our afternoon meeting at 2:45 today, a little early, because Coach Lombardi had to go to an AFL-NFL meeting in Miami. He came into the meeting room—wearing a blue shirt, a tie, dark pants and glasses—turned to Dave Hanner and said, "Everybody here, Dave?"

"Well, I got forty-two," Hanner said.

"How many you supposed to have?" said Lombardi.

"Forty-two," said Dave. "But I might have miscounted." He checked the room again. "I think I've got everyone here."

Lombardi turned and faced us. "OK boys," he began, then stopped and rubbed his hands together for several seconds, obviously thinking about what he was going to say. "This may be the last time we'll be together, so . . . uh . . ." His lips actually began to tremble; his whole body quivered. He looked like he was about to start bawling. He never finished the sentence. He sat down, facing the movie screen, right next to the projector, his back to all the guys, and said, "Let's break up."

The defensive players left the room, going off to their own meeting, and Vince stayed with the offensive team. He didn't say a word. He just put on the projector and let it run, not even bothering to run the film back and forth until late in the movie. I don't think any of us concentrated on the film; we were all wondering what playing for Green Bay would be like without Lombardi. I don't particularly want to find out. It's been hell to play while he's been there, but I don't want to play if he's not around. I wondered how many of the old pros on our club could keep going without the driving force and will of Vince Lombardi. I hope we don't have to find out.

"What did you think of Vince's statement?" Donny Anderson asked me, after the meeting ended.

"Looked like there's no question about his retirement," I said. "I've never known the man to get emotional over nothing. It looked like a clear indication to me that this is going to be his final football game."

JANUARY 13

We had a short workout this morning, the last one before the Super Bowl, and while he was taping me, Bud Jorgensen, our trainer, said to me, "Well, Jerry, how many does this make?"

"How many what, Bud?" I said. "Seasons?"

He nodded.

"End of the tenth," I said.

"This is the last one, huh?" Bud said.

"Yeah, Bud, I guess it is."

I don't really think it's my last season, but I took a look around the locker room and I looked at Fuzzy and Max and Henry and a few of the other guys who're thinking about retiring, and I got very nostalgic, very sad. I'm going to miss those guys.

I remembered that I used to play every game as if it were my last game, and I wished I could get back that old concentration. I thought again about Vince retiring—I was still in a state of shock from his comments yesterday—and I realized I might be playing my last game for him tomorrow. I want to make it a perfect game. I don't want to have one bad thing, not even one medium thing.

We played our regular volleyball game, the King Ranch Bullies against the Cicero Sissies, and we were tied 8–8 when Vince blew the whistle for the start of practice. We tried a few plays, and Gilly got off late once—he missed the count—and Coach cussed him pretty good. If Vince's going out tomorrow, he's going out strong.

My wife's been here the past few days, and so has Chandler's. Tonight we're putting the girls in one room, and Donny and I are sharing one. It's better for the girls to be away from us tonight. We're always grumpy and grouchy the night before a game.

JANUARY 14

I was tense this morning, much more than I had expected to be. I had so many things to do. I had to help Barbara get packed and off. She was going right back to Green Bay after the game. I had to get my own stuff packed and sent to the airport for my trip to Los Angeles. I'd bought thirty-five tickets for the Super Bowl, and I had to make sure they were all distributed. I must have had a thousand different distractions, and, after our pregame meal at 10:45, I got up, left the dining room, went to meet my wife in the coffee shop, and completely forgot about the meeting that we've had after every pregame meal for ten years.

I was sitting in the coffee shop talking to Barbara when I suddenly remembered I'd left my tape recorder in the dining room. I rushed back and tried, unsuccessfully, to open the door. It was locked. I knocked, and somebody unlocked the door, and I walked in, and there was the whole offensive team, right in the middle of the meeting. All the guys gave me a funny look. Coach Lombardi gave me a look that wasn't funny at all. He didn't say a word. He just scowled. The meeting lasted another ten or fifteen minutes, and I hardly heard a word, my mind wandering to all the things I'd done to get ready to leave. After the meeting I hurried down to the lobby, checked out, paid my incidental expenses, and climbed aboard the team bus about twenty minutes before it was supposed to leave. Five minutes later everybody was on the bus. We were all tense.

When we got to the Orange Bowl in Miami I dropped my stuff in the locker room and strolled out to the field for a little look at the pregame festivities. I saw the two big statues, one marked Oakland, the other marked Green Bay, breathing smoke. I just wanted to kill a little time, settle down a little.

In the locker room, for the first time all season I decided to leave my tape recorder running during the pregame talks. If I got caught by Lombardi, I didn't think he'd suspend me at this stage of the year.

Bob Skoronski spoke first. "Let's not waste any time, boys," he said. "Let's go out there from the opening play. They're a good football team, boys. If we lose, boys, we've lost everything we ever worked for. Everything. I don't have any damn intention of losing this ball game, and I don't think anybody else here does."

"Fellas," said Willie Davis, "you know as well as I do that when we went to camp in July, this is what we had in mind. This game. This game is going to determine what's said about the Packers tomorrow. Fellas, in another sixty minutes, we can walk in here with another world championship. Fellas, it's recognition, it's prestige, and, fellas, it's money. So let's go out and have fun. Let's go out and just hit people. Let's just go out and play football the way we can."

"My impression of this ball club," Forrest Gregg said, "is that they're the type of people who like to intimidate you. Watch those linebackers, those linemen, the way they're hitting people late. No sense getting upset about it. They're gonna do some pass interference and holding and stuff like that, but let's not get upset about it. Let's go out there and play our brand of football. Let's face it. They're a little bit afraid of us right now. Let's put it to them from the very first whistle and put it to them every play."

"It's the last game for some of us," said Max, "and we sure don't want to go out of here and live the rest of our lives letting these guys beat us."

"Let's play with our hearts," said Nitschke.

Then Carroll Dale led us in the Lord's Prayer, and we broke up with whoops and hollers, and we ran out on the field and loosened up, and then we came back inside for our pads and our helmets and a few words from Coach Lombardi.

"It's very difficult for me to say anything," Vince said. "Anything I could say would be repetitious. This is our twenty-third game this year. I don't know of anything else I could tell this team. Boys, I can only say this to you: Boys, you're a good football team. You are a proud football team. You are the world champions. You are the champions of the National Football League for the third time in a row, for the first time in the history of the National Football League. That's a great thing to be proud of. But let me just say this: All the glory, everything that you've had, everything that you've won is going to be small in comparison to winning this one. This is a great thing for you. You're the only team maybe in the history of the National Football League to ever have this opportunity to win the Super Bowl twice. Boys, I tell you I'd be so proud of that I just fill up with myself. I just get bigger and bigger and bigger. It's not going to come easy. This is a club that's gonna hit you. They're gonna try to hit you and you got to take it out of them. You got to be forty tigers out there. That's all. Just hit. Just run. Just block and just tackle. If you do that, there's no question what the answer's going to be in this ball game. Keep your poise. Keep your poise. You've faced them all. There's nothing they can show you out there you haven't faced a number of times. Right?"

"Right!"

"RIGHT!"

"Let's go. Let's go get 'em."

We rushed out of the locker room and onto the field, and all the speeches were a lot better than the way we played the first half. The first time we got the ball, we moved fairly well. They threw the five-two defense at us, and they threw a few other defenses at us, and we found out fast that they weren't going to give us any special trouble, that we could move the ball against them. Physically, they weren't quite so awesome as our NFL opponents. But we made a million mistakes, stupid, high-school mistakes. Kenny Bowman called his block one way and blocked the other way three or four times. He hadn't done that more than twice all year. We all made silly little blocking mistakes.

We scored the first two times we had the ball, but both times only on field goals, which was a little unsettling. Then Boyd broke into the open, and Bart hit him with a long pass, and we were ahead 13–0. We got lazy and careless, the way we always seem to when we build up a lead. Oakland came roaring back, hitting real hard, and scored a touchdown. Chandler's third field goal gave us a 16–7 lead at the half, not a terribly impressive margin.

Between the halves there wasn't much we could discuss. Our plays were working fine; we just weren't executing them right. A few of us veterans got together—Forrest and Ski and Henry and me and a few others—and we decided we'd play the last thirty minutes for the old man. We didn't want to let him down in his last game.

Oakland never quit. The year before, against Kansas City, the game was settled by half-time even though we were only winning 14–10. In the second half, the first time we lined up for an extra point—which is generally the perfect time for a defensive man to take a swing at your head or smack you with a forearm or just give you his best shot—the Kansas City kid playing opposite me leaned on me, uttered a loud groan and applied about as much pressure as a good feather duster. I knew the game was over.

But Oakland played just as hard in the second half as it did in the first. Right near the end, when we had the game locked up, we had a short yardage situation. The play was going to go between Gregg and me, and I figured it might be one of my last plays for Lombardi, and I wanted to make it good. I got a perfect block on Dan Birdwell, knocked him down. He jumped up—he hadn't spoken to me all day—and said, "Helluva block, Kramer." He patted me on the rear and said, "Way to go." The next play, Birdwell practically killed himself to beat me. Zeke rolled out to the right, and I took Birdwell that way, and he slipped off me and got Zeke. He was still going all out. He hadn't slowed down a bit.

The game ended 33–14, with Oakland in possession of the ball. We had been planning for the co-captains, Skoronski and

Davis, to carry Vince off the field, but Willie was playing when the gun went off, so Gregg and I, the two men closest to Coach, just lifted him up and started running out on the field. He was grinning at us and slapping us and he hollered, "Head for the dressing room, boys," and we headed for the dressing room, clutching the man who'd made us the Super Bowl champions for the second year in a row.

When we had all reached the dressing room, Vince gathered us together. "This has to be one of the great, great years," he said. "I think it's something you'll always remember. You know everything happened to us. We lost a lot of people. Thank goodness we had the boys who could replace them and did a helluva job. And those who were not hurt played a little bit better. Boys, I'm really proud of you. We should all be very, very thankful."

We got down on our knees, and we began, in unison, "Our Father, Who art in Heaven, hallowed be Thy name . . ."

We finished the Lord's Prayer and we all began slapping each other on the back and hugging each other, and, once again, the cameramen and the reporters poured in.

I sat in front of my locker, and I talked and talked and talked. I talked about the mistakes we made during the first half. I talked about the spirit of our team. I talked about Lombardi. I saw the fellow who wrote the article in *Esquire* about Lombardi, and I cussed him out a bit. I told anecdotes and I told my opinion of just about everything, and after a while I noticed that most of my teammates were dressed and were starting to leave the locker room. I was still in my uniform, still perched in front of my locker. I really didn't want to get up.

I wanted to keep my uniform on as long as I possibly could.

EPILOGUE

Fuzzy crowing about the two greatest guards in the history of the National Football League . . . Max telling Coach to throw one in his diddy-bag . . . Bart threatening to kick Steve Wright in the can . . . Tommy Joe talking about Cecil Barlow's cow . . . Ray Nitschke wearing a toupee and shades . . . Hornung . . . Currie . . . Tunnell . . . Taylor . . . Jordan . . . Quinlan . . . Davis . . . Adderley . . . Gregg . . . Chandler . . . Hart . . . Ron Kramer . . . on and on and on . . . all the guys I played with for the past ten years. That's why I play professional football.

That's why I'm going to keep playing professional football.

I know now that for me the main lure of football is the guys, my teammates, the friendship, the fun, the excitement, the incredibly exhilarating feeling of a shared achievement. When I look back upon the 1967 season, before I remember the block on Jethro Pugh, before I remember Bart's touchdown against the Cowboys, before I remember our victory in the Super Bowl, I remember a very special spirit, a rare camaraderie, something I can't quite define, but something I've tried to capture in this diary.

A few years ago I was flying to California for the Pro Bowl game with Frank Gifford and Forrest Gregg. Forrest was talking about retiring to go into college coaching, and Frank had just returned to the New York Giants after a year in retirement. "Forrest," Gifford said, "don't quit till you have to. It'd be a terrible mistake. You'd miss it too much."

Gifford's remark hit me. He had everything going for him—a promising television career, financial security—yet he still wanted to play so badly. I think I understand now; I think I understand what Gifford missed, what I would miss. I feel right now that I'm ready to play another five years, maybe a couple of years at guard, then a few at tackle, where you don't have to run so much or so fast.

If anybody had told me a year ago that I'd be thinking about playing five more years—even three more years—I'd have told him he was crazy. I figured then that 1967 was my last season or, at best, my next-to-last season. But the 1967 season was a revelation to me. I felt physically better than I had in five years. Finally, I'd come back from my injuries and my operations. Finally, I wasn't groaning and aching every single day. Finally, professional football wasn't a chore. I know that I complained often during the season, that I went through periods of depression, but, ultimately, I enjoyed myself. I enjoyed the whole season.

It was a beautiful season, almost a perfect season, marred by only two disappointments. I regretted my deal with Kraft; after the season, Kraft decided not to compensate us for our losses. And I regretted my failure to make the NEA All-Pro team, the one selected by the players; I did make the UPI team, but I learned in

January that Gene Hickerson of Cleveland and Howard Mudd of San Francisco had beaten me out for the NEA team. Outside of those mild setbacks—and the fact that I endured my eighteenth consecutive year of football without scoring a touchdown—I had a lovely season.

While I was touring the banquet circuit a few weeks ago, my wife happened to sit with Dave Hanner at a Cub Scout meeting. Dave told Barbara the coaches had been analyzing the 1967 movies, taking them apart, choosing plays for teaching reels. "Jerry had his best year," Hanner said. "Never saw him play any better."

I disagree with Dave. I think I played my best football in 1961, but I definitely played better in 1967 than I did in 1966, and I played better in 1966 than I did in 1965. I'd like to keep up the trend in 1968.

I've been spending the winter running back and forth between banquets and business, talking football almost every day, exploring the possibilities of a television career, looking into a nationwide chain of restaurants, doing nothing more strenuous than a few rounds of golf and an occasional game of handball. I've been on the road most of the time.

I was out of Green Bay the day Lombardi announced that he was retiring. I can't say I was shocked. But I did feel saddened. He was our most valuable player, and I'm going to miss him, even his screaming and his ranting. I have a lot of confidence in my own ability, and I think I would have been a good football player even if Julie Andrews had been my coach, but I don't know if I would have been a champion without Vince. He made us think like champions.

Vince is still general manager, and I know he's going to be popping his head into the dressing room and onto the field, and he's still going to give us dirty looks whenever we do anything wrong.

Phil Bengtson is our head coach now, and Phil, who came to Green Bay with Lombardi in 1959, as the defensive coach, has always been a cheerful, easy-going guy. I've always called him "Uncle Phil" or "Coach Phil." He'll change a little now; he's got to change. I could sense a change when, a few days after Lombardi retired, I came home to Green Bay and stopped by the coaches' office.

"Congratulations, Phil," I said. "I'm happy to hear about it." I didn't start calling him "Coach" right away—I guess, for a while at least, that's still reserved for Lombardi—but there was a glance, a look that passed between us, that made me feel things are going to be a little different. Phil's the head man now, and he's not going to be a nice guy all the time. He can't be a nice guy all the time.

I'm not worried about Phil's capabilities as a head coach. Nobody can question the job he did with our defensive team. He made our defense the finest in professional football, and he instilled in his defensive players an almost murderous desire for perfection. I remember in the National Football League championship game when Ray Nitschke, after tackling Don Perkins of Dallas for a two-yard loss, leaped to his feet and kicked the air viciously, almost kicking Perkins. Nitschke wasn't mad at his opponent; he was mad at himself because he had failed to execute the tackle perfectly, exactly the way Phil Bengtson had taught him.

Four more months, and back to grass drills. Back to the nutcracker drill. Back to Sensenbrenner Hall. I'm actually looking forward to it. Only the bright memories remain, and I feel great. Nothing hurts me—yet.

JERRY KRAMER
Green Bay, Wisconsin
March 1968

REMEMBERING DICK SCHAAP

TRISH MCCLEOD SCHAAP

In the early sixties, Dick Schaap went to Green Bay to write an article for the *Saturday Evening Post* about Green Bay Packer player Jimmy Taylor. When he arrived at the dorm room shared by Taylor and Jerry Kramer, he found Kramer seated on his bed reading poetry aloud. A few years later, when Schaap was asked by a publisher if he knew of a football player who could keep a diary that Schaap would then turn into book form, Kramer was the obvious choice. It was the beginning of what Schaap described as one of his most treasured friendships, one which spanned several decades, several marriages, a dozen children between them, and several more collaborations, *Farewell to Football*, *Lombardi*, and *Distant Replay*.

The camaraderie between urban cowboy and city slicker made a person feel good to be in their presence. They laughed, reminisced, told stories, sang each other's praises, played golf in each other's tournaments, and thoroughly enjoyed each other's company as few men allow themselves to do.

Dick Schaap lived to enjoy being an honorary Green Bay Packer and was posthumously inducted into the Lombardi Legends. He grew to love the Packers team of that era with a passion and admitted, when it came to these icons, his hands were not journalistically clean.

Jerry Kramer and Fuzzy Thurston may have been the last two people Schaap recognized before he slid into a final coma and died two days later. At his memorial service on January 17, 2002, in the Cathedral of Saint John the Divine in New York City, Kramer was among the dozen friends from the world of sports and entertainment who delivered humorous and passionate eulogies to an audience of more than two thousand.

DICK SCHAAP (IN VIDEO)

I started going to Green Bay in the early sixties by train. Not many reporters could find Green Bay then. On one of my early trips, I met Jerry Kramer, sitting on his bed in the dorm, reading poetry out loud. Real poetry, not "There was a young lady from so and so." When a publisher asked me to ask a football player to keep a diary, I asked Jerry Kramer. He said yes. Neither of us suspected that Jerry's diary would lead up to an unforgettable game, the Ice Bowl, or an unforgettable block with time running out and the Packers down by three points. I remember Kramer telling me Vince Lombardi's theory, that the Packers never lost the game, but sometimes the clock ran out when the other team had more points.

JERRY KRAMER

Dick had come up with the title in his mind, *The Day the Clock Ran Out*. And it looked like we were going to run out of time. They replayed The Block over and over and over, and pointed me out, and I got some publicity, which was rare for an offensive lineman. But thank God for instant replay. And Dick goes, "That's it. That's the title."

Dick Schaap was a friend of mine. [We] came from different parts of the universe it seemed like. It seemed like an unlikely friendship. In the beginning, we worked on and off for thirty or forty years. It's awfully difficult to express in a few words what that friendship was all about. Friend, pal, buddy, co-conspirator on occasion. One of the good guys. Trish, Carrie, David, Jeremy, and Michelle: Thank you for sharing him with us. I know he was gone a lot. And I know he traveled a lot. I know he was involved a lot. And I know he gave a lot of little pieces. Thank you. We appreciate you sharing him with us. I think we loved him as much as you did.

I got him to come to Idaho. Now, our worlds were, like I say, poles apart. But I got him to come to Idaho a few years back. I had a ranch. Now, in Boise, Idaho, at that time was about seventy-five thousand people. Which was the biggest city in Idaho. And much too big for me, so I lived about forty-five miles outside of Boise. I always felt sorry about the people that lived in New York, and I would tell Dick about that. And he would always tell me he felt sorry about the people that lived in Idaho. But we had a wonderful relationship. But he came to the ranch to spend a week with me, and I took him up to the Sawtooth Mountains and the high country, where lakes are gin clear and the air is crystal clear and it's got the high mountain peaks and it's virtually uninhabited. Dick would say, "This is nice. This is nice." I took him down to the

Snake River Canyon that's about six thousand feet deep and you're looking at about three billion years of geology. And there's a roaring white-water canyon in a sensational part of the world. And Dick would say, "This is nice. This is nice." I got him a pair of cowboy boots and a cowboy hat and put him on a horse. His eyes got very, very big—but he didn't say "that was nice."

A few months later we were here in the city. We come out of his apartment—it's an asphalt jungle, a cacophony of sound. The carbon dioxide. The city. The traffic. The people . . . New York. Dick throws his arms open wide, and he looks up at the sky and says, "God's country, this is God's country!"

There had been an article written about Coach Lombardi the week prior to the Ice Bowl. And it was a very derogatory article. It belittled him and made fun of him and caused a great deal of pain in his family, and his mother had been talking to him and was crying on the phone. And we heard about it, and I had made up my mind that if I had a chance to say something, I was going to say something about Coach Lombardi. And I was interviewed after the Ice Bowl and it was a rare occasion, but I did have a moment to say something about Coach Lombardi. I said people didn't really understand him. They didn't know him the way we knew him. That he was a really beautiful man. Never had the occasion to use that term again, until today. Dick Schaap was truly a beautiful man.

ABOUT THE AUTHORS

Jerry Kramer was a right guard for the Green Bay Packers
from 1958 to 1968. During his time with the team, the Packers
won five National Championships and Super Bowls I and II.
He was inducted into the Green Bay Packers Hall of Fame in
1977, and his jersey has been retired. He lives in Boise, Idaho.

Dick Schaap (1934–2002), a sportswriter, broadcaster, and
author or coauthor of thirty-three books, reported for *NBC
Nightly News*, the *Today* show, *ABC World News Tonight*,
20/20, and ESPN and was the recipient of five Emmy Awards.

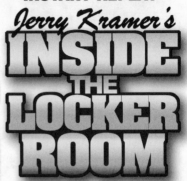